HI! MY NAME IS LOCO AND I AM A RACIST

BAYE MCNEIL

A HUNTERFLY ROAD BOOK

Hi! My Name is Loco and I am a Racist

For Aiko

CONTENTS

ACKNOWLEDGEMENTS

I owe a debt of gratitude to a number of people who have helped during the writing and editing of this book. I begin by thanking my hosts, the people of Japan, particularly in Yokohama, Saitama, Kawasaki and Tokyo. If not for them, there would certainly be no Loco. Loco is as much the product of my love for this land and its people as he is anything else.

I also want to thank the readers of my blog for their support over the past three years. These guys hung in there with me and encouraged me so much. I don't think I would have had the confidence to even attempt this project, let alone complete it without them. As I've told them before, I'll say it again: "You all have been a blessing!"

And speaking of blessings, I have to also send out big love to my friends and family, my Mamas and Babas, my teachers and role models from The East Family and Uhuru Sasa Shule. I never realized how much they'd done for me until the writing of this book, for which so much of what they invested in me came to bear. I am so proud to have been a part of something so magnificent. The Creator, indeed, has a Master Plan and these are the people who made me aware of that and set me on the course that has brought me to this point! Aluta Continua!

I am also thankful to Amanda Taylor who helped me so much and in so many ways. With every editorial session with Ms. Taylor this manuscript improved and, as stubborn a head case as I can be, that's saying something. Also big love to the Katalist herself, Kateria Niambi; she also helped me out a great deal with the editing. And, to Coach Doug Reed! Thanks, my brother, for your editorial help and for always having an encouraging word when we spoke. It meant more than you know.

A special shout out to the staff at WIP Internet Café in Jiyugaoka, my home away from home, where I did the majority of the writing. I know I must've been their best customer, and these guys are the reason I kept coming back.

And last but certainly not least, to my mother, Waridi Stewart, whose love has borne me my entire life and whose creative ability to take nothing and turn it into not only something, but something beautiful, has always inspired me to do the same. I love you, Ma!

INTRODUCTION

GOING THROUGH SOME CHANGES

A caterpillar forms a chrysalis around itself and, before long, a lovely butterfly emerges. Is the caterpillar aware at the start of the process that by its end it will have transformed from one of the more loathsome looking larvae into the recipient of often extraordinary beauty? That instead of inching around destroying trees and pestering farmers, it'll magically take to the air and become one of the most adored creatures on Earth?

Probably not, right?

No more than that good man who drinks one too many shots of scotch after a rough day at work; a day during which, at his supervisor's discretion, he had been screwed out of a promotion he rightfully deserved over an unfortunate drunken incident at an office holiday party that resulted in a couple of embarrassing minor injuries and a severely damaged copy machine; an event that managed to overshadow his otherwise stellar performance record. It was all he could do not to cry into his shot glass right there at the bar.

Just a caterpillar on a barstool, encasing himself in malted barley.

Later, while driving home, his faculties mildly impaired but not much more than usual, sobbing freely in the privacy of his SUV over that first home he'd promised his wife (that he now won't be able to afford), and the bedrooms of their own he'd promised his two rapidly growing kids (that he won't be able to provide), he drifts over the tear-blurred double-solid lines dividing the road. Then, SMASH! He collides head-on with a Prius carrying a family of four headed home after a fun evening at a family entertainment center, killing the husband and critically injuring the wife and kids.

He's released from the hospital a few weeks later in splints, bandages and stitches, and suffering from headaches due to the severe concussion he'd suffered, only to find himself on the business end of a judge's gavel, sentenced to no less than five (no more than ten) years for vehicular manslaughter.

Deservedly, many would say.

While serving his sentence, he is routinely beaten and gang raped (among other things) until he eventually submits to being some brute's bitch. This continues until the day of his release.

He emerges eight years later, a free man, a different man, a *changed* man.

His wife has changed, too. She has a new man (and a new house) and his kids have a new father (and their own rooms) and he has nothing but the clothes on his back, a smoking habit he didn't have before he was convicted, a sphincter that has never really healed properly (thanks to a mentally ill prison surgeon's ineptitude), and the painful memory of having been some animal's play thing.

Perhaps he uses this horribly all-too-common experience to spur him to never before imagined accomplishments. Maybe he writes a book or screenplay about the experience that becomes a best seller or a hit movie starring Jamie Foxx and Brad Pitt (who gives a tour de force Academy Award winning performance as the skinhead rapist).

Maybe our caterpillar turned Monarch butterfly uses his newfound fame and success to establish an organization to fight on behalf of abused prisoners everywhere or to combat mental illness in prisons worldwide, earning him further acclaim and even a Nobel Prize nomination.

Or…

Maybe our larva becomes a Death's-head Hawkmoth, and blames his supervisor for everything that has befallen him since he was unfairly passed over for promotion, seizes him leaving home one morning and strangles the man to death with the T-back panties he was forced to wear in prison. Then, he lies in wait counting the days (536 of them) until his former prison husband's release from jail, with his own version of the *Shawshank Redemption* burning a hole in his soul. The mounting pile of instruments he's collected especially for the occasion is an assortment so grotesque that even a dentist would blanch. He proceeds to abduct and torture the rapist, slowly and medievally, extending it over a two-week period.

Once the degenerate has suffered immensely and is deader than most people would wish on their worst enemies (deservedly, many would say), and unable to handle what has become of the proud provider, husband and father he once was, our tormented moth takes a flying leap off of the highest point in the vicinity. He doesn't flutter on wings the Creator has used as a canvas. He doesn't glide on nature's breath. He plummets to the earth below, cursing the Creator the whole way down, and cracks the concrete with the force of his landing.

You hear about this kind of shit all the time…certainly more so back in the States than here in Japan, but here, as well (just replace a tall building or bridge with a subway platform, and the concrete with a speeding train entering a station). And it's usually as a result of some kind of change.

You just never know how things will turn out. The only thing that is a certainty is that change is inevitable.

I've gone through some changes, too.

And, when I read over some of the essays and stories I've written over the years based on my mind-altering experiences here in Japan, and some of the thoughts I've had and shared with the world, I either smile, adoring the proof laid out before me that I am a talented writer and somewhat gifted thinker, or I cringe and say *I need my goddamn head examined and a shit load of meds.*

Seriously, though.

I mean, what does a butterfly perceive when it happens upon a caterpillar slinking up the bark of a tree to munch on leaves? Is it the same perception it would have upon encountering a chrysalis?

Does it have the thought, "*Damn*, I've come a long way"?

Doubtful.

Post-metamorphosis, the butterfly – in addition to being a flying work of art and a motif in many musical, visual and literary masterpieces – is a surrogate/sex slave fluttering about knocking up female flowers on behalf of their immobile beaus. It's a timeless, endless, thankless instinct that keeps the butterfly way too busy to get narcissistic and reflect on change, I bet.

Besides, even before making that famous transformation from revolting to revered, the caterpillar already has the capacity to change. It adapts to its environment, often taking on the appearance of the vegetation it feeds on. If some bug specie decides that caterpillars make a tasty snack, within a handful of generations, those caterpillars will produce a toxin that will make that predatory bug's progeny think twice.

Why?

To survive!

That poor guy in a prison cell, who eventually surrendered what he'd come to think of as his manhood to human predators, did so for the same reason.

Which begs the question, how have *I* adapted to survive among the predators and other ills in my environment? Sometimes I watch myself as I go through the typical day, like a spider poised in a web in the corner of my mind. And from that vantage, I can see that Japan has been *my* chrysalis, and that I have undergone some adaptations.

Some are toxic.

Some hold the promise of pretty wings.

*****

Hi! My name is Loco, by the way. That's not my real name, of course. Just a pseudonym I've taken on for so many reasons I could fill a book…in fact, I've gone ahead and filled a book. I'm a native New Yorker, born and raised in Brooklyn. I currently live in Yokohama, Japan, where I put my degree in English to use teaching junior high school kids and a dozen or so private students how to speak my mother tongue. My hobbies are reading, watching movies, taking pictures of trains & stations, social networking, and playing basketball with my boys on the weekends, but my passion is writing. I do it every day, even if only in my head…

And, oh yeah…I'm a racist.

The book you're about to read is a selection of stories and reflections. Half are from my experiences before coming to live in Japan, and half are on those I've had over the course of the eight years I've resided here. Some of these writings were originally part of my blog, *Loco in Yokohama,* which I've kept for the past three years. All have contributed to my current state of mind in both subtle and profound ways.

The dream of writing a book about life in Japan — which I would wager is shared by every writer or wannabe writer who has ever lived here — is one I'd put on hold until now. Why was the dream deferred? Well, because the *Japan Book,* written by an English instructor, whether fiction or non-fiction, is practically a cliché. So I told myself that if I couldn't find subject matter related to my life in Japan that hadn't been covered so thoroughly that I could cut and paste it from ten books written the previous year, then I wouldn't do it.

Fast forward almost a decade.

A decade spent in Asia learning about myself and teaching about my world, tearing down shrines of ignorance and erecting temples of understanding, learning the true measure of love and the true meaning of loss, indulging hate and enduring what *really* violent thoughts can do to a mind reluctant to act on them, discovering the writer I had the potential to be and uncovering the obstacles that lay in-between living my dreams and having them deferred.

It's been *quite* a ride so far. One I wouldn't trade for anything.

During my time here I've paid careful attention to the work of other foreigners living here — mostly the content creators — via the books they've written and the blogs they keep. I've watched their videos and vlogs, and listened to their radio shows and podcasts. I've run into them in person in the streets, and met / tweeted up with them at bars and cafes around Yokohama and Tokyo. They come in various flavors of humanity, different races, cultures and nationalities.

Most of the successful and popular Japan-based creators tend to stick with "positive" stories and light material; shrines and temples, anime and language study tips, food, fashion, festivals and females. Others might delve into the creepy and the kooky, mysterious and spooky (of which there is plenty - some even fascinating), but the woolly mammoth in the room has often gone ignored; or worse, denied. Creative folk, either knowingly or not, seemed to be unwilling or unable to deal with what I felt to be the most glaring of issues here.

It made me feel a little paranoid, to say the least.

I questioned whether what I was seeing was real or a figment of my imagination. Was I suffering from delusions of persecution? They're not exactly unknown among expats here, that's for damn sure. Maybe *that* was the reason I saw the behemoth while many did not, or could not.

Some of these content creators would, on occasion, partially acknowledge it with their right hand, but somehow manage to dismiss it with the left. A post of theirs might read something like: *"I sat down on the train today and this Japanese guy sitting beside me suddenly stood up and stormed off into the next car, looking back at me angrily as he walked away. That's rather odd, I thought. But then my nose informed me what the issue was. I was wearing a new aftershave, and Japanese people are sensitive to foreign fragrances. I was also wearing blue jeans and a sweatshirt, and Japanese are very particular about these kinds of things. They prefer a more professional attire, especially when it comes to foreigners, and rightfully so. I'm glad I didn't jump to conclusions like some other bloggers do. It was all my fault. I felt really bad for having disrupted this guy's peace of mind. I hope I see him again tomorrow so I can apologize."*

Others, though, were either oblivious or in total denial; like contestants on a wacky game show where they're made to wear blindfolds and try to guess objects from their *feel*. Hand one contestant a freshly used condom and, despite the "lubrication" and "ribbing," they'll invariably say it's a balloon, inflate it and make a balloon animal just to prove their point. Hand another contestant a dildo, and they'll stroke it like a sculptor does clay, and say, *"I know this shape, especially here at the tip and here around the base. It's so familiar, Wait! I've got it! It's an o-miyage (souvenir) from a Japanese penis matsuri. I wrote my doctorate thesis on these fertility festivals. It's a quirky time-honored tradition that dates back before America and its bloody Black Ships came and tarnished this great country! Am I right?"*

It's that kind of crazy up in here!

Well, in October 2008, I said "enough of this shit!" (I think those were my exact words), started blogging, and proceeded to give that neglected prehistoric pachyderm some overdue attention. Reaction was mixed, but the reception was mostly considerate. Over the course of several months I was fortunate enough to build a readership, practically one reader at a time. It seemed some people had been dying to talk about the mammoth and were ever on the lookout for a suitable venue. *Loco in Yokohama* came along and met this need head-on. I've been blessed with some of the greatest readers: thoughtful, intelligent, critical and challenging; a burgeoning writer's wet dream.

Others were not so thrilled that I had the audacity to tell *my* stories. These *Happy-Go-Lucky Guys* (I call them) did not take too kindly to my negative words about *their* beloved Japan. They viewed and treated bitter malcontents (they call me) as a plague on two houses: That of the Japanese, and their own.

To be fair, some of these Happy-Go-Luckies were truly oblivious to the mammoth for, though they might occasionally smell the piles of dung it leaves everywhere, it did not reveal itself to them in its full glory. The Japanese would generally behave differently in their presence, for reasons that became clear the longer I stayed here, got to know people and observed the goings-on. One reason being that the reception whites receive in Japan is a bit different than the reception some other ethnic groups receive, especially Chinese and those of us of a darker hue. (Invariably, these Happy-Go-Lucky types were

Caucasians who think Japanese are colorblind and treat all foreigners equally). Some of these guys and gals will defend this notion by any means necessary.

The comments they'd leave on my posts would run the gamut, ranging from YouTube crude: *"You niggers make me sick with your constant whining! Kneel and suck it like the rest of us, and be glad no one's throwing a rope around your neck."*

To disbelief: *"You seem like a nice guy, Loco-sensei, and pretty intelligent, too. So I just can't understand how you can be so off when it comes to Japanese people. They're so harmless and polite. Maybe you're just a little over-sensitive, or misunderstanding them due to the language and cultural differences. Perhaps if you studied Japanese..."*

To something approaching solution-oriented: *"You apparently have an excess of energy, evidenced by your long, fascinating post, so why don't you put it to more productive use and do something about it? The onus is on you to change their minds. Writing blog posts in English just isn't going to cut it. Get out there and show them that black people aren't all the same. Some are really good people, smart and kind-hearted, like you. For God's sake, Loco, be a game changer, not a complainer."*

To dismissively condescending: *"Some people come to this magical and mysterious land with unstable minds and a certain amount of dung already encrusted in their nostrils. And, please forgive me for pointing this out but, particularly Negroes...ahem...I mean, people who are descendant from that dark, feral continent. Personally, I believe you people are born with trace amounts of dung in your noses, thus you smell it wherever you go. The further you travel from your own kind, the more pronounced the smell becomes. I'm pretty sure I've read a scientific study or two that has proven just that. So, I must conclude then that what you smell is your own stench! Why don't you go back and live among your own kind, where everything naturally reeks of dung, cause then you'll be more comfortable, no? And leave the Japanese to the people who understand them, accept them and love them for the adorable, unadulterated child-race that they are."*

With assurance that you'll find yourself in the minority of a minority, and the target of baffling conjecture and derisive censure from the majority, I began to understand why people avoided talking about the beast. It was easier to just live and let live, and tread the path of least resistance with a clothespin pinched on your nose.

But, I don't get down like that.

I welcomed these attacks. I wanted my ideas and assertions to be challenged. How else would I learn? How else could I grow as a writer and a thinker, and more importantly as a person? I took the hits, and believe me, they hurt sometimes. The downside of writing from the heart is that your heart is exposed, and nothing makes for a more attractive bulls-eye. But, the upside is, it's the only way to really reach people, anyway. So, I was, and still am, thankful for these castigations for they inspired me to embark on an exploration of how I came to hold the positions I do.

I thought long and hard about whether these pooh-poohers had a point. Had I come to Japan predisposed to see racism where it didn't exist? Had my experiences in America *disabled* me, rendering me ill-equipped to navigate through the racially opaque currents of life in Japan? Was it *I* who was the racist and, with vision tainted by this dark social impairment, saw it everywhere around me?

I needed to know if I was asking the right questions. *And,* I needed answers!

Distressed, I asked myself the most difficult question first:

Am I a racist?

And those feelings I had been harboring for years about many of the anonymous Japanese people I encounter on a regular basis all came to bear, and collectively, in an ensemble of brutal honesty, choired back at me a resounding, *"meh, who isn't?!"*

The indifference in the answer scared the shit out of me, and launched my exploration, in earnest. And, in what had become typical Loco fashion by that time, I started a series of posts related to my lifetime in the shadow of the race question, and gave this series a sincere yet provocative title: "Hi! My Name Is Loco and I am a Racist!"

The series was a *qualified* success! How did I measure this success? Well, for one, it was a frank discussion with, essentially, the world! Word of this series spread and readers chimed in not only from Japan and the U.S., but from developed and under-developed countries far and near with their thoughts on race. And, in the end (some 40 posts later) I had a much better understanding of myself and of the world around me.

Were all of my questions answered during this series? Unfortunately, not. Certain issues just don't easily avail themselves of resolution, racism prominent among them. Did I learn some of the right questions to ask? You bet!

Everything else – the increased attention to my blog, the accolades and *attaboys* – while gratifying, was just gravy. I knew my background wasn't your average person's, not even your average New Yorker's, but I was overwhelmed by how much interest it generated. And a good number of these readers damn near demanded that I write a book about this issue, promising they'd buy a copy.

Write a book about *this*??? Yeah, right! How could I write

a book about racism? Who the hell am I? I'm no scholar. I'm just a guy with a blog and a fairly interesting perspective and background.

So, initially, I dismissed the idea.

While I was writing the "My Name Is Loco..." series, I hoped I could exorcise these dark feelings within me, or at least confront my fears by dragging the little gremlins out of the closet and exposing them to the light; part catharsis, part analysis, part self (shock) therapy.

But, as I wrote my way down memory lane I noticed that there was a racial thread that had run through my life from childhood until the present; that race had not only played a significant role in my upbringing but a traumatic one. And, though I felt better having acknowledged and somewhat addressed my racism, I knew it wasn't going to be remedied by merely blogging about it. It was going to take some time and some doing.

And, that it might indeed make for an interesting book.

One I'd like to read, at least.

So, I had a change of heart and, after three years of blogging, I dusted off that publishing dream and got down to business.

The book you're about to read is the result. And all you guys who promised to buy a copy, here's your chance!

Amazon may be bursting at the cyber-seams, and the shelves of your local library may be warped with the weight of books by expats living in Japan, but there's NOTHING like the one you're about to read now.

Not even close.

*****

It is _not_ human nature to be racist. But, unfortunately, I'm still open to the idea that I might be wrong. I have not seen or heard any conclusive evidence (aside from a bunch of pseudo-science emanating from sources with a clear agenda of divisiveness) that we racists are born this way and that we will die this way, but not before passing our legacy of fear and hatred on to our children. I say "unfortunately" because if that _is_ the case, if this affliction is part of our DNA, then we are doomed! How do they say it? Rearranging deck chairs on the Titanic? That's _all_ of us! Just another species, like that woolly mammoth, soon to face annihilation at the hands of the same species that has given so many other species economy class tickets to extinction: our own. We're just a handful of holocausts, genocides, ethnic cleansings, and manifest destinies away from a man-made Armageddon.

Sorry to be all doom and gloom just then, but I'm sick of living in a world where so many people are forced to dwell in some form of denial because this issue threatens to tear asunder the very fabric of the world we're living in. Aren't you? Sure, it promises to tip the scales of class, power and privilege. But, so what! And, yeah, it has the potential to unleash forces of darkness that will dim even the most luminous signs of hope. But, no reward without risk, I say.

I'm of the mind that tackling racism – beginning with ones _own_ susceptibility – will ignite a beacon of light that will shine in dark rooms and even darker alleys of the soul, and guide humanity a leap closer to that promised land Martin Luther King dreamed about and the _Imagine_ nation John Lennon sang about; an aspiration I'd like to think the majority of us share.

For, to me, _this_ is the issue that defines us.

I wrote this book because I wanted to offer up my experience in hope that it will inspire others to tell their own stories, perhaps even question their own ideas about race.

Personally, I think that racism is like a virus; not necessarily a terminal one like HIV, but a chronic one like hepatitis. And that, with constant vigilance and conscious abstinence, it can be managed and perhaps one day even cured. The insidious nature of racism, though, is such that the very moment you let your guards down and get complacent, even for a moment, it can become acute and leave you *ass out!* At least, that's been my experience.

I've written this book because I feel it's my responsibility as a human being to use my meager gifts to at least *try* to make the world a better place. Truth, I believe, is a good starting point. And in this book, through some soul-wracking, I've endeavored to arrive at some rather elusive truths; at least they were for me. I'll leave it to you to decide if I've succeeded or not.

*****

To my way of thinking, there are three different types of racists. By no means are these types hard-and-fast, though. They are as follows:

1- The Shit Kicker: This person is a racist due to having bought into the pseudo-science, media distortions, and the heirloom of misinformation, stereotypes and prejudices handed down to them by their parents or indoctrinated into them by the society in which they live. And, as a result, walk this planet with a feeling of racial, ethnic or cultural superiority.

The shit kicker believes that there are different breeds of human and this breeding is signified by color or ethnicity. Their most distinguishing feature is that they are often inclined to *actively* participate in both covert and overt actions that demonstrate they've completely succumbed to these beliefs; the worst of which are the flagrant use of racial slurs and epithets to demean and divide, race-based exclusivity and other discriminatory practices, lynchings, genocide, and so on...basically the darker qualities of human nature that can be seen in the world on any given day.

2- The Posers: These are people who, like the shit kicker, have been brainwashed, but only partially so; their brains are stuck in the spin cycle. They've been spoon-fed the same malarkey but, as a result of multicultural / multiracial experience or education, have not surrendered to delusions of grandeur and superiority. They'll likely have "friends" of various races, may even date (though marriage would be a stretch) outside their race, acknowledge that all humans, essentially, have the same capacity for good or evil, and recognize the inarguable truth of human equality.

However, their minds and hearts have but so much resistance to the constant bombardment of misinformation and propaganda, and living amid the resulting debris has had a detrimental effect on their capacity for reason and objectivity. Some have been traumatized by the preponderance of flagrant ignorance, fear mongering, hate crimes, and discriminatory practices that continue to be pervasive. Others retain a hardly manageable level of jealous possessiveness for privilege or entitlement they enjoy as a result of racism, or envy privileges and entitlements they associate with another race.

Nevertheless, they're in a position to deny their racism (to themselves and others) because *some of their best friends are* such and such a race. But, they're not above tolerance of, and may even use on occasion, the language of racial distortions and distinctions. They may feel a varying level of shame and guilt at this tolerance, but over time they often acquire the ability to alleviate it by accepting their *victimization* as an unavoidable consequence of living in a world they believe has always been divvied up on the basis of race.

3-The Oblivious: These people believe that they see all human beings as equals, although there are (to their minds) clear disparities based on race, culture and ethnicity. They can't see the contradiction in this position. They simply hold on to these beliefs as if they were self-evident. Thus they have no clue that they are racists.

After all, they're good people, kind to animals, children and the elderly, charitable, a profound desire for a peaceful world free of hate, and they'd certainly *never* intentionally harm another person based on race. Thus they feel the world would be a better place if other people could be more like them. But fate has seen to it that they can't. They can't because of these *natural* differences. It's unfortunate, hell, it's a *damn* pity. But, it's the natural order of things, and, with few exceptions, there's nothing that can be done about that.

To the Oblivious, a Poodle, a Doberman Pincher, and a Golden Retriever are all dogs, of course, but clearly one cannot be expected to think of them the same way, treat them equally, or expect comparable behavior from them. So, why should humans be any different? The key to racial harmony, from the Oblivious perspective, is acknowledgment, acceptance and tolerance – if possible – of these differences. And, in the Oblivious mind, these beliefs do not constitute racism. To the contrary, they often qualify as an enlightened world view or, at a minimum, basic common sense.

And, just in case you're wondering, I'm a poser!

Before I continue, I think I need to make something clear.

There's a stigma attached to the label *racist*. The word has been demonized. It has come to represent one of the lowest forms of human degeneracy, akin to pedophile, Nazi, troll, telemarketer and bill collector (OK, maybe not the last two, but you know what I mean). Demonizing racists is not solution-oriented. It only chases the problem underground and encourages denial, in all its forms. This is what shuts down discussion and introspection, and why when some of you saw the title of this book, it made you feel uncomfortable. I think, with the amount of racism running rampart in the world today, we need to remove that stigma, and see it for what it really is. It's not some dark aberration that only people lacking in morals and common decency are subject to. I think it's more akin to adulterer, hypocrite or liar. Certainly not admirable people, but for damn sure these are the people in your neighborhood, in your office, in your carpool, in your living room and maybe even in your mirror…and they ain't *all* bad.

Some of the greatest thinkers and heroes in the history of mankind were racists. George Washington was a racist, and so was Thomas Jefferson, just to name a couple. But, these men played crucial roles in the formation of, as President Obama so eloquently said, "…a union that could be and should be perfected over time." These men did extraordinary things, and that's *part* of the reason they are not remembered only for being racists. I'm sure they had the capacity to love and the need to be loved just as much as people do today. So, when I say, "I am a racist," please keep in mind that racists have a long history of achievement and beneficence toward humankind.

*****

I don't pretend to be totally objective (if that's even possible). This book is a body of empirical knowledge gained one hard knock at a time, laced with an innate awareness that, I admit, is not batting a thousand. It has led me astray on a number of occasions, but retains my trust. For I've learned a great deal through these failures.

And school ain't out just yet. The chrysalis is still about me. I'm still learning things about life and about me, every day. Some lessons are pretty straight forward, but most I learn the way fools learn to be just a little less foolish, and children just a little less childish. The way winners say is the *only* way, and I hope to God they're right, because I learn things increment by painfully tiny increment…in other words, the hard way.

Going through changes this way may not be ideal, but one thing's for certain: I'm less likely to forget what I've learned, for these lessons will have left an unsightly imprint on my thick skull, cankers on my damaged heart, and scar tissue on my solace-seeking soul.

And, maybe, just maybe, *this* is the material that butterfly wings are made of, and why they're so awesome to behold.

CONVERSATION #1

I Don't Want To Believe

This conversation took place during a lesson at a cafe in Yokohama between me and a Japanese private student.

Me: How are you doing today?

Private Student: ...I'm...I'm chotto, wakannai...(I don't know)

Me: Are you ok? You seem troubled. How was work? Tough day?

Student: No, I was not busy. It was quiet day.

Me: That's good.

Student: Demo, saa (But) This morning on the train...

Me: Ohhh no! Not Again? Chikan? (Subway pervert)

Student: Oh no no no! Not this time...

Me: What happened? Another suicide?

Student: No, not suicide. Chotto matteite. (Give me a moment)

Me: Ok

Student: On the train, it was crowded. And there was a black guy.

Me: Uh huh.

Student: He was sitting anoo...muko...across to where I was sitting?

Me: Across *from* where you were sitting...

Student: Yes...across from me. Nobody sit next to him.

23

Me: I see. So, what happened?

Student: That's all. That happened.

Me: Oh…Oh? Did it upset you?

Student: Hai! Yes, it upset me very much. You have told me this happens to you but…

Me: But what? You didn't believe me?

Student: I believe you. But I don't want to believe.

*****

I

AN EMPTY SEAT ON A CROWDED TRAIN

T he doors slid open on the nearly vacant subway car and a mass of passengers piled in. All the available seats were filled in a wild flurry.

Well, *almost* all.

People either spurned the empty seat or ignored it as if it were occupied.

A cute little girl – all of four or five – spotted it, and made a blind dash for it. Her mother, almost violently, yanked her away just as she reached it, hissing, "abunai!" (dangerous). As Mom dragged her away, the little girl glanced back at the seat, looking for the danger her mother perceived but she had not. Where was it?

Two curious eyes quickly scanned the area near the empty seat, slowing upon the people on either side of it. One was a woman about her mother's age with pretty hair, a stern face but with soft features. A little tense, but very normal looking, the girl probably thought. Her eyes then darted to the far side of the empty seat, and the person seated there was…well, it was definitely a person, but unlike the people she encountered regularly; he was huge, with *dark* skin, like that funny guy on the TV commercial with the talking dog for a father…a friendly face, but not happy like the TV guy… a little sad…or maybe angry…

Then she felt her head being manually turned away from the dark man, by her mother. But, she couldn't resist her curiosity and turned back to take another look. And, in the artless expressions of a child, curiosity gave way to a dreadful comprehension. *Oh! I see what scared Mommy! Now I understand why she hurt my arm! She was afraid…of him! He must be a bad man!*

And, just like that, an innocent child became the newest

recruit to the cult of *Different Therefore Dangerous.*

The roughest days are those when I'm forced to bear witness to the birth of a racist, to watch as a child's mind is perverted as a matter of course. It's enough to break your heart.

Let it go, let it go, I chanted to myself several times in succession, like an incantation, while shaking my head like the action might help jar the image of a child's crossing to the dark side from its fixed position. I must've looked loco to the other passengers.

There was a time when a scene like that would make me want to holler. Now it just makes me feel uptight. Has my skin toughened or have I steeled something inside of me against this kind of tactless cruelty?

As the train pulled away from the station, I closed my eyes and took a couple of deep breaths, willing myself to uncoil my mind and unclench the grip I had on the handrail beside me. Behind my eyelids was a tranquil sight: black, beautiful emptiness.

It was a peace I knew would last only as long as my eyes were shut.

*****

Back when I was fresh from the States, the empty seat was troubling, but silently so, like a sullen mute thinking hateful thoughts transmitted through cold eyes and pouted cheeks, and I could live with that. Besides, I was easily distracted by all the stimuli in my new environment. Everything in the subway car held my interest, from the advertisements, to the design of the car and the contrast of shapes and sizes with the ones I was accustomed to back home. I was in my element. I've always adored locomotives, and the discrepancies I discovered fascinated me! I was a kid in a candy store, and the abundant eye-candy at every turn only served to emphasize that. My adventure was underway; a whole new world, full of wonders, raced by outside the train's windows.

But, soon enough, as is always the case, the awe began to wane. The candy in my environment started tasting too sweet and getting stuck in my dental work. I wanted it to melt in my mouth, but instead it melted in my hands. I rolled with it, though. This was to be expected. Life certainly hadn't been a sweet shop before I came to Japan, so I knew very well how to get by without it.

But, without distractions in every direction, the mute seated beside me, disguised as an empty seat, kept coming into view. *"What's with this thing, anyway? And what's wrong with these people that they so often find sitting beside me verboten?"* But, I'd dismiss these questions before they could take root. I was in a new society, I told myself, so naturally things were different. And the amount of eccentricity I'd encountered thus far in Japan almost made the empty seat into just another cultural quirk among many. Taking a tablet called: "this is *not* America," once-a-day helped a lot, too.

Besides, the mute didn't insist on the same level of attention I was paying everything else. It just *knew* it would eventually get it. It reminded me of an over-confident opponent in a chess match, eight, nine, ten moves away from another notch in the belt, as it sat there looking back at me. I could feel it waiting for me to make a move, one of a couple of moves it anticipated I would make, so it could cut my defenses to pieces, and cry, "mate!"

But, I refused to engage.

Then, one day, out of the blue, the mute pulled a Helen Keller and found a voice! Or perhaps I'd given it a voice. It sounded like mine: same lilting intonation, same baritonal Brooklyn bravado accented with ghetto elitist.

"What's wrong with you, Loco? It scolded. What do you care how these people get down? So what they've chosen not to sit next to you! Big fucking deal! That's their prerogative! You've got better things to think about than where people plant their asses, don't you? Life is short, my brother! Don't waste it sweating what these characters do! It ain't worth it, yo!"

I didn't know where this was coming from...I wasn't sweating anything! Why did I feel the need to tell myself *not* to do something I wasn't even doing? I agreed wholeheartedly with this assessment. *Of course* I had better things to think about...duh! I had a language to learn, and stories to write. There was money to be made, and girls lined up for a taste of the outside world I represented. *Fuck* I care about an empty seat. Yet, the obvious was being overstated for a reason.

This denial continued for a while, as I tried to keep my life filled with things that made denying the empty seat the attention it was due a prerogative.

Maybe a year later, the seat started condescending, on my behalf. Just like it knew how much I hated condescension! That should have been a red flag. An inanimate object knowing my triggers so well should have raised all kinds of alarms. But, it didn't.

"Cut them some slack, Loco. They're a simple people," the empty seat whispered. *"Closed-minded, arrogant, ignorant, unsophisticated, and unaccustomed to the ideas you personify! You're gonna have to accept that fact! Embrace it, even. Keep in mind this is their tiny island lair, and they're a homogeneous race only a handful*

of generations from both isolation from the civilized world and nuclear devastation! You, on the other hand, are the product of advanced citizenship, direct from the thriving and throbbing cultural center of the known universe, living among modern day savages who actually think they're advanced! Your presence here spits in the face of their delusions and desires. Of course they shun you. You are the present and the future! They're history! Literally, a dying breed desperately clinging to rapidly decomposing ideas. No wonder they're afraid of you. They don't know you are the light at the end of the dark tunnel of ignorance in which they dwell! They think you're a bullet train racing toward them! You represent the change they most fear!"

That bit of abasement boosted my self-esteem and pacified me for a spell. Hell! I *was* a fully actualized adult living in the *real* world. *They* were dense and callow babes in the woods. I was more than different. I was *better* than them! I rode that wave of superiority to shore whenever I needed to. I smiled at the empty seat, knowing it was a sign that my feet were planted firmly on the moral high ground. *You know you're hitting the right chords when people either hate you or love you,* so I must be doing something right, I told myself, because I had my fair share of both.

Then, a couple of years later, and without any preamble, the seat took a different tack. One of those chess moves where you emotionally prepare yourself to lose by envisioning your finger tipping over your king in surrender.

What it did was, it stopped echoing my thoughts and started eerily amplifying what I imagined to be theirs. It would explain, apologetically: *"It's nothing personal...we just find you threatening, that's all. You're an over-sized member of a notoriously loud and ostentatious people. Besides, it's common knowledge among us that you have an odor we would find disagreeable and frankly unendurable. It is not our intention to offend you, mind you. We'd just prefer risking offense to jeopardizing our well-being or peace of mind. Sure, that's not especially kind, and goes against our famously polite nature, but it is reasonable, isn't it? After all, we have no experience dealing with your kind, and we don't speak your language, so we default to* better safe than sorry. *It's just our way."*

I'd never heard such plain spoken and obtuse disparagement. Nothing in my self-proclaimed superior background had prepared me for such absurdity. The empty seat had judged me, handed down a decree that I had no hope of appealing. An echo of the *guilty* verdict seemed to issue from the seat and rebound off the walls of the train car and the scornful faces of the passengers in an endless reverberation of treachery, and I really wasn't sure how to respond to it; or even if I should respond to it at all.

Contentment vanquished, my smile withdrew defensively into my heart like the head of a turtle into its shell, and in its place I'd don a scowl and wear it like a mask over my sadness. I'd glimpse it from time to time reflected in the windows I used to peer out of at a new playground for my imagination, and in the eyes of my fellow passengers when they would dare to meet mine. Indignation became a weapon I'd brandish on the people around me (because I'd look pretty foolish aiming it at an empty seat, now wouldn't I)?

But, the empty seat would not be intimidated by my angry mien. It had evolved from spiteful to tyrannical. It would settle for nothing but utter surrender. *Kowtow or suffer my wrath,* it sneered, insolently laughing at me and my attempts to maintain some semblance of self-respect and dignity.

I almost held my ears when it pumped up the volume, and broadcasted the condemnations of a subway car full of

Japanese, saying: *"We don't like you. We don't trust you. We think you're a bad person, a pitiful person, an inferior human lacking morality. You steal. You habitually womanize and rape. You commit violent acts against innocent people – like us – as a matter of course. Everybody knows your kind embraces the baser human instincts. That's why you've been cursed with that dark skin; makes it easier for us to identify you. You're dangerous to our personal safety and our very way of life. And, moreover, there's a good chance you carry some incurable Western plague, virtually non-existent in our island paradise until you and your ilk came along. You must know by now that your presence here is not welcomed! Why don't you make Japan a paradise again...and take your black ass back to the jungle or ghetto that produced you!!"*

"SHUT THE FUCK UP ALREADY!!" I yelled at the empty seat, clearing almost half the car at the next station.

The empty seat smiled, and cried, "Checkmate!"

That was the day Loco was conceived. The day I realized I needed an ally, even if I had to procreate him.

Like Freddy Krueger, who was known as "the son of a 100 maniacs" because his mother was locked in an asylum and gang raped by the patients, Loco was the son of 100 empty seats sodomizing my self-esteem.

*****

I opened my eyes as the train pulled into Akabane Station in Tokyo. Many people got off and just as many filed in. The seats that had been made available by exiting passengers were, with a surge, snatched up. It was like an aggressive game of musical chairs, only imagine the game if there were dozens of contestants, one chair, and they were not allowed to touch one

32

another.

Two salarymen and an Office Lady (OL) were on a beeline for the empty seat beside me. The woman was in trouble, though: Chivalry hasn't died here. It's never lived here. In fact, the opposite of chivalry has been the order of the day since randy Samurai roamed the streets of Yoshiwara.

On final approach, the OL noticed the jockeying salarymen and hit the brakes. Then, one of the salarymen looked up, at me, and rather startlingly by-passed the seat and plowed his way into the mass of boarding passengers. They spread for his thrust like a sphincter and clasped shut once he'd passed through.

The other rushing salaryman noticed the first's odd behavior as he turned to sit down, a bit baffled by what had transpired. As his ass drew closer to the bench he happened to glance to his side, perhaps to make sure he wasn't about to sit on someone's lap or belongings, and realized, with unambiguous alarm, why the other guy had behaved so oddly.

He froze a moment in mid descent, looking like he'd had a sudden back spasm or like he'd seen a turd in the seat beneath him, before snapping back to an erect position. I came to hate him in that moment; an impotent hate. As much as if I were bound and gagged and while in this helpless state he'd spat in my face. I could almost feel his spittle dripping from my chin. His contempt was such that his eyes never touched me again as he strode away. He was immediately engulfed by a mob of his brethren who apparently shared his aversion to the empty seat beside me. Several glanced at it, then subsequently at me, but not one approached it. I came to hate them, too. Their unanimity put their nameless Asian faces on my shit list.

As much as a person can get used to harboring such thoughts, I'd gotten used to it. But, I habitually check to gauge how other people feel about it, always hoping to catch a look of surprise or disgust, or any acknowledgment from anyone. Even one soul would have done wonders at that moment. Sometimes I get lucky and someone will look at me with the barest hint of commiseration. But, that morning, it was not to be.

The eyes of the quicker people, those who were quite skilled at avoiding being caught staring through a creepy intuitive anticipation, seemed to find the ubiquitous cell phone, manga comic book, appointment book, or make-up mirror of immense interest. Quick, yes, but a fraction of a second too slow for my taste. Some of the slower rubberneckers awkwardly found things in the vicinity of my person captivating…like the advertisements above my head, or the window behind me (the one with the shade drawn to ward off the morning sun's glare) or the toes of my shoes, or the hand of the man standing nearest to the standing room in front of me that also remained vacant, or, hell, the atomic particles in the space between us, the vacuum of air that encircled their heads, eyes glazed in a pseudo Zen-like state of ultra-unawareness.

It was kind of creepy, actually. Like they'd photoshopped me *and* the empty seat out of their reality.

I used to wonder what the seat must say to these people sitting around pretending not to see it. Its emptiness is as plain as my presence, so there's no way they cannot acknowledge it on some level. They *are* human. Surely it speaks to them, as well. I imagine it must be a learning experience, a moment of self-discovery. I'd like to think the empty seat challenges them by saying something like, *"I can tell by that post-frontal lobotomy expression on your face that you probably didn't know this about your fellow citizens, did you? Well, now you do, so what now?"*

I put life on pause for a second and looked at the forsaken

seat beside me. It was physically ugly, as well, made of this greenish-blue streaked polyester fabric, darkened by age, dust, and the residue of thousands of sweaty Asian asses; stains and odors that will never come out.

My eyes slid over to the woman seated on the opposite side of this ugliness. She sat a little stiffly like if there were a partition made of bedrock between her and it. She had an attractive face but every time her eyes drifted my direction she would have a nervous fit and start repeatedly finger brushing her hair out of her face, tucking it behind her ear (from which it would fall back to its previous position almost immediately) while ever so slightly inching further away, like the partition was hot.

I used to break down sometimes and place my bag in the seat, or spread my legs so that it didn't gape so much. You know, to try and make it less obvious, therefore less affecting. Or, make it appear to others that it was empty on account of my being an inconsiderate asshole – an assessment far preferable to the ones playing out in my head. Other times, in a desperate effort to hold on to the good mood I'd begun the day with, I'd decline to look in its direction; *out of sight, out of mind* being the logic there. But, that rarely worked either. My pains to pretend it didn't exist only made it stand out in sharper relief.

This day I decided to try something new. I just sat there admiring the enormity of this black hole of humiliation, inviting it to take its best licks. Maybe then I could just move on. I glared at it, with laser intensity. *Give me your best shot!* I gazed long enough for the seat to start to transmogrify, to shed its relationship with reality and forge one with the surreal. Like the melting wax of a burning candle, feeding on the flame. Only I was the flame it was feeding on. I blinked my eyes stupidly, and looked away hoping to break the spell. Only, now, I could

35

still feel *it* feeding on me; gorging on my goodwill toward men.

It was, as I had requested, giving me its best shot!

Within moments it had consumed my capacity to see the people around me as anything but a collective, a hive mind, a swarm of nasty little worker bees, each with a teeny-tiny stinger, pricking me in turn.

A subway car full of pricks!

I needed a distraction.

Then I remembered my kanji cards. Kanji is one of the three types of writing, not including English, used here. It's an ancient style of writing, used by the Chinese for centuries before it made its way across the sea separating these two historical foes.

I used to find studying kanji very gratifying. One of the few things more aggravating than the nonsense I have to put up with on the train was the loss of my independence. Back home in New York I was very independent, of course. I could read, write, and speak English fluently. But, here in Asia, that little girl who just learned the reason why I'm a scary person – cause Mama knows best — was probably more literate than I was.

So, I whipped the cards out.

Kanji is one of those Asian knacks that many Japanese assume to be as indigestible by Western brains as rotten soy beans (a Japanese breakfast staple) are for Western stomachs which, I got to tell you, motivated me all the more to tackle it. Just to see the crestfallen mock-surprised look on their faces when I read a Japanese newspaper would make it worthwhile.

The train pulled into another station and I looked up to see where we were. As more people piled in I noticed a boarding salaryman spot the empty seat. I could see the surprise register on his face for an empty seat is a rare sight on a rush hour train.

Then our eyes met, and something lit up in his.

Oh fuck!

At that moment, several people were hovering around my seat trying desperately to appear unaware of my presence in their midst. Like subway performers doing some sort of synchronized miming. The objective seemed to be for the team to coordinate their movements in such a way as to suggest that they were centered on a sumo wrestler, but if one were to look at the wrestler directly it would mean death to all team members. I was the wrestler. Unfortunately, they weren't going to live out the day cause one bitch kept neurotically sneaking a peak over her shoulder at me while adjusting her handbag from my seated reach.

This salaryman that had spotted me, after having shoved his way through the mime troupe, now stood over me smiling and, in passable and highly audible English, asked could he sit beside me. It was as if he believed the empty seat was a stool at a crowded bar that I had been holding for a friend who hadn't arrived yet. He looked convincingly unaware that the seat was a megaphone through which the people in the vicinity shared their viewpoints on how the world should be.

I looked up at him and shrugged.

He took that for a yes.

He had no way of knowing that by this time, I had given up on Japanese people. I used to feel a gleam of hope when someone sat beside me. I'd take notes to see if I'd done anything different. Maybe there was a pattern. Maybe there was something I could do to encourage more people to take the plunge. But after years of inconclusive experimentation now I just wonder why the person broke ranks.

The empty seat (and my position beside it) seems to

attract certain types of Japanese people. I've met a number of interesting people as a result of this magnetism for some of the brave souls who've filled it have also worked up the courage to speak to me. And eventually divulge that they have either traveled abroad, or have earnestly studied English at some point in their lives, as if they understood that their taking the seat was something I'd be curious about.

Not to suggest that no one "normal" (that is, without an agenda) ever sits beside me. Of course they do. And sometimes it's done so naturally that it makes me wonder if I'm delusional.

However, the most frequent occupants, unfortunately, are the guys or girls who are just fascinated with *anything* foreign. Gaijin Freaks, my girlfriend, Aiko, called them. It feels really creepy being someone's fetish, I got to tell you. These fetishists are mostly male and they *really* make my skin crawl.

This guy kept glancing over at my kanji cards. I knew he was going to try and strike up a conversation at some point. But still he managed to startle me when he abruptly yelped in mock surprise, "You studies kanji, don't you? Waaaa! That's very wonderful!!"

I used to be under the impression that I wanted to fit in, assimilate as it were, and that *politeness* was one of the keys, so I muscled a smile onto my face and aimed it at him.

"You are American?"

I nodded, my face still poised for a yearbook portrait.

"Oh, where in America you come from?"

He was getting all giddy like he'd finally found a receptive gaijin, and all the time, work and enormous fees he'd invested, studying at schools like the one I was headed to that day, were about to pay dividends.

"Hawaii," I lied.

He looked stumped for a moment like I'd replied *Addis Ababa*. Either he wasn't sure that Hawaii was in the U.S., wasn't aware that black people lived in Hawaii, or maybe Hawaii just wasn't foreign enough for him – Hawaii being the number one travel destination for Japanese visiting America. Or, maybe it was something deeper. Like maybe his grandfather had been a fighter pilot in some Japanese bomber squadron and used to brag that he personally sank a destroyer in Pearl Harbor, so Giddy-san felt a pang of guilt sitting next to a black Hawaiian. Whatever the reason, some of the glow in his eyes dissipated.

I felt bad about having lied to him, then. His disappointment was so palpable. But, at the same time, I didn't care how he felt because I wasn't in the mood to be his or anyone's object of worship. I'd prefer the humiliating empty seat to a person who'd only sat there to practice his English or mentally ejaculate all over me.

"I see," he nodded. And kept nodding, like he was thinking of something to say and nodding was the mechanism that set his thoughts in motion. The nodding was getting annoying so I returned my attention to my kanji and hoped he would leave me be to study. I pretended to concentrate.

"Oh, that is very difficult kanji!" he said. "Even *we* cannot read kanji sometimes!"

The kanji character I was holding at the moment was the kanji for eat. I cut my eyes in his direction.

"*We* who?" I asked, because 'we' had to be some unfortunate people by my estimation if they didn't know how to read that character.

"Eeeee?" he gasped. "Wehooo? Is that Hawaii language?"

I almost laughed. "I mean, who is this 'we' that can't read this kanji?"

"Oh!" he shouted, and laughed. "*WE* is Japanese."

39

I looked around the crowded subway car at *WE the Japanese* and wondered how many of them couldn't read the card in my hand. Some of them were watching the guy beside me so intensely that they hadn't noticed I was watching them. He didn't seem to care, though, so preoccupied with explaining to me about this *WE*. Or perhaps he just didn't care so much what this *WE* thought.

So, I sat there with a shit-eating grin listening to him explain, in painful English, why reading kanji was so much more difficult than reading English. A spiel I'd heard dozens of times since I arrived here. How the English alphabet has only 26 letters while there are thousands of kanji characters. A not-so subtle way of saying *Japanese brains are able to process and retain so much more than western brains* it seemed to me.

I kept smiling, though, having gotten somewhat accustomed to being inundated with the Japanese perspective, and feeling the futility of responding substantially. To explain to him why his simplified conclusion was insultingly inaccurate would require either a higher level of Japanese on my part or a higher level of English on his. And that had been the case each and every time I'd been accosted with this bizarre claim.

"I'm so sorry," I said, cutting him off. "But I have a kanji test today and I'm going to need every bit of my limited brain capacity to pass it, as you well know. So I need to study now!"

He looked taken aback, at first, and then began bowing and apologizing for disturbing me. And, again, I felt bad for lying.

At the next stop, he stood, apologized again, and bowed to me on his way out.

There was another mad revolution of passengers and all the empty seats were taken.

Well, almost all...

2

AN AUSSIE, A KIWI, AND A COLORED GUY

When I first came to Japan, I lived with an Australian and a New Zealander. Both guys were very cool, very funny, and *very* white.

Over the years I'd worked through my race issues, so I didn't think anything of it. Ok, make that, I didn't think *much* of it. But, while celebrating our first night together in Asia, listening to some tunes and getting to know each other over a dozen cans of beer, I learned I still had some residual kinks to work out, when I told Joe: "Eminem's pretty talented for a white boy, but I wouldn't even mention him in the same *language* with Rakim, NAS and Biggie!"

Joe (he was the Kiwi) hadn't even mentioned Eminem, who, though white, was the most popular hip-hop artist that year. He'd just asked me who were the best rappers in my opinion — one of those innocuous type questions that white people tended to ask me unaware, in most cases, that it was a trigger. To Joe, mine was simply an opinion he valued because not only was I, well, black, but I hailed from NYC, the hip-hop capital of the world.

What made it worse is that Joe had just nodded and rolled with my racist hiccup, like he'd expected me to hold that kind of prejudice against Eminem.

And to top it all off, it was an obese lie!

Though I wholeheartedly believed that Eminem wasn't quite at the level of Rakim, NAS and Biggie at the time (who just happened to all be black) he definitely warranted mention alongside them, as far as lyrical ability was concerned. And, if I were really being honest, I would have said that he was much more talented and far cleverer than most of the other black hip-hop artists out there.

And, just like that, I learned I still had some racial wrinkles that could use a little spray starch.

*****

So, how did I come to live with two white cats?

I'd taken this job with an English Language school called NEON that was as ubiquitous in Japan as Starbucks are in Midtown Manhattan, making the company one of the top recruiters of foreign workers countrywide. It follows that they tried their utmost to make relocating to Japan as painless as possible.

The upside of this support is that they provided us employees with apartments at relatively reasonable rates that didn't require us to go through the rigors, expense and humiliation of doing so in a language and a culture unfamiliar, and unfriendly, to most of us. For example, a Japanese landlord is entitled to a non-refundable gratuity, equal to a month's rent, in addition to the deposit, and are notorious for legally rejecting foreign applicants based primarily on the fact that they are not Japanese.

The drawback of NEON's assistance, however, is that you often find yourself in a roommate situation with absolute strangers, thrown together randomly, and forced to find a way to get along.

Not that it should matter. People are people (I told myself) but I'd never met any New Zealanders or Australians before we shared this three-bedroom apartment.

If it weren't for *Lord of the Rings,* New Zealand wouldn't have even existed in my world. As for Australians, yeah, sure, I was a big Mel Gibson and Russell Crowe fan, loved Olivia Newton John in *Grease* and that song of hers, *Magic,* still gets hummed in the shower occasionally, and Crocodile Dundee was cool. But, that was pretty much the extent of my knowledge about Australian people.

That didn't stop me from having it in for them, though.

You see, Australia's aboriginal people appear to favor people of African descent, and I grew up in an environment where everything of African descent was placed high on a pedestal. Injustices committed against native people of any race were intolerable, as well. Though I'd never done any research into the matter, I was predisposed to believe the Aborigine in Australia were treated by its European assailants about as well as America's *settlers* treated the aboriginal population it encountered. Such is the nature of invasion and conquest.

It didn't help any that Greg, the Australian, while regaling Joe and I with otherwise fascinating tales from *Down Under*, was the kind of guy who managed to somehow innocently refer to black people as "colored" and not-so innocently refer to Aborigines as "Abos" characterizing them as "useless uneducated drunks who wanted nothing more than to be separate from civilization."

Another way of saying savages.

*****

I was the only black person at the NEON branch where I taught initially.

Most of the Japanese students had never experienced being in close proximity to someone of African descent so I was something of a celebrity to some of them and, to put it mildly, a curiosity to others. Even to some of my fellow English instructors (mostly Australian, British and Canadian) I was a novelty, as much for my race as for my place of birth. Most had never met a genuine New Yorker before.

I'd be lying if I said I never experienced this phenomenon before. Even in NY, at some of the companies I'd worked for, I was the only black person to ever hold a particular position or work in a certain department, which often required me to "represent" an entire race. So, as a NEON instructor, I would occasionally suffer flashbacks, like a Vietnam vet suffering from post-traumatic stress disorder.

Every night I left this trying environment and went home to two loud-talking, heavy drinking, guitar playing roommates. I didn't really have a problem with them at all, though. Everything probably would have continued as such if we had been living in what's known here as a Gaijin House (apartment building or house where only foreigners live). But we were living in a mansion (a Japanese apartment complex) where we were one of three apartments rented by foreigners while the remaining apartments were all rented by Japanese.

And *they* had a problem with us. How do I know? Well, you'd think I'd know this because of the dirty looks I received, or the knocks on the door and walls in the night, or hate mail from anonymous parties slid under the door, or "Go Home gaijin" painted in graffiti on the door, or any number of heads-up like that.

Nope.

This is Japan.

If I happened to run into one of our Japanese neighbors and if, upon seeing me, they didn't manage to scurry back into their apartments in time or in any direction aside from mine, they would display a brand of kindness that would leave me with the impression they were going to submit my name for president of the Tenant's Association.

Instead their complaints went to the landlord, and the landlord went to our employer, who in this case was the guarantor for our apartment. And our employer in turn would call and bitch us out.

Or, rather, bitch *me* out!

My cell phone rang one afternoon in those early days and on the other line was some British accent with an attitude telling me testily that *I* had better follow the rules as laid down in the rental agreement I'd signed (basically instructing us to behave as if we were mutes because the walls may not be made of paper like they were in earlier times in Japan, but they weren't much thicker), or face dire consequences.

Rules I had been following not so much to a "T" but as much I ever follow rules I feel to be a little on the anal side.

Rules my roommates, however, did not so much break as never even acknowledged.

After the call I got more than a little vexed, though. There's something about being reprimanded by the British that I could never really stomach. Intentionally or not, they always seemed to be condescending or patronizing. And NEON management was swarming with them. That night I caught up with the Aussie and the Kiwi in the living room, living it up as usual. I marched in and called a meeting for the following night. They'd said "cool!" That they, too, had been meaning to get at me about something. Which, to me, implied that they had already huddled about me.

Mind you, the two of them didn't know one another either when we moved in.

What the fuck??

"Fine, whatever."

*****

I arrived home the following night to find my roommates sitting in the living room. I gave them a distracted "what's up" in greeting, slid my room door open, went in and slid it shut behind me.

I was tired. A NEON day had the potential to be torturous. Teachers avoided me, or interacted with me ultra-gingerly, because they'd come to realize (with a heap of help from me) that they had no idea how to speak to me without saying racially off-color and often offensive shit. And the Japanese students had no idea how to speak to *anybody* but other Japanese. And had an irritating tendency not to ask questions to learn about you, but rather to have the ignorant notions and stereotypes floating around in their heads confirmed. But, for a steady paycheck and to maintain my visa status I had to kneel and suck on it more often than anyone should ever have to kneel and suck on such a thing. So, yeah, I was beat.

I turned on my computer and was planning to do some writing about the daily grind to purge it from my system, when I heard Joe call me from the living room.

"Yeah?" I replied.

"We're meeting tonight, right?"

"Oh shit! I forgot all about it!"

I came back into the living room and the two of them were watching me. Joe looked high or drunk, but he often did. Greg looked dark.

"You wanna go first?" Greg offered but with a tone that suggested he had something burning to get off his chest and if he didn't get it off right that second he would spontaneously burst into flames and take half of the apartment complex with

47

him.

"Nah, you can go first." I said. "But, let me just say something before you do. I want to thank both of you for taking the time to meet this evening and I apologize for forgetting about the meeting, even though it was my idea. Lucky thing I came straight home, eh?"

They both nodded, Greg's eyes glared impatiently.

"Ok, well, I don't think we need to make any rules for this meeting. We're all, well, I believe we all have respect for one another and won't get too carried away. But I should tell you, I come from a place where people in general are pretty direct. And I intend to be direct. I invite you both to do the same."

"Ok," Joe said. "You stink!"

"Yeah," Greg added, "Do all colored guys smell like shit, or is it just you?"

"What!?"

"YOU STINK!" Greg reiterated loudly, like I was hard of hearing. "Every time you open your room door you stink up the whole house!"

I couldn't believe what I was hearing. Not to mention how I was hearing it. I mean, men stink. Hell, people stink, in general. That's why man made deodorant and cologne and douche and perfumes and incense and what not. People produce some god-awful funk, and as evolution went on I guess we just got used to human stench, as long as it wasn't extraordinarily reeking. And I didn't reek! I showered daily, sometimes twice. I wore Speed Stick deodorant and Polo cologne. My foot odor might have been an issue, but since we'd moved in my shoes had been in the entrance area and I monitored the smell carefully, marking the improvement my shoe-removing life in Japan had garnered.

I was pretty sure my hygiene was not the issue here, but for the life of me I couldn't figure out what it was.

"I don't know what you guys are talking about," I cried. "I don't stink, and neither does my room!"

"You can't *smell* that shit, mate?" Joe asked incredulously. "Smells like you have an animal in there."

"Yeah, a dead animal!" Greg added with disgust. "You're not doing some dodgy religious shit in there, are you?"

"I...I..." I was flabbergasted. I couldn't even respond. I'd told them to be direct but damn! I was wholly unprepared for the intensity in their voices, the venom in their words. I wondered if they were pulling some elaborate gag. It was either that or my room really did stink to high hell.

Looking at their faces, I was leaning towards the latter.

"I don't know what to say."

"Try saying you're gonna stop doing whatever the hell it is you're doing in your room that has the house smelling like a zoo," Greg said.

"Listen, there must be some mistake!"

Joe, the more reasonable of the two, asked what it could be. I told him I didn't know. He shook his head.

*****

Joe and I had actually arrived at our new apartment on the same day, having ridden on the same train from the Tokyo headquarters of NEON. I saw him that morning, at the other end of the car, struggling with his duffel bags and guitar. I had only one suitcase. My other stuff was to be delivered by the airport the following day. In my free hand I had a map and a layout of the apartment and my roommate's names. I'd noticed

49

on the train that he did too, which is how I figured he was either Joe or Greg and we were headed for the same address. That, and there were no other foreigners on the train. But, I'd be damned if I was going to help him. Usually I would have, but that day we were racing, or at least I was. He hadn't cared I would later learn.

The three-bedroom apartment we would eventually occupy was empty. There was a five-and a-half tatami mat room (a tatami mat is made of a type of straw and measures about three feet by six feet), a six tatami mat room and an eight tatami mat room — the master bedroom I presumed. This master bedroom was next to the living room and also had a door that led out to the backyard, according to the layout. I wanted that room! Smoking was not permitted in the apartment according to the forms I'd signed at the office so, for convenience, and for size, I wanted that room! I tried to reserve it with the company, but I was told the rooms were on a first come/first serve basis!

"You guys can move in as of the first of April."

The first of April found both Joe and I on the Saikyo line headed out to Saitama. April Fool's day found me running through a train station with my suitcase in one hand a map in the other and looking like the poster boy for the holiday. Joe was not far behind, looking like Kurt Cobain, naturally grunge. He had long unkempt hair and clothes that looked like he'd actually survived a few years of a heroin binge in them.

I couldn't figure out the Japanese on the map I had so I asked the staff to point me towards the taxi stand. I hailed the first taxi I saw and pulled on the back door. It wouldn't open. Once I'd let it go, though, it suddenly sprang open like that car in the Harry Potter movies, or like someone with an attitude was going to jump out of the back seat. I almost tripped over my suitcase getting out of the way. No one got out.

I could picture Joe just strolling along lackadaisically.

I hopped in.

"Take me here!" I said to the driver, jabbing my finger at the map. "Please! Here! You know here? We go here! Koko! Koko!" (Here, Here)

I knew very little Japanese that first day. So I used a lot of hand signals and English from cheesy westerns. He glanced at me and then at my hands and then at the map then back at me and nodded, "Hai, hai, shitteiru, shitteiru." I turned and reached to pull the door closed and it lurched at me.

"Fuck!"

I turned to the driver and he had a little smirk on his face as he pulled off. I was most definitely the April fool.

The apartment was about two minutes by cab from the station, I would later discover. I'm pretty sure that driver took about 15 minutes, though. I kept asking him if he was sure where he was going.

"Hai hai hai hai," he replied.

Finally he pulled up in front of an apartment complex and the door opened on my side. I realized then that it was automatic.

"How cool is that!" I said. I paid him and got out, practically on the run. The complex was on a long road but I could not see Joe anywhere.

Fuck, did he beat me?

The apartment was on the first floor. I lumbered down the long hallway and finally I reached it. The door was still closed and locked. I whipped out the key they'd given me at the office and opened it slowly, listening for life within. Nothing, no sounds.

YES!

I'd studied the floor plan so well I knew it by heart. The two smaller rooms were on either side of the hallway leading from the front door. I peaked in both as I proceeded towards the master bedroom. No Greg. No Joe. The rooms were smaller than I thought they would be. The company had provided us with a futon to get started, and both rooms had them, rolled up in the center of the waxed and glowing hardwood floors.

A little further down the hallway there was a toilet room on one side of the hall and a shower room on the other. I found that interesting. I'd never seen a bathroom where the toilet had a room to itself. A little further along was the rather spacious eat-in kitchen, with a couple of appliances provided by the company. I'd have to go through the checklist to make sure all the items were there. The living room was next to the kitchen and a faux-leather couch was there as well as a TV, TV stand, and a large sliding glass window/patio door that looked out at a backyard full of grass and weeds.

To the right of the dining room was a wooden sliding door. The other two bedrooms had regular doors. I smiled. Mine was the most "Japanese." I slid it open and a smell wafted up into my nose like a goddamn…

*****

"Oh shit!"

"What?" Joe asked, jumping at my sudden jolt.

"Come here, both of you." and I led them to my bedroom door, slid it open and pointed down.

"Smell that!" I said, pointing to the tatami mat. They both slowly knelt down and gave it a whiff.

"That's it!" Joe said

"That's the fucking smell!" Greg agreed. "It's this straw stuff? Damn, how can you sleep with this smell?"

"I got used to it after a couple days. I don't even think about it anymore."

"Damn, mate," Joe began. "I'm sorry, I–" and he broke out laughing. Greg also apologized for jumping to conclusions and regretted some of the things he'd said.

"No biggie! If either of you were stinking I would have gotten at you the same way, trust me."

"Well, I guess we can wrap up this meeting, and go get some brews!"

"Not just yet," I said.

The colored guy had something to say.

*****

I used to work for a financial printer in NY — a big one. The company printed prospectuses as well as quarterly and annual reports for many Fortune 500 companies. I eventually became a customer service rep, but I started out as a proofreader. And, yes, proofreading legalese *is* as excruciating as it sounds.

There were a handful of us working in the department. The proofreaders, as a rule, were always doing this job to make ends meet while we pursued other endeavors, generally creative ones. There was Andy, who was really a screenwriter and director and is now out in Hollywood living the dream. There was Joel, who was putting the final touches on his manuscript. He eventually got it published a year after I met him and it did pretty well as I recall.

Then there was me and Aaron. I was happy just to have a

well-paying job at the time, and Aaron had been proofreading since damn near the fifties and wasn't going anywhere unless it was on a stretcher or in a hearse.

Aaron was a great old guy, with a sharp mind and a sharper wit. He'd lived a full and interesting life. He'd often divert us with sumptuous stories of how he'd proofread and copyedited various famous writers' works, and how half the prissy bastards' grammar was poorer than his granddaughters'.

One day he told us about how he'd once even proofread a *colored* writer's work.

"…I forget his name, though he was a pretty famous colored guy, and a helluva writer!" he'd said.

The rest of the proofreading staff shifted uneasily in their seats with Aaron's use of this anachronism, smiles glued to their faces, like you might do if your grandmother farted while she was talking to you.

Andy, always good for a laugh, said "Don't you mean, *Negro* writer? My God, Aaron, live in the now!"

We all cracked up, except Aaron. He didn't get it.

And *he* was American!

*****

So how in the world was I going to get Greg to get it?

I mean, political correctness and sensitivity to minorities in speech is mostly an American idea, I thought. I had no idea what Australians thought of American proclivities or where they stood on the issue, but if Greg's use of "colored" and "Abos" was any indication, their racial sensitivity lay somewhere between Japan's and South Africa's. So I sat there trying to think of a way to tell Greg that though I assumed he meant no offense by its use, I'd prefer he didn't refer to black people as Colored, or Negro, or Niggers, or Afro-Americans, or Abos, or anything other than black, or people of African descent (though I have no idea where the Aborigines in Australia came from originally, if anywhere) or African-Americans, or whatever nationality the person happened to be. That his use of 'colored' was more distressing than the threatening call from the main office about the noise, and even more upsetting than his allusions to some kind of animal sacrificial religious ritual taking place in my bedroom.

This was a very complicated subject. Short of explaining the U.S. history of racism and racial bigotry and the impact of slavery and Jim Crow, and such, how could he possibly get it?

So I decided to go light first.

"Have either of you received a call from the main office?" I asked them.

"No," Joe said, "But, I lost my phone the other night."

He was on his third phone in as many weeks. His M.O. was to get as drunk as possible as often as possible and challenge himself to get home safely with all his possessions and body parts intact. He failed constantly. He often came home minus some blood, skin, cash, even a tooth once. And that's the times when he made it home at all. Sometimes he'd crawl into the house in the morning after having slept on someone's lawn or on the ground in front of the train station, after having missed the last train, waiting for the morning's first train.

Greg was worse. Greg didn't even bother to come home and shower up. He went straight to work that way. Straight from some street corner or friend's house, or gutter, grab some Mintia (Japanese Tic-Tacs), brush the grass out of his hair, throw a little water on his face and try to stay awake and employed.

Sometimes he vanished for days, on a binge. His office would call me inquiring about his whereabouts. "Hell if I know." He'd show up a couple of days later looking like a hobo, smelling and smiling like a wino.

"They called my school, I think, but I wasn't there that day," Greg said.

"Well, the thing is," I began. "They've gotten complaints about the noise from our landlord, and they threatened me over the phone, talking about we'd be evicted if it continues."

"What kind of bloody noise?" Joe asked, looking a little puzzled.

"What the hell?" Greg yelped.

What the fuck!! You know good and damn well what kind of noise they're talking about, both of you do! I wanted to yell. *You fuckers come home every night pissed and play the guitar like this is a recording studio, or blast Red Hot Chili Peppers like you want to introduce the whole neighborhood to rock, or bring a mob of Aussies up in here for laughs and brews, shits and giggles, and all in the living room, just outside my bedroom, regardless of the time.*

But I didn't yell. I kept my cool.

"You think they can hear you?" Joe asked, looking up at the ceiling, and at the walls. "I reckon they must. I can hear you even in my bedroom down the hall with the door closed, mate."

"Hear *who*?" I asked.

"*You*, dude! When you have one of your Japanese girls in there. It's like a war zone."

"Yeah, I almost opened your door to make sure everything was alright one time," Greg said, laughing loudly. "I thought you were killing her!"

"What the hell are y'all talking about?" I was perplexed.

"You!" Joe said. "I mean, I don't like to talk about what a man does in the bedroom but, you!!" Joe was shaking his head. "Yeah, we gotta nickname for you, mate...don't we Joe?" "The Machine!"

*****

I wasn't prepared for the level of verve I would have for the girls here in Japan. And, I don't think any man can really prepare himself for the onslaught of attention Japanese girls eagerly pay foreign men here. If a guy had had the same ratio of beautiful girls coming on to him or finding his charms irresistible back home then maybe he'd have developed the ability to manage his libido. I'm sure celebrities can identify. I certainly couldn't.

I didn't understand why the two of them weren't enjoying the fruits of their notoriety, though. I eventually chalked it up to the fact that they were too busy getting loaded to get laid. They were both pretty handsome guys. Joe was even cool, in a bohemian way: young, smart, blond, blue-eyed, a Japanese girl's wet dream in the flesh. And Greg had this rough outback Marlboro-Man thing going (or maybe that was just my image of him), and he could play the six-string guitar like nobody's business. I mean, when I say he played the guitar as a complaint, it's only because he'd do it loud enough to disturb the neighbors and at all hours of the night. My qualms had nothing to do with his ability.

But, I couldn't be the source of the noise that was generating ill will among our neighbors. It had to be the foreign sounds, I thought. Hell, everybody has sex, even Japanese. I hear them occasionally; the thin walls do go both ways. But, I rarely heard televisions or radios or loud talking, even on weekends. Not at night, anyway.

And I told my roomies just that.

"Come on, now, Machine," Joe said with a smirk. "That noise coming out of your room is not usual."

"Yeah, man, it sounds like you're slaying them with your big, black pocket monster," Greg added. "I know all you guys are packing heavy!"

"Whoa!" I snapped. "Ok."

"What?" Greg snapped back. "You trying to tell me that you're not as big as a..."

"I said WHOA motherfucker! Whoa means chill the fuck out with that shit!"

"What's your problem?" he asked genuinely alarmed by my reaction to what he probably thought was a compliment.

"*My* problem?" I cried, looking at the two of them in turns. "*My* problem?" I repeated.

They both sat there looking at me, stunned into silence at my outburst. I still hadn't found the words to address this issue, though. I had actually planned to postpone any discussion of it until I had. Going into it half-cocked didn't seem wise, considering the harmony of our living arrangement hung in the balance. And they were actually really cool guys and I'd heard NEON roommate horror stories (kleptomania, assaults, property damage, and so on), so I knew I could easily be doing much worse.

But, things had come to a head.

"Listen fellas," I said. "I don't know how things are in Australia and New Zealand, or even in Japan for that matter, but I know how…how I'd like things to be in this apartment, in our home."

They were still watching me, a little on guard, Greg more so than Joe. My outburst had put him on edge, and I could tell he was a fighter. I pictured him, through my Crocodile Dundee-tinted lenses, as one of those guys who punched people in the jaw as a greeting back home, where bar brawls were probably nightly entertainment. Joe looked serene but pensive.

"I'm a little sensitive when it comes to racial...um...let's just say racial identification," I began, and I knew I had stepped on a slippery slope, especially when their eyes started bulging. "For example, the words Nigger, and Colored, even Negro... they just don't sit well with me. You follow?"

"What about black?" Joe asked. "Is black okay?"

Thrilled that I'd reached one of them I said almost excitedly, "Yeah! Black is, how do you say it, *Sweet as!*"

"Sweet as..." Joe said, smiling. Everything was *Sweet as* with him. It was his favorite phrase.

"What's wrong with colored?" Greg asserted. "That's what we call our neg...er...our black guys back home. They don't seem to mind."

"What can I tell you, man? I ain't Australian," I said as calmly as I could, for I could see Greg was still tense. "I'm from a place where calling a black man colored — especially if it's coming from a young white guy like *you* – you might as well be saying, 'I *really* need a serious ass kicking! Are you busy?'"

They both fell out laughing. I wondered if they knew I was more than half-serious.

"I got you," Greg said after a couple of minutes once he'd caught his breath.

"I got a question, though," Joe said through his teary-eyed laughter. "You know I like hip-hop, so—"

"So you want to know why do a lot of the hip-hop artists say

Nigga all the time?" I asked, anticipating where he was going. "That's a difficult question. And I'm afraid I can't even answer it. I mean, maybe they like to embrace the horror. Or maybe they think by overusing it they're defusing it. You know, trying to make it harmless. Or maybe they are so young that they have no idea how painful the word used to be. Maybe they're just ignorant. Talented, rich, influential, but ignorant. I really can't answer that question."

"Oh." Joe sighed, looking bummed out. "That's kind of fucked up."

"Yeah, we're gonna sit here feeling sorry for Dr. Dre and Snoop Dogg...I don't think so," I laughed. "I gotta better idea. Let's go get some brews and wake up the neighbors. We can finish this meeting next time."

"Now you're talking!" Greg said.

CONVERSATION #2

Keep Your Mind On The Money!

This conversation took place at a cafe in Yokohama with a potential student. This was a trial lesson. The student was attractive, tanned, long black hair with dyed tan streaks, heavily made-up and sparkly with glitter. She was wearing leopard skin patterned tights, a low-cut blouse with a whole lot of cleavage showing…

Me: Hi, my name is Loco…you must be Emi?

Emi: Yes!

Me: It's nice to meet you!

Emi: Oh Yes!

(Takes a seat…)

Me: Ok…so, a little about me…I'm from America, from New York. and I've —

Emi: Eeeee! New York? Sou desuka… Kakkooii!! (Is that right? Very cool)

Me: (Smile) Yeah…so, yeah, I've lived in Japan for–

Emi: You like hip-hop?

Me: Ummm **(Geezus. OK Loco, stay focused…keep your mind on the money)** Yes, I do!

Emi: Eeeee…(nodding, grinning and giggling)

Me: So…and, um, I teach English at a Junior High School in Yokohama. My hobbies are reading, watching movies and playing basketball. And I like to–

61

Emi: KaaakkoooIIII!!! (Coooooool)

Me: Listen, Emi, why don't you introduce yourself, in English.

Emi: Eeeee? dekinai yo! (I can't) Please ask question to me, ok?

Me: Ok, fine…So, what is your job, Emi?

Emi: I am part time office worker…and dancer.

Me: Oh really? Wow! Like a hula dancer, or–

Emi: You know pole dancing?

Me: Ummm, yeah. You mean like *Flashdance*?

Emi: Sou sou sou sou sou! I am pole dancer!

(Keep your mind on the money)

Me: That's, um, very interesting!

Emi: I dance at Roppongi and Shibuya and Ginza…

Me: Wow! So, why do you want to study English?

Emi: I want to meet cool American black guy…but I can't speak.

(Keep your mind on the money)

Me: Ummm, right, I see. Well, I hope I can help you. (I pull my English text-book out of my bag)

Emi: Eeeee! Iyada! (Frowns at book) I want to study English, but I want to study slang…

Me: Slang?

Emi: Yes! Like hip-hop slang, and New York slang,…

Me: Well, I don't think you're quite ready for… **(Keep your mind on the money)** …actually I don't think that's gonna be problem. When do you wanna start?

Emi: Anytime!

*****

62

3

THE EROTICISM OF EXOTICISM

Whenever I meet a new Japanese girl, sooner than later, they get around to asking me some variation of *The Question*: What are the differences between Japanese girls and American girls?

It's a loaded question.

Back in my early days in Japan, if I'd had my wits about me, I would have done what clever politicians train to do, and that is to not accept the premise of questions where the premise is a presumption. In other words, if you answer the question then you are acknowledging that there are indeed differences between American girls and Japanese girls. But, I wasn't thinking clearly when I first arrived here.

I was enchanted.

When asked *The Question*, I'd never question *The Question*. I'd look right into the doe-like eyes of my *josei* (girl) du jour and say, with a straight face, "Japanese women are sweeter," mostly to keep my answer simple yet complimentary.

A more thorough and frank answer would have been, 'I think Japanese girls are the fucking bomb! In general, they're prettier (in a prepubescent kind of way), sexier (in a dumb blond kind of way) and are just fiendin' to be feminine, like pre-teens dressing up in Mama's clothes. They're passive and pliable and just dying to be led around and told what to do, which taps into some psycho-sexual sadistic thing dwelling in my psyche, I suspect. They taste great, they're less filling, they smell better, and are lower maintenance than their American counterparts. They require little to no game (effort) whatsoever, like top shelf call girls (even dressing the part) only relatively free of charge. They are awkward, giggling, disease-free, confidence-free aphrodisiacs incarnate.

Enchanted is an understatement. I was actually in nirvana

in them days; quite removed from reality.

I remember a Twilight Zone episode about a book lover, who was taunted and harassed for his passion by his wife and friends. One day, he found himself alone in a bank vault when a nuclear explosion destroyed the city. He survived, thanks to the thickness of the vault, only to find he was the last man standing. He was about to kill himself out of despair and loneliness, when he found that the library had (miraculously) also survived the atomic bombing. He was happy as a pig in shit until, in a particularly cruel Rod Serling twist, he drops and breaks his glasses.

That's fucked up, right?

Well, my glasses broke, too: the rose-tinted lenses through which I adored Japanese women, that is. Now I can see the truth behind the curtain of stereotypes about them.

The truth: They're just people. And people are people.

I learned some outrageous stereotypes about Japanese woman before coming to Japan. Mostly I'd heard them from the mouths of my predominantly black friends...folks who should have known better about the dangers and inherent inaccuracies when stereotyping. The women would make dubious assertions like, "You can't handle black women, so you're gonna get with one of them submissive ass Japanese chicks, right?" or "Better hope you don't catch nothing, cuz I heard them bitches don't know how to say no!" And, black guys? Well, they weren't much better. "You're moving to Japan, yo? Oh man! You gonna have a ball! Those Japanese motherfuckers ain't packing shit in their boxers so I know them Japanese chicks got to be starving for some real dick!" or "Man, I hear them Japanese girls are easy as fuck! You gonna make a killing!"

Only after my head began to clear of all these notions (which took a bit of time) was I able to see the truth.

Are Japanese girls easier? I'd have to say, the answer is an *equivocal* yes, they are! However, I submit, they are no easier than their American counterparts under the same conditions.

Case and point: When I was a teenager growing up in Brooklyn, I was a sentimental young man with some romantic notions about the fairer sex. Love songs made my heart race and rejection broke it. I used to write tear-stained pages of poetry and short stories about love and loss. I had a stack of notebooks filled with this stuff, like the guy who had previously owned the house where *Brad Pitt* and *Edward Norton* squatted in Fight Club. (*I am Jack's medulla oblongata; I am Jack's complete lack of surprise*). Mine was more like, "I am a red tear in the duct of a dying man."

That's the kind of stuff I wrote after Tanya tore my heart from my chest and played hacky sack with it.

Tanya was my high school sweetheart, sort of. She was this light-skinned cutie from Bed-Stuy who inexplicably managed to emerge from the Projects exuding purity and sweetness so uncorrupted you'd think she was raised in, well, in Japan, or a nunnery. Only, Tanya's high school sweetheart was not me, but this cat named Lance. She just pal'd around with me. I was like her Forrest Gump.

"Run, Loco, run."

And, I ran my ass off…right behind her whenever she'd let me.

Lance was a lying asshole, but we all were so that didn't make him special. What *did* make him special was his heritage: he was half-Jamaican, half-Chinese. He had half-slanted eyes, was half as dark as me and had half-straight hair that half the girls in the school went half-bananas for half a chance to run their fingers through.

He was my boy, though. We used to get zooted together on the regular. That is, until Tanya went *entirely* bananas over him. Then, naturally, I hated him.

So what he was exotic! Well, half-exotic, anyway. Why should that matter, I used to wonder. Who was the one writing poetry for Tanya? Sure as hell wasn't Lance! Did I give her my undivided attention? Well, when I wasn't smoking blunts and drinking 40s, you bet your ass I did. Did I make it clear that *if this world were mine I'd place at her feet all that I own* (inspired by Marvin Gaye and Luther Vandross)? Yes, indeed I did. Well, kind of. I mean, I never actually said it, in so many words, but I'm pretty sure my actions (and volumes of cursive verse I never actually showed her) implied it loudly enough. But, did she give a damn once Lance had cast his half-slanted eyes on her? No. Did Lance even give a shit about her? No. Did Lance talk to her on the phone every goddamn night and listen to her drone on and on about totally mundane shit? No. Did Lance drag his ass to her church on Sundays and watch, in bewildered amusement, as her mother suffered sanctified seizures all over the goddamn place? Hell no. Did he hold her sheepskin coat when it was clearly too hot to be wearing one but, since they were fashionable, she wore it any fucking way? No.

Fucking Lance, lucky bastard...all *he* had to do was just be!

Was Tanya an easy mark for Lance? Yep! A pushover. Why? For essentially the same reason Japanese girls are easy marks.

Here in Japan, virtually every non-Asian guy is Lance. We are all lucky bastards. We are all exceptions and thus exceptional. We represent a chance for Japanese girls to feel different, to do things out of the ordinary, to be distinctive. We're human theme parks that hold the promise of a ride on the wild side.

We're a chance to learn about something aside from that which is known all too well.

Never underestimate the eroticism of exoticism, I've learned.

And, though there was enough negative stereotyping going around to keep black guys at pariah status in most circles, there were some benevolent rumors circulating, as well. Somebody had pumped these girls' heads so full of unsubstantiated information about *me* that my actual input became redundant at best and counterproductive at worst. They knew all they needed to know about *me* to make an informed decision and, in a satisfactory number of cases, had somehow concluded that *I* was indeed desirable.

Never underestimate human susceptibility to hype and stereotype, I've also learned.

So, Tanya, you heart breaker you. I hated you for a long time. But, now, I ain't got nothing but love for you. I realize that anyone can be vulnerable to the exotic factor...even me.

And, so, I am Loco's utter lack of surprise that you let Lance run up in that thing when I offered you my eternal love.

I sympathize, and I forgive you...

...bitch.

*****

Yeah, I was vulnerable to the call of the exotic, but it slowly began to dawn on me that libido and exoticism were not the only forces at play here. There was more going on than your usual *lust trumps morals* scenario. This realization was like waking up after a wild night of wanton and reckless gallivanting, going to take a piss and having it burn so much you find religion in the urinal.

In other words, uncommonly unpleasant.

I used to hang out with this cat named Damon. He was one of a handful of black guys I'd met in Japan willing to hang out with other black guys, who wasn't as boring as watching rice grow. He was Canadian but his street credibility was earned in Toronto's cousin down south, Detroit, where he apparently spent quite a bit of time (for some reason that eludes me to this day). The Motor City was the arena where he acquired his "American" accent and street knowledge, according to him. I tried to tell him that, to me, Detroit only meant *Motown, GM, Ron LeFlore* and *the Bad Boy Pistons* that whipped Jordan, Bird *and* Magic Johnson's asses, but he thought I was just playing, and I let him go on thinking that.

"Ron, *who?*" he'd asked.

We were getting our drink on at a bar in Ebisu, Tokyo, when I turned to him and asked, apropos of nothing, "Why do you think we do this shit?"

I was drunk, but not that drunk, and so was he. He cut his eyes at me, suspiciously, and then nodded towards two Japanese girls who'd just entered the bar. Then, he winked at me like God had mysteriously answered my question on his behalf.

I shook my head and took a swig of beer. This was gonna be one of those nights. I could feel it. But, I'd been entertaining the desire, of late, to at least talk about it a little. Up until that night, finding some promising prospects in pumps with the Japanese facsimile of a bump had been the unsung mission. And we were nothing if not focused. But my focus had diminished of late, and Damon had picked up on it.

"Are you turning gay on me, nigga? Look at this buffet up

69

in here! And, you gotta ask?"

"For real, though."

He took a sip of the beer he'd been nursing and checked himself in the mirror behind the bar. I was surprised he didn't keep a mirror in his attaché case – one of his accessories. He needed an attaché case like a dog needs condoms. He also had at his disposal all the latest hi-tech gadgets Japan had to offer: iPod, top of the line cell phone, PSP, etc. In addition, he had conversation pieces. Stuff he'd picked up for its *kawaii-ness* (cuteness). The kind of crap Japanese girls tended to get a kick out of, and served to neutralize some of that fear most of them had of anyone darker than a cafe au lait (which he barely was). Little doodads that gave the impression he had a soft creamy center to his caramel exterior. He flaunted one of those creatures from *Monster's Inc.* on his key-chain, Nemo could be found dangling gleefully from his attaché case handle and Anpanman stickers adorned his phone, which lay on the bar so he wouldn't miss a text from his girlfriend.

He glanced at me, realizing I was watching him.

"They came here for us, nigga! Time to represent!" he said, like that was end of the discussion. "You with this, or what?"

He was already getting up off his stool. Damon had a very commanding way about him, but he usually reserved that aspect of his nature for those white boys in the office. With me, he'd usually ease back on his ego throttle due to the street cred he perceived me as having; my being a New Yorker and all.

I glanced over at his prey for the moment, the two girls who'd just walked in. We were in a Gaijin bar, frequented by foreigners and the Japanese women who adore them, so there was no doubt why they'd come. It was just a matter of who got to them first and had even a minuscule amount of game…

unless it was some white boys. They didn't need any game at all.

Damon was ready to make a move, and was waiting on me.

Two white guys were hovering, I noticed, giving the girls a chance to at least take their seats before they swooped in. Damon noticed too and wasn't about to let them do that. He'd told me tales of being cock-blocked by "corny-ass crackers" on several occasions.

"Nah, you go ahead." I said, deciding I wasn't up to the chase.

"Awright, suit yourself," he said, undeterred, as he turned their way. But, just as he took a step towards them, the two white guys moved in; two real cornballs at that. One wore a retro Space Invaders T-shirt, and the other, a black leather vest over a white T-shirt. Damon stopped in his tracks and wheeled on me. I could see in his eyes he was rummaging through his pimp playbook for this scenario: *How do you cock-block two Charisma Cornballs and not come off as being so aggressive you scare the shit outta the J-bitches?*

He struggled with the strategy for a hot 20 seconds or so and probably concluded that though the accomplishment would fit nicely on his pimp résumé, to do so solo would require more effort than he'd gotten used to expending on J-girls. He was spoiled. We all were. In Canada he'd have never let it go at that, from what he'd tell me every chance he got.

"Fuck it, they'll be more," he said. And he was right of course. There was always more of where that came from in Tokyo. The night was young and we'd hardly spent 1000 yen, yet. So, he sat back down.

"So, what the fuck is *your* problem?"

"Nothing," I yelped. "Just not up for the bullshit tonight."

"Then why the hell you come out?" He snapped, irritated. "You *know* what I'm about!"

That was true, and I started feeling bad about cramping his style.

"Sorry, bruh. My bad."

"You feel guilty, don't you? Man, I told you about that shit. This ain't no Judeo-Christian society here. So, you need to leave those Judeo-Christian values with the Jews and Christians. When in Rome, you knowhutumsayin? These bitches just want to fuck, and so do we. It's a match made in Ebisu! You can't be applying all that Western bullshit you got up in your head to these bitches. Trust me. I talk to them. I *know* them. I understand them better than these Japanese motherfuckers do!"

"Is that a fact?"

"NiiiiGaaaa!" he sang, exasperated. He hated to be doubted and felt his supremacy, as far as knowledge and experience with Japanese girls was concerned, to be irrefutable; a true connoisseur.

"You practically just got here, son. I've been up in this piece *four* years already. I'd consider myself an imbecile if I didn't know these bitches better than they know themselves. And, trust me, son, *you* are what they're all about! *You!* Not these corny-ass white boys and definitely not these faggot-ass Japanese motherfuckers. *You*, Nigga!"

By "you" he meant himself. He was even looking at the mirror when he said it.

"Listen, I feel you, but–"

"Take those two characters," he said, cutting me off, pointing at the two white boys conspicuously, and hoping they'd notice. He was still a little salty about their interception. "Sure, they're sorry-ass white boys and these bitches definitely go for that, but–"

"Yo, Dee, bust it!"

"Huh? Bust what?" he looked around like danger had walked in the door. I almost laughed. Sometimes Damon didn't understand my slang. Granted, it was New York slang and kind of old-school, at that. And hard as he tried to front like he wasn't, he *was* Canadian.

"I mean, check this out," I said, rephrasing. "I feel you on all uh that, but…well…I kinda met someone and…"

"So what! I got a girl, too," he said, shaking his head. "Man, haven't I taught you anything?"

"Taught *me*?" I spat, putting down my beer, screwing up my face. "Yo, Son, don't get beside yourself! You ain't said nothing I ain't heard a thousand times from a thousand wanna-be pimps on a thousand corners! Niggas in New York come out the womb kicking the same shit you kicking. You ain't taught me shit!"

"Yo, Chill Loco!" he pleaded. "Why you getting all uptight? I'm just fuckin' with you!"

"Cuz you don't listen! All you do is run your fucking mouth!"

"Alright, fuck it," he said. "So, what was it you said? Something like, 'why do we do this shit?' right? See, I be listening to you."

"So answer the fucking question!"

"Cuz pussy is good," he droned, like he was explaining 1+1=2. Then he smiled. "Mo' pussy is mo' better!"

And I laughed. Mostly because, unawares, he was quoting something I'd said a few months back, but partially because it was almost impossible to get some "real" talk out of any of the black guys I'd met in Japan. I felt silly for even trying.

73

"Seriously, though," he said, suddenly, with a straight face. "Tell me this Japanese pussy ain't the fucking bomb! I mean, I ain't no Charisma Man. I don't know about you but I used to get mad pussy back home, too…and not the skanks, either. Quality pussy, from all kinds of bitches: White bitches, Black bitches, Mexican bitches, even Chinese bitches. but there's something about these Japanese bitches that just makes banging them more…more *something*."

Couldn't have a conversation with Damon without him finding a way to mention that he *wasn't* a Charisma Man (and his uncertainty about your status), and that he'd always had more than his fair share of women. The Charisma Man was that guy who didn't get any love back home, but became a super lover in Japan. His constant assertion of this, to me, spoke to his insecurity on the matter and made me wonder whether he was being on the level or not.

But, of course I knew what he was talking about when he said Japanese girls had a certain "something." I used to call that something the J-factor.

But, at the moment, I was trying to deconstruct the J-factor, trying to understand it better.

"Maybe you hate them," I said, hoping to shock him.

He actually thought about it for a second, shocking *me*.

"Maybe," he said, and shrugged, like its relevance was inconsequential at best. "How Snoop Dogg say it? 'I don't love them hoes!'"

And he laughed.

"I mean, look at them!" he ordered, scanning the bar. "What's to love?"

As I looked around I caught a reflection of myself in the mirror…and got stuck there. I looked good! Like Damon, I was in a suit and tie, as well. It was basically the NEON uniform, and I hated every moment spent in it, but I looked sharp as hell. The suit was grey wool and the tie a pink and burgundy Polo paisley. My hair was freshly cut and my beard and mustache were neatly trimmed. And, I was glowing like the oversexed bachelor I was.

And, that's when it hit me. I was one of those detestable Charisma Men Damon disparaged at every opportunity, in the flesh.

I mean, underneath that glow, I was pretty average looking; plus kind of thick in the middle with an over-sized head. I smoked too many cigars and drank way too much coffee. I'd sooner under dress for an event than overdress. I detest fashion, actually. I do have a developed sense of humor, given to zaniness at any given time but, character wise, I have flaws galore, and the more debased of them (selfishness, laziness, and promiscuity) I hide beneath a veneer of boyish charm, artistic integrity and an earthy sagacity.

Before I came to Japan, unlike Damon, I'd had my moments, but nothing even remotely close to the degree of action I got here in Kawaiiland.

"What if I told you *I* was a Charisma Man," I blurted out like it had been a truth just dying to be unleashed on the world. Damon looked at me like I'd confessed I liked getting sodomized with lit candles.

"Nigga, don't...man...don't be telling people that shit," he stammered, looking around like someone might have overheard. "That kind of honesty? Man, Macks just don't get down like that!"

"I ain't a Mack."

"I know, but–" he said before he could catch himself. "Well, anyway, don't worry; your secret is safe with me!"

"What secret?"

"That you're a, you know, one of them," and he nodded towards the two white boys, Space Invader and Vest boy, who'd beat him to the punch. They were taking pictures with their cell phone cameras, posing with the two girls, one hand making "peace" signs, the other all over the place, testing to see how touchy-feely the girls would let them get. Apparently, the answer was quite!

"Mannnn" I sighed. "If I had a secret, you really think I'd tell yo' ass?"

"Fuck is that supposed to mean?"

I didn't know it then but that was the question that derailed our "friendship." I mean, for a "pimp," Damon was, like myself, actually a pretty sensitive guy. And I do have a tendency to come at people who condescend to me with both barrels blazing, a defensive knee jerk kind of reflex. Sometimes I'm even unaware of it. Like this time. I hadn't even realized the severity of what I'd said. I thought it was common sense. If you want to keep a secret you don't tell the cat with the biggest mouth in the office, even if he is your boy.

"Nothing, man."

"Alright, Mister *Charisma*," he said, snarling sarcastically. "Let's see now: You done gone and found yourself a J-girl worth more than her Louis Vuitton handbag, am I right? So now you gonna preach at me about how we ought to be respecting these bitches, right? How I'm dead-ass wrong for taking advantage of these stupid ass hoes, right? How I'm a *classic* misogynist, and how I need to check myself because misogyny does as much harm to me as it does to these hoes, or some shit like that, right?"

My face must've registered mild surprise because he smiled like the devil. Damon loved that kind of reaction. He lived for it. He sets you up with all his Motor City street talkin', where profanity, "bitch," "ho" and "nigga" find their way into every other sentence...then he slips in a word like "misogyny." A word that is as far from his usual "I'm kicking it with my niggas" vocabulary as Toronto is from Detroit, and fancies himself impressive.

I, on the other hand, (and probably the greater evil of the two), feel a peculiar need to show I can be as potty-mouthed as the next guy by modifying my vocabulary according to my company; dumbing down, or niggering it up, as it were, so I won't stand out. A survival instinct I've been honing ever since I was a pre-adolescent bookworm to avoid looking and sounding like I thought I was the smartest guy in the room, or lacked the capacity to *keep it real*. Ironically, this is an instinct that has taken a welcomed hit here in Japan because I rarely speak in plain English, let alone speak to people who would question my *authenticity* because of a lack of profanity and colloquialisms.

Weren't we a pair!

"See nigga," he said. "I ain't one of these stupid ass motherfuckers out here running around Asia, dick first, without an inkling. That ain't me!"

He'd said it like he knew I had doubts about him.

"I have four older sisters! And we're all college-educated," he added. "They know how I get down, so they get at me all the time with the same bullshit you kicking! Talking about how I don't respect women cuz I don't respect myself, and if I keep this up I'm gonna forget *how* to respect all together, let alone love, and what am I gonna do with myself then? And all that kinda bullshit! As if a nigga don't respect hisself. Picture that shit!"

A waitress came over and asked did we want another beer or something. Damon, still mid rant, looked at her with eyes that could rape before he caught himself, threw on his *I'm as harmless as a Pokemon* smile, and said, "no thanks."

I ordered a beer. When she walked away he turned back on me, and glared.

"These Japanese bitches ain't got no respect for us no how. In fact, ain't none of these Japanese motherfuckers got any respect for anybody but Japanese! And, the worst part is they don't even fucking know it! You live here, nigga! Tell me, I'm wrong! I got too much respect for myself to be respecting fools that don't respect me. My moms didn't raise me to kiss *no*body's ass. Youknowhutumsaying?"

He actually waited for me to acknowledge the question. I was accustomed to ignoring "youknowhutumsaying." My older brother used to use that phrase every other sentence and it used to drive me nuts!

"I hear you, man," I said, halfheartedly. I mean, I did want to talk but I wasn't expecting a rant. Especially one that made sense.

"And they can't be trusted at all! These bitches will fuck *anybody* any time. Fucking don't mean a goddamn thing to them but an orgasm and a shower. They ain't laying around wondering if you respect them afterwards. Bitches back home be on that bullshit, but not *these* bitches! They don't give a fuck about that! Am I *right*?? Ain't no morality standing in the way of a good fuck over here. They ain't going to church tomorrow, or ever! And they know the big Buddha ain't got nothing against them letting some big dick nigga run up in that booty!

And I *DIG* that shit! Tell me you don't, Loco, and I'll call you a fucking liar to your face...cuz you told me you did just a few weeks ago!"

I took a swig of brew and held my tongue. I didn't know what to say, anyway.

"I know what you thinking, and you're right. A few of them *do* have a clue how to treat people who ain't Japanese. But the masses? Shit! The masses have their heads in their asses! My girl is an exception though! She cooler than a motherfucker. And got mad respect for the black! At least *now* she does, thanks to me. But it took me about a year before I got it through her thick Japanese skull that *all* niggas ain't like me! After we jumped that hurdle – and that's a *huge* fucking hurdle here, as you know by now – that's when shit finally started getting real. Now she ain't fit to live here. She can't even stand her own people anymore. Now that she can see these motherfuckers through *my* eyes, she ready to move back to Canada with me!"

He was starting to depress me. I almost regretted starting the conversation

"Listen, Loco, I can see you going through some shit. And, trust me I've been there. All I'm saying is I ain't here, and you ain't here, to be bigger fucking men and prove our moral superiority. And we ain't here to teach these racist motherfuckers how to be part of the human race, either. We're just here to teach English. That's all. And they wouldn't have any use for us otherwise. So we might as well take advantage of the few privileges our Gaijin status grants us. And one of them is easy access to these bitches!"

I glanced up from my beer and noticed more than a few Japanese people were surreptitiously looking at us, in that pseudo-sneaky way they have about them. His rant had drawn attention. I'm sure that was part of the reason he'd done it so loudly. He loved the attention. While most of the Japanese probably couldn't catch all that he was saying, the foreigners could definitely understand him. And, though, unlike the Japanese, they pretended not to be tuned in, I knew they weren't missing a word of this. I didn't know whether to feel embarrassed or not. He was saying a lot of the things I've thought (in nicer terms) and felt about Japanese people, and the women in particular, and it would be hypocritical of me to try and deny it.

"That's what I'm saying," he said, like my silence was acquiescence, which it probably was. "They just want a little exotic flavor in their lives, is all, and I give it to them...WELL! We're just big dicks to them. So, why the fuck I gotta respect them? Why black women always be on some bullshit? Like I can't do both: get all the ass I ever wanted and keep my self-respect. You on that shit, too, ain't you?"

"What? I didn't say shit!"

"Yeah, but you were thinking it!" he snapped. "I know how you think! You ain't no mystery, Loco. You think cuz you from New York you –"

"Whoa, whoa, whoa!" I hollered. "Hold up! Don't put words in my mouth. Where I'm from ain't got nothing to do with nothing, so don't change the subject. All I said is maybe you hate them."

"So what if I hate them! This ain't no moral dilemma. A nigga like to bang hoes. *Especially* these Japanese hoes! You got a problem with that?"

I did take issue with that, actually. But I wasn't exactly sure why.

"Listen, Damon. I'm just trying to figure out my own

motivation, understand my own thinking. I don't give a fuck what you do."

"Yes, you do!" he shouted, scorching me with his eyes. "You know, Loco, I never told you this shit before, but you got a judgmental way about you. It puts me on the defensive way too often, and I *don't* dig that shit at all. Nigga, if you ain't with this shit, don't judge me. Don't hate the playa, hate the game, nigga! If you don't wanna play the game no more, cuz you found you some silk in all this polyester over here, cool! I'm happy for you. If you think you gonna lose your soul, or lose your self-respect, or whatever dark thoughts you're wrestling with over there, fuck it, stay at your crib and jerk off to J-porn with that mosaic shit on it. Whatever gets you off, nigga. I feel you! I love me some J-porn but, personally, I prefer the real motherfucking thing, and *here*..." He waved his arms at the room, expansively. "...*Here* is where it's at: *Real* bitches looking for some *real* niggas!"

I looked around the bar, again. More girls had arrived since we'd started talking. They'd arrived in pairs and trios, mini-skirts and boots, hot pants and pumps. Looking like they wanted to have fun, looking for something different, something exciting, something exotic, and this Gaijin bar was the place to find it.

They were looking for us!

Damon followed my glance as I zoomed in on a quartet of foot-long fluttering eyelashes around black-lined eyes focused on the two of us. They were awfully cute. Cute as those I'd choked my chicken to many a night, both here and in the U.S., and a *big* part of why Japan is endurable, I confessed to myself, disturbingly.

"You see what I'm saying!" he said, like the view had

verified all he'd imparted, confirmed his frame of mind. "Now, if you don't mind, *this* Mack here would like to get his dick wet while he's still in the prime of life!"

"Fuck it, let's do this!" I almost whispered, like the words had escaped from some secret place, deep within the chasm of me.

"*That's* my Charisma Nigga!" Damon roared, pounding me on the back. "Let's go *represent!*"

*****

"They are not a moral people," Patrick said. "At least not moral as we see it."

"As *we* see it?" I asked, incredulously. I couldn't imagine he and I saw anything similarly, but I didn't say so. I just wanted to know how he'd become the most notorious charisma man in Tokyo...at least as far as NEON was concerned. His exploits were whispered far and wide. His accomplishments were legendary.

"They're piss poor peasants, practically barbarians, closer to animals than they are to us," he said.

I couldn't believe my fucking ears!

You don't believe me, do you?" he asked, like he was accustomed to having his assertions challenged, so he came prepared to present proof that would satisfy even the fiercest opposition that Japanese people were sub-human.

"OK, answer me this: what separates humans from animals?" He asked, and folded his arms across his chest.

I was speechless and wasn't about to engage in this discussion, not seriously, anyway. I just looked at him, trying to decide if he were yanking my chain or not.

I'd seen Patrick several times with different Japanese girls in various locales, and all of them were clearly out of his league. Like this one time I'd run into him at a Starbuck's in Shinjuku. He was with a Japanese cutie, flawless in every way, by all appearances. He was sitting there confidently gaming away with his patchy, almost ring-wormy looking haircut, blotchy skin, wearing the same busted ass suit he'd be wearing every time I saw him. He'd had her locked in a conversation and she clearly couldn't understand what he was saying well or, I believe, she'd have fled the scene like she'd had an appointment for a magazine photo shoot cross town. But, on the contrary, she was beaming at him and looked like she wanted to have his little half-Japanese babies right then and there.

"Patrick!" I'd shouted.

With some effort they both yanked their eyes from one another and looked at me. He registered surprise and embarrassment, and all of the confidence he'd had just moments ago vanished, transforming him before my eyes into the sniveling, nervous, twitchy, shifty eyed Patrick that almost made me ashamed to share his race...the guy I'd see at the office from time to time.

"L-L-Loco!" was all he'd stammered.

I'd felt bad, responsible for the depletion of his confidence. So, I decided to keep it moving and pretended to be in a rush. I figured I'd catch up with him another time to find out the details.

And that "another time" happened to be this day, which found us working at the same satellite NEON location. We'd gone to McDonald's together for lunch and over Big Mac sets I inquired as to his method of procurement. I wanted to know how this guy, who made even me feel debonair and irresistible by comparison, was able to overachieve as he was infamously doing.

Only to be told that it had something to do with Japanese being akin to animals???

"Come on, man," I said. "You don't really believe that shit, do you? You? As a black man, you ought to know better than that. After all the shit blacks have gone through with white folks thinking like that about us...*please* tell me you're kidding."

He laughed.

"All I know, Loco, is what I've learned and what I see."

He paused and took a sip of his drink just as a couple of office ladies were passing by. One was about to take a seat at the empty table beside ours but the other, after taking a glance at us, called to her – with a little urgency – that there was another table across the room. The other couldn't understand the urgency until she glanced our way and noticed us. Then she rose and hastily followed after her companion.

Patrick then turned back to me like he'd forgotten I was there.

"Look around us," he said. "It's the lunch rush, right? So, why do you think every table in here is occupied except for the two on either side of us?"

I just looked at him and waited for the answer I knew he would supply in due course.

"You probably think it's cuz Japanese people are a bunch of racist fucks, right?"

"No," I said. "I mean, it could be that...but, who knows?" I said, playing devil's advocate. I hated to get into whining sessions with foreigners here.

"I used to think like you," he said, like a pompous mind-reading fuck. "I used to think that Japanese were racists, or xenophobic, or whatever you want to call it. But now I know

84

better."

"OK," I said, still wondering what this had to do with animals. "So, what's the real reason, Patrick-sensei?"

"If you were to move away from someone the way they just did, so blatantly, what do you imagine would be going through your mind?"

"I wouldn't do that...well, I should say, I wouldn't do that unless there were special circumstances...someone I was trying to avoid on purpose and wanted them to know it, or maybe a homeless person stinking to high hell or something like that. But, I wouldn't do it otherwise. Not without cause."

"Why not?"

"Because that's a fucked up thing to do to someone," I snapped, almost losing the objectivity I was holding on to by a very thin thread.

"Why?"

"Cuz I wouldn't want anyone to do that to me. You know, that 'do unto others' thing."

"*Exactly!*" he said, like I'd made his point. "You'd have to have a reason. You wouldn't do it without one."

"Okay." I said. "I'm sure they had a reason, too."

"Are you?" he asked. "Why? Cuz they're shy? Cuz they're afraid of people who look different than themselves? Cuz they're afraid of the unknown?"

"That's what everybody says."

"Listen, Loco," he said in an exasperated tone like he was trying to be patient with me. "I have a very high regard for human beings, and I think humans have a rather high capacity for rational thinking, don't you?"

"Some do, yeah."

"I believe this is what separates humans from animals–"

"So, you think Japanese don't have a high capacity for rational thinking?"

"What do you think?" he said, like he was teaching a course.

"I think you've been here too long." And, I laughed. But my heart wasn't in it. And Patrick knew it. He smiled and took a sip of his coke, eying me with a look that said *you get me motherfucker.*

"Okay, big deal! They moved. That's their prerogative, isn't it?" I asked. "I mean, I'm sure they had a motive...it's like fight or flight, right? They decided to fly instead of fight. Whatever feelings of fear or threat they might have experienced have been neutralized by moving. The way I see it, that's basic human instinct."

"I agree, and I disagree," he said. "I think fight or flight is a basic *animal* instinct...and maybe children. But not complex enough for mature humans. I think human motives should by directed by our morals. Or, at least, there should be a concerted effort to utilize them."

"How do you know they didn't?"

"Come on, Loco...you saw them. You see it everyday here if you're eyes are even partially open."

"Morals, eh?" I said, watching him closely. "You don't think you're being a little too — "

"Fuck no!" he snapped. "For me, I think, doing the right thing for the right reason pretty much sums it up. Assuming they are rational beings, if they had even considered our dignity as humans for a second they could never have concluded that moving was the right thing. Any other motive is beneath contempt."

"But those are Western morals, dude," I said, though I didn't feel as confident about what I was saying as I was displaying.

"You can't apply that shit universally, can you?"

"*I* do," he said. "I have to. It's the only way to protect my dignity from the onslaught of offenses over here, in the U.S., hell, anywhere."

"Huh?"

"You see," he explained. "I only allow humans to offend me, *adult* humans. And once offended, I respond appropriately, dependent on the offense. But, children and animals don't offend me. Japanese adults don't behave like rational humans and they certainly have no more regard for my dignity than a child or animal would. So, I don't see why I should recognize in them something they can't recognize in me. To prove I'm the bigger man? At what price? And for what purpose?"

"So, basically you're a predator and Japanese animals, particularly the females, are your prey."

"Something like that," he laughed, hideously, though he probably didn't know it.

"That's really twisted," I said. "If I understand you correctly, you're punishing them for lacking the morals you value."

"Exactly! So?"

"But, you've let this idea you have of them being animals transform *you* into an animal! Haven't you? I mean, by treating them this way you're compromising your own morals, aren't you? Or did I miss something?"

He thought about it for a second. It was a short second, measured in fractions like those marathon timekeepers do.

"You missed something," he blurted.

"What?"

"You missed the fact that, if I don't see them as human then the guilt you're trying to play on doesn't exist."

He laughed, again. Only this time he seemed to be forcing

the issue a bit...my words had cracked his shield a little. But only a little. Not enough. Not nearly enough.

"I'm no more an animal than a cattle rancher is. Or a chicken farmer," he said with a dark smile that could have been a snarl. His lips spreading, yellowing crooked teeth bared. There was no smile in his eyes, though. His eyes were as cold as the eyes of a shark, and as dark as his logic. "Or maybe a big game hunter. Yeah I like that, better. I'm just a sportsman, Loco. Pure and simple."

4

GANBATTE

(For Aiko, my honeysuckle rose)

Flowers droop and sigh when you're passing by
And I know the reason why
You're much sweeter, goodness knows
You're my Honeysuckle Rose — Fats Waller

We first met in late Spring. I was riding my bicycle around Urawa City, in Saitama, mainly exploring and looking for some trouble to get into, when I rode by this hostess bar. Standing in front of it were three girls, all of them enticing. None of them looked over 20. Two of them had that Harajuku *gyaru* look: tanned, sparkly, streaked hair and heavy make-up. But the third one was stunning even without the adornments. She was dressed in a *yukata*, a light summer kimono, and her hair was pinned up revealing her lovely neck and cheeks.

As I passed, I gave them a little smile of acknowledgment and they, being business girls, gave me some cheese in return. I was half a block away when I heard their voices call after me. I almost crashed in my haste to respond to them. I turned around and cruised back trying to look less eager than I felt. I had been in Japan only a short time then, and as I mentioned before, the *yellow fever* was raging. In fact I was so beguiled that I hadn't even noticed that I was being hailed in English...and fairly good English, at that!

It was the girl in the yukata that was doing the talking. I rolled up beside her and she began to pitch the business.

"Only 5000 yen (about $50) and you can sit and drink with me!"

I told her straight out she must be mad, that back in the States we rarely pay that much without a guaranteed happy ending. She laughed out loud.

"This is not America!"

I asked about other services and she said that a roll in the hay — with another girl, of course — would cost about $5000 US. Now it was my turn to laugh out loud, which drew the attention of the other girls.

The boundary between hostess and client was broken. She did so with a smile that no amount of money should be able to produce, a look that promised more than one night with her could ever fulfill. I could see how she got the job. Her whole essence promised "I am the one you won't ever forget!"

Though we were both talking a mile a minute, we established without saying that not only was I not a potential client, but that there was potential for something to grow between us. So the conversation shifted from a pitch to something typical of what would take place between two people digging one another.

At first she'd given me her stage name, but after the biz talk had ceased she confided her name was Aiko.

"I'm a university student," she said. "I'm studying psychology."

I wasn't surprised, I told her. Many college students, even in the U.S., do similar jobs to make ends meet.

"Maximizing your assets," I said, winking, and she laughed.

It was so refreshing to finally have someone Japanese laugh at my jokes.

Of course, she didn't know all of my cultural references. But, she was very perceptive. She had an uncanny ability to smell humor and intuit meaning. And, as it had been back in the States, this was what won me over. She simply laughed at my jokes. She actually *got* me.

We talked until it became clear to her co-workers and the others standing around – including a middle-aged guy with such a fierce look in his eyes that, even though he was laughing and smiling as he coaxed men into the club, he totally looked *not-to-be-fucked-with* – that we were not talking about business.

"That's my boss," she said. "He's actually a nice guy!"

"Yeah, I was just thinking, what a sweetheart he must be."

She cracked up! Her laughter filled that alley, lined with houses of ill-repute, with more genuine joy than such a place should ever have. Before I left, we exchanged info and promised to keep in touch. I rode away on such a high that I sang all the way home.

Now, at the time, I was seeing this other girl, Reiko. She too could speak English, but was way too *Aussie-ized* for me. She'd lived in Perth, Australia for a couple of years before returning to Japan and discovering that she no longer had any interest in Japanese men. I'd met her my first weekend in Japan at a club in Roppongi. She was drunk, I was horny and curious, and we connected as people do. A couple of days later we did the deed, and for my first taste of Japanese loving, it was incredible, mentally anyway. Otherwise, it wasn't much different than the tastes of home. After the mental charge I'd jacked myself up with wore off, which didn't take long at all, my eyes were once again roving.

A couple of days after I met Aiko, I gave Reiko back the spare keys I had to her place. She took them and the bad news relatively in stride. She'd cried. I wiped her tears and told her I'm sorry. She shrugged and sobbed, "syougannai" (Oh, well) and I never heard from her again.

I hooked up with Aiko the following week and we went for a stroll around my neighborhood. A tree-lined walkway led to a park with a lake, surrounded by a garden path. We strolled along it, in the darkness, talking.

She told me about her love for singing. She was a jazz singer, had a little band with her classmates. I was and still am a great connoisseur of jazz so we had a lot to talk about. We also talked a little about the history of jazz. I knew quite a bit more than she did, so she listened, rapt, with eyes that devoured my words.

Later, we discovered we also shared admiration for Noam Chomsky and discussed some of his ideas. And movies! We both loved film. She knew director's names and filmographies as well as I did and we chatted about them, too. We had walked around the park about ten times without really noticing.

It was well after 11pm by then, and she ought to have been headed home, for the last train to her station was around midnight, but neither of us wanted to stop. We took a seat on a bench and sat in that park, hand-in-hand, talking all night. I was annoyed by the bugs and she was afraid of the bats, and we were both taken aback by sounds and movement coming out of the shadowy areas of the park, but we used these frights to pull ourselves closer together. The sunrise found us in the same place the stars had left us.

A couple of weeks later I convinced her to be my girlfriend. For me it was an easy call, but for Aiko it was far from that. Her decision-making process was very different from mine. For me, girlfriend meant assurance that I would have the companionship of the most interesting person I'd met since I'd been in Japan, and that we'd probably be having sex sooner than later. But she took the boyfriend title *very* seriously, much more seriously than I did.

I'd told her that I just wanted to have fun, and isn't that what being boyfriend and girlfriend is all about? But, Aiko had started college late and was 24 years old already. And, in Japan, that's approaching spinster status, she'd informed me. When I laughed at the absurdity of that she'd cut me a look that told me she didn't find anything funny about her predicament. Many things had to be considered before saying yes, and she spent a couple of weeks considering them all. Even when we were together she'd fall silent sometimes, and just look at me.

She had the kind of mental engine that molded her face into a mask of beautiful brilliance when she was pensive.

I hadn't known it then, but in the time between the walk in the park and her simply saying, "OK, I'll be your girlfriend," was when I fell in love with her.

After she said yes, that's when things started getting rocky, though.

She quit her hostess job (I didn't insist she did but I had insinuated it enough) and got a part-time job answering phones at a call-center, a big-time pay cut. She had been making more than girls her age earn full-time working part-time as a hostess, and had gotten used to having money. Now, she was broke all the time, and hated it. "See what I do for you," she'd said. "I've taken a vow of poverty."

After the honeymoon period, which was very sweet, we'd fight and argue as couples tend to do. Most of ours were about her suspicions as to my whereabouts and what I was getting into when she wasn't around. She knew about the girls in Japan and their affinity for foreign guys, so she'd always send emails that said, "where are you?" and "why does it take you so long to respond? Are your friends more important than me?" and "Are you with some other bitch? I know you are!"

She knew her people, well, and she knew me too, better than I knew myself apparently. She was right most of the time. Her emails and calls would catch me in the middle of all kinds of trifling shit.

From my arrival in Japan, I'd been suffering from an obsession with Japanese girls. And getting involved with Aiko had only slowed down my momentum a little. Unaccustomed to the amount of attention I was getting from women, I'd become something of a womanizer. I was finally sowing my oats crazily the way I never had (but wish I had a chance to) in America. I had regressed into an almost adolescent mindset of conquest for the sake of conquest, for the belt notch, for notes to compare with cats like Damon, and to tell my boys back home in Brooklyn.

I had actually, for a brief time, entertained the thought of writing a book about this obsession many Japanese women have with Western guys (particularly white guys), the corrupting influence it has on the soul of foreigners, and its implications for the future of international relations — or some crap like that. Seriously, I did. I'd even momentarily proselytized myself into believing that I was a cheater with some sanctified purpose, like research; a missionary for the Church of Latter-Day Debauchery.

But, with Aiko, things felt different from the start. She wasn't like the other Japanese girls. I didn't have to sit there and endure incessant questioning about what Americans think about Japanese this and Japanese that, or what black people think about this and that, until I wanted to rip my ears off. And she didn't have to sit there patiently smiling and listen to me drone on and on about how, yes, some things are different but we have many more things in common. It went without saying. When we got together we actually *talked*!

We were very good together. We had so much in common. We both wanted to travel and study. She had a very strong interest in exploring the psychological impact of this focus on cultural differences. In other words, she was fascinated, and borderline obsessed with the fixation among many Japanese with Western culture, as well, at the expense of Japanese culture. She was totally disgusted by their inability to see the individuality of foreigners, their tendency to overlook the

Gaijin's glaring demerits blinded by their focus on their exotic qualities. She labeled these people "Gaijin Freaks."

She'd decided to make a documentary exploring this phenomenon. But, before she could do that, she had to explore it on a personal basis, I believe. I wondered if that was a major factor in why she'd agreed to be my girlfriend in the first place. Maybe I was *her* research. But, I was so thrilled to be around her I really didn't care what her reasons were.

I told her that I had come to Japan with the intention of writing a book about my experiences in Tokyo and Saitama, comparing and contrasting the differences in culture with that of NY. She loved the idea and we decided to work together to accomplish our goals. We bonded in this way, and so our discussions on the matter – which were often heated – were also enlightening and educational for both of us. We went on like this for several months, seeing each other a couple of times a week, talking, fighting, loving, and learning from each other.

She helped me with my Japanese and I helped her, when requested, with her English. However, most often my assistance was not sought directly. She resisted for some reason I always had difficulty putting a finger on. Perhaps it had something to do with the stigma that girls in Japan live under – that they fuck with foreign guys in order to get free English lessons, or as some kind of status symbol (English ability and capacity to interact with foreigners being a sign of a "globalized" mentality or merely cool). But, whether she intended it or not, her English got better and better the more time we spent together, to the point that she hardly used Japanese at all.

*****

One day I told her, out of the blue, that I needed a break; that I had some serious concerns about our relationship. And it's true, I did, but not enough to stop seeing her like I had. She never knew this but it wasn't because of her, but because I had a fever blister on my mouth and I was embarrassed to see her, or even go to work. I called in sick for almost a week. I don't know exactly why – maybe it was because of its placement on my lip, in the most conspicuous and intimate of places – but I cowered in my house for days, avoiding all human contact. Even the Aussie and Kiwi were concerned about me. I told them that I was OK, but I was pretty damn far from OK. I felt disgusting.

I could have handled it better. In my heart I knew it was just a cop out though, this fever blister business. When I looked in the mirror I saw the ugly little cluster, sure, but I also saw the ugly little man in the mirror. This blister was the Creator's nasty little way of making a point.

Point taken, I said to the mirror.

It was easier before I met Aiko and got all emotionally entangled. Back in NY I'd cheat on girlfriends and if conscience ever stood in the path of lust, you better believe there was going to be a hit and run that night.

But, there was something about the nature of the cheating I was doing in Japan that exacerbated the guilt — something dark and spiteful. It was different than what I'd felt when I cheated back home. I wasn't even sure at the time if I was feeling guilty over the cheating or over the spitefulness with which I did it. All I knew for sure was that I was dealing with an element that I had never dealt with before.

Aiko couldn't make any sense of this sudden flip. I had expected a dramatic episode: tears, hysteria, showing up at my door uninvited, demanding to see me, and the likes. One ex-girlfriend had even come to my door with a gun while I actually had another girl in my bed! I'd experienced all of that many times back in NY and my ego secretly always kind of dug it. I don't know. It just made me feel more like a *real* man, needed and loved. But, from Aiko, there was none of that nonsense. She just said, "Fuck you! You are so stupid," and promptly hung up on me (and yes I was so manly I'd done it over the phone). I probably could've come up with a better line than "I need some time," but I'd gotten so upset over the blister that Aiko's feelings had been moved from my passenger seat to the backseat. Selfish and, as she'd said, stupid would best describe me at this time.

A couple of weeks later, during which my lip had healed up and my fever had gone into remission (I'd gone without any J-factor and was feeling pretty good about myself), I tried to resume relations with Aiko. But, as I should've expected, my behavior had changed her outlook on our relationship. She took me back, but there was no hoopla. I told her I'd missed her and I was sorry...that I'd fucked up. She'd responded with the Japanese equivalent of, "it's *all* good, boo!"

She was still in love with me, though. I knew that much. But now she was leerier. She became much more independent, which is *really* saying something. She'd always done whatever she wanted to do. I was just fortunate that *I* was what she 'd wanted to do most often, so her headstrongness worked out in my favor. But, from the time she took me back, she began hanging out without me a lot more than she used to. She took to texting me incoherent messages from drinking parties with her university friends, calling me up, shit-faced, from Chinese night clubs in Omiya (her ex-boyfriend had been Chinese) slurring in Japanese while refusing to use English, and even doing goukon (group blind dating parties). She'd told me that back in high school, she used to do *yarikon* occasionally, which is like a Japanese drinking party with a guaranteed happy ending. I hoped she wasn't going that route again, but Aiko was as loco as I in many respects (which is why we hit it off so spectacularly) so I wouldn't have put it past her.

On top of that, she started teaching private Japanese lessons. She wanted to do research to better understand foreigners, and make extra money on the side, she told me one day, so she asked me to help her make an ad in English. I did, and she placed it on a language study website frequented by expats, along with a photo of herself, and the responses poured in.

She began to have unusual conversations, in Japanese, with one of these students she'd taken on. At first, I thought she was losing her goddamn mind! She was holding lengthy, giggly chats, in *my* house, sometimes even in my bed, with this guy. I didn't realize she was *trying* to make me jealous. I just thought it was some strange Japanese shit! I'd seen enough social oddities that the culture shock worthy had become damn near the commonplace. Nothing really surprised me anymore. I learned to just roll with everything, making mental notes of the contrast.

But, jealousy...*this* I didn't roll with well.

It had been years since I'd felt jealous, or even possessive over a woman. I couldn't rightly recall what jealousy felt like, actually. I didn't know what to do with it. One moment, I felt like stalking her, so I could catch her in the act...but then what? Hurt her? Hurt some guy? Get arrested and end up in some Japanese jail, with a bunch of Yakuza trying to *tattoo* my ass? And, in the next moment, I was telling myself *I'm too cool for this shit!*

I started hanging out with Damon, again, prowling the Gaijin bars, picking off Japanese girls like a predator. And I also resumed my role as English teacher / *foreign fuck you'll never forget*, with first one NEON student, then another... pretty soon I found myself in one of those crazy flukes of life, teaching a class seated across from four ladies, two of which I was currently doing, and one, a married jukujo (late 30s-early 40s and totally hot), who'd just given me her email address on the down-low. Loco was up to his old tricks. I practically lived in the love hotels of Shinjuku and Shibuya.

But, my jealousy was not alleviated. In fact, it got worse. I found out, the hard way, that *I* wasn't *too cool for this shit!*

When I would call Aiko, she wouldn't answer, and if I texted her she'd respond hours later, or even the next day sometimes with a "Sorry, I was out with my friends and drank too much! What did you want?" or some shit like that.

This jealousy actually scared the hell out of me. I was even studying kanji motivated mostly by my determination to read her text messages (which she knew at the time that for me it was like Neo looking at the Matrix encoded, so she didn't even bother to be sneaky). Eventually, I convinced myself that I couldn't possibly love her. If I did, how was I capable of doing the things I did on the side with these other women?

So one night I broke up with her, in typical Loco fashion: cruelly. I was never good at breakups. I told her, "I can't stop you from fucking anybody. All I can do is trust that you don't." At the time, I didn't think these words were *that* harsh, but she found them to be devastatingly indicative of my lack of emotional investment in our relationship. And, with a thud, we were done.

I took on another girlfriend, one of the girls that I had

been cheating on Aiko with who'd shown promise as far as a future together was concerned. We began to see each other more regularly, and I proceeded to try to replace Aiko with her, transfer my feelings for Aiko to this new vessel. In my mind, at the time, Japanese women had become that uniform. They basically behaved the same, thought the same, felt the same, looked the same, and fucked the same. I thought it didn't matter.

I realized I had been slowly dehumanizing them, not simply to rationalize my sexual exploits but with spite in my heart. For every day I had to suck on the humiliation of the empty seat beside me on the train, and every other paper cut of degradation I endured, I imagined I was vindicated. This revenge fucking did wonders for my libido and prowess, as well.

Aiko's stand-in lasted for about four weeks – four hellish weeks – during which I began to feel, see, taste, hear, and smell the difference between this other girl and Aiko, between ALL the other Japanese girls I'd known and Aiko.

Meanwhile, Aiko had taken up with that student she had been all giggly with on the phone at my house, she informed me via text message.

"He's a really nice guy!" she told me one night when I called her *just to say hi*. I wanted to kill him, and I missed her so much I found it hard to breathe. I told her as much. She told me to get over it. "You had your chance! But you prefer your little *Gaijin Freaks*, deshou? Well, enjoy yourself!"

A couple of miserable weeks later I called again and asked her could we be friends, but what I really wanted was to feel her energy, her vitality, her gentleness, her anger, and fury, again. She told me she'd have to ask her boyfriend for permission (she was vicious). But after a few days she called back and said, "Sure, why not."

So, we became friends, of sorts. We talked endlessly the way we always did. Sometimes our conversations would get so good she'd sadistically bring me back to reality with a gush over how happy she was with her new beau, and how it was too bad I hadn't been able to appreciate her the way he does. She bragged how he calls her every night just to see how she's doing, and always takes her to cool places. How they'd gone to a very expensive onsen in Hakone…and how he was teaching her German (he was from Germany). It made me jealous as hell. The thought of this Euro-trash with his hands all over my baby! I cried at night in my little tatami cave, looking at pictures we'd taken together and cursing myself for being such an idiot.

Despite the pain, I maintained my friend disguise while I tried to subtly undermine their relationship, which soon progressed to not-so subtle attempts. But Aiko, stubborn as she was, and sharp as a tack, resisted me with calmness and nonchalance, which only fanned my desire.

After a few weeks of this though, she'd worn me down and made her point clear enough so that even someone as slow on the uptake as me could understand: We were kaput! So, I gave up, at least with the aggressive stuff. And, we *really* became friends.

I told her one day, "Feel free to talk to me about anything, even him." And, she did. I took it like a man, anything to keep her in my life. I became calm and resolute too. I figured, it was all for the best. I'm such an asshole I would probably fuck it up if we were to ever get back together anyway.

Not a month as true friends had passed before Aiko called me one night and said she missed me and that she did not feel about her boyfriend the way she felt about me, indicating for the first time, that she was open to discussing reconciliation.

I had been walking back from the 7-11 when I got the call. I was halfway home, with a bagful of junk food, ready to couch potato the night away. I stopped there in the street and we talked for two hours! I fell in love with her again that night, or maybe it just deepened.

But, still, it was not love like I had known before. Maybe love is different with every person, every relationship. Or, maybe I have some serious emotional issues that make me incapable of feeling and behaving the way I've been taught that you're supposed to when you're in love. I really don't have the answers. All I know is that night I felt more satisfied with myself than I had in my entire life. Maybe it was as simple as she had chosen me over him, a victory over an adversary. Victory feels good doesn't it? And I felt great! I felt perfect. I contained my glee as best I could, though. Kept it out of my voice, but I did do a silent little end-zone dance in the streets of Saitama, scaring the hell out of people passing by. I told her, "If you take me back, I promise you won't regret it."

"Don't talk about that now. I need –"

"Take as much time as you need...I'll be here!"

A couple of weeks later, we were back together, with a renewed resolve to make it work. She sent the German packing (she'd said, but personally I think she'd scared him away with her energy and aggressiveness. She was a dynamo and from her descriptions of him, he seemed too mild-mannered and conservative for her) while I cut out the philandering and focused more on studying Japanese and making money.

It had been over a year since we'd met. Our routines were basic but very nice. On Saturdays, she'd meet me at Starbucks in Musashi Urawa where we'd have coffee and talk about psychology, or Jazz, or we'd help each other with language stuff. Sometimes we'd go to izakaya and have dinner, and smoke and joke, or fight and argue, but we were together as much as possible.

One time I'd told her how rude it was for restaurant staff people to ignore me the way they do, and only interact with her, even if I'm speaking Japanese. And she agreed it was rude, so sometimes she'd pretend to be Chinese (she could even speak some Chinese) and shrug when they spoke to her in Japanese, forcing the staff to deal with me so I could get some practice in. She was so great!

Sometimes we'd go to the movies, or go play pool. Then, we'd go to my house and make love and talk until it was time for her to go home. She'd stay over occasionally but that would cause arguments and fights with her parents. Other times I'd go over to her house and have dinner with her family. She had an older sister and a younger brother. Her mother, a devout Jehovah's Witness – well as devout as Japanese can be – adored me. And her father, well, it was hard to get a read on the man, but he smiled once. He was a descendant of samurai, Aiko told me, in possession of what she called the *Bushido* spirit, which I think she possessed, as well.

My spirit is derived from my mother, which is more of a nurturing, emotional spirit. When we fought, it was her fire, her stubbornness, her pride, that bore her. She was not passive, not weak, not angelic or baby doll like, and yet she was soft, and pliable, and sweet and tender and delicate. I was temperamental and moody, but able to bring her around whenever she went off the deep end, with some sound advice or a rocking hug. She loved my hugs.

I used to give her "promise" coupons when I fucked up. Like sometimes when I got mad at her headstrong ass, I'd call *her* a Gaijin Freak. After all, she'd gone from a Chinese boyfriend, to me, an American, to a German, and then back to me. "Sounds like *you* are one of your gaijin freaks to me!" I said to her one night, and she kicked me out of my own bed, and wouldn't sleep with me until I gave her a coupon that promised something like, "Once a week, for a period no longer than one month, the bearer is entitled to any form of pampering I am able to provide (within reason), including but not limited to, *full body massages, meals of her choosing prepared and served,* or *an all-expense paid visit to a nail salon.*" And she loved it! I'd always keep the promises, conspicuously. She loved the simplicity of promises being kept. She was a very simple girl on many levels, and I loved that about her.

In the summer of 2004 she asked me to feel something growing under her skin on her leg. It was a lump. She went to the hospital and they said it was a tumor. They tried to remove it but could only remove part of it. She spent a couple days in there and all of her friends came to see her. She was a little depressed about being in the hospital, but kept a smile whenever her friends were around. I spent as much time as I could with her. Once she was released, she had to go back and forth to the hospital throughout the summer (and she hated it) while the doctors tried to ascertain whether it was malignant or not. They never did.

The following summer, in 2005, a new tumor came, this time on her back. It was followed soon after by a third, on her other leg. But, she did not want to spend another summer in the hospital, so she decided to spend it with her friends, and with me. But once the summer was done, she could no longer put it off. There was pain. She called the tumors her children. They were like little fetuses springing up all over her body. By that winter, I had lost count; 10 or 15 tumors. She had to be hospitalized repeatedly. Test after test neither confirmed nor denied their malignancy, she told me, frustrated as hell with her doctors. They decided to treat them like malignancies, and began her on anti-cancer drugs, rounds of chemotherapy, and pain medication.

*****

The Japanese have a word that they use in the way Americans might say, "hang in there," "keep your head up," or "break a leg," though it isn't a cultural equivalent at all. You hear it all the time here, and before long you find yourself using it, sometimes even appropriately.

The word is: Ganbatte.

I learned what ganbatte really means on February 27th, 2006.

I was on my way to the hospital to visit Aiko before work, when I got a frantic call from Aiko's best friend, Pei-Pei, telling me that I needed to hurry to the hospital because Aiko had fallen into a coma in the night. I was already en-route so I just continued on my way, trying not to panic. Even though I knew in the back of my mind that there was a chance she wouldn't beat this thing, somehow, through all of it, I thought for sure that she would. She was coming to NY with me in June to meet my friends and family…she wasn't going anywhere before then. Some miracle would occur and kill those tumors, I thought. Each time I went to see her, watching her slowly deteriorating physically and emotionally, I still refused to believe that cancer could kill a life force as strong as hers.

When I arrived at the hospital, her older sister was alone

106

with her, distraught. She saw me and screamed in joy. She spoke in Japanese a mile a minute, so I couldn't follow, just grasping at familiar words and body language. I gathered that she had been waiting for her parents who were on their way, but that she was worried that Aiko would die before they arrived. She said that I should talk to Aiko because the doctors had suggested that even though she was comatose she could still hear us. I looked down at my baby. She was struggling to breathe, and there were tubes everywhere. The cancer had spread to her lungs and brain weeks earlier, so the coma should not have been a surprise.

The night before, I had sent her a text message telling her I would see her in the morning. She'd replied "OK". I asked her did she need anything, she said "iranaiyo." (she didn't). It was late when she replied, 1:27am, so I asked her what was she still doing awake, hoping against hope that it wasn't due to the pain she had been enduring ceaselessly for the past three months or so. She replied, her last words to me, "Neyou to shiteru" (I'm going to sleep). And my beloved did just that. I replied, "OK, sleep well," and a little kissy smiley icon.

My last words to her.

If I'd known that was going to be our last exchange I would've said... I don't know what, just something more.

I knelt down beside the bed and began to talk to her, hoping for a reaction to my voice, but inside not wanting her to respond nor to wake up. I wanted her pain to end. I fully understand euthanasia now. But, Aiko wasn't going anywhere, not before the rest of her family arrived.

Her little brother arrived with his girlfriend followed by Pei-Pei. Her mother came moments later. Everyone took turns encouraging her to hang in there because her father, the leader of their clan, would arrive soon. Her mother implored her, holding Aiko's hand and saying over and over again, "ganbatte, Ai-chan. Ganbatte!"

But, Aiko didn't need to be told, I think. She was her father's daughter through and through, and wasn't going anywhere without his blessing.

Her father arrived a few minutes later in a panic. I moved from beside her to make way for him. He called to her. The whole family joined in, congratulating her, "Father's here, Ai-chan! You did it! He's here!"

I left the room for the family for a while, and went and had some coffee and a smoke. The doctors had told us that though her heart was young and strong, her lungs were weak and so she could only keep breathing on her own for the next several hours or so, the rest of the day at most. I called my job and told them I wouldn't be in, and returned to the room.

When I returned her mother told me to talk to her, so I did. They had set up her iPod and speakers to play her favorite music, some jazz ballads and what not. And then that Christina Aguilera song, *Beautiful*, came on. She loved that song. I sang it to her and, for a moment, she seemed to respond to my voice. She took a deep breath, and it just slowly slipped out of her.

I sang, "You are beautiful, in every single way..." while I waited for the next breath.

It never came.

But, she'd had a very high fever so she still felt so warm and alive. I caressed her cheeks and rubbed her bald head where the hair had begun to grow back. She looked so beautiful I felt the song was about her.

She died in my hands.

I didn't accept it. No one had noticed it but me. I wasn't

even sure I'd noticed it. I hoped I was mistaken. I got up and her sister took my place beside her. She realized Aiko wasn't breathing and cried out.

The doctor came in, checked her vital signs, and looked at his watch.

3:37pm.

*****

On March 1st, she was to be cremated, so I went to Aiko's home first thing that morning for the last viewing. She was in a box on the floor in the living room. Her face looked so beautiful and alive. I couldn't believe she was gone.

Pei-Pei, who was Chinese, but could speak English and Japanese fairly well, translated some of the goings-on, but most of what was said to me and about me will forever be a mystery – except that it must have been good. This woman who I treated so haphazardly sometimes had nothing but great things to say about me to her friends and family. I was treated with so much... priority, it was overwhelming. I might have been her husband, and indeed I felt widowed. Her father, whom I thought didn't like the idea of his daughter and I dating, was surprisingly full of warmth and compassion for me.

Her friends came to me and, through Pei-Pei, told me about all the wonderful things she'd told them and how happy I'd made her.

I used to call her a negative person, a pessimistic, glass is half-empty kind of girl, but she'd told me that I had changed her: made her more positive, more optimistic. God, I don't see how I can be given the credit for that. I was leading her in that direction, but not by example. I'm such a hypocrite. What did she see in me?

After an hour or so they closed the box. I touched her former body one last time before they did. Her father's pillar cracked a bit, as did her mother's. They had been a fine mix of solemn and jovial since my arrival, like a New Orleans celebration of the recently departed.

When her father had picked me up at the train station, with Aiko's little cousins from Osaka in the back seat of the minivan, he had told them to greet me in English, and they all shouted, "Hello!!" when I got in. I laughed along with her father, saying, "Hey y'all" and the jovial tone had been set.

But, that all ended when the casket closed.

They loaded her into the back of a hearse and we were off to the crematory. Some of the joyfulness returned during the ride, but again I couldn't understand most of it, so I sat, looking at Saitama pass by out the window, wondering where Aiko's spirit was at that very moment.

We arrived at the crematory. It was obscenely gorgeous; like a New York museum, surrounded by manicured trees, burbling brooks and gardens maintained to an almost inhuman perfection.

In a room designated for this purpose, we viewed her body one last time through a glass-covered box, her face framed in flowers, and her casket filled with the things she liked — as per Japanese tradition. It reminded me of some ancient Egyptian queen taking her treasure with her to the next realm.

When her mother had told me about this tradition a couple of days earlier I'd had a hell of a time thinking of something to place in the box. I had decided on my Ken Burns' Jazz DVD set and my Jean Michele Basquiat book. We both loved Basquiat's art and were crazy about the history of Jazz. But when I'd presented these things the family had said something to indicate it was too much. That stuffed animals and little trinkets of that sort were the norm. I had given her a stuffed Snoopy doll the first time she'd been hospitalized and she'd slept with it in her bed ever since, so I'd placed that with her instead. I'd put it by her leg, but her father moved it up next to her face so that through the window in the casket I could see *my* queen, Aiko, and the Snoopy doll, ready to make the journey to the next realm.

I'd also written her a letter the previous night. I wrote that I was so sorry I hadn't been a better man for her, and that I lied and cheated and abused her trust. I told her that I couldn't think of anything she wanted because she wasn't much of a material person, more of a doer, and so the best thing I could do was promise her that I'd do my best to honor her memory by being the kind of person she'd shown me how to be by example: a doer. "Ganbarimasu!" I wrote.

This letter I also placed in her casket.

After a while we were led through the immaculate crematory by a staff person who was guiding the casket on an electronic cart. We followed him to the oven rooms, and the casket was placed in one of these ovens. A few words were offered and a switch was thrown, and like that, her body was incinerated.

We were then led to a private waiting room and served tea and whatnot. I tried to talk with Aiko's friends and family but I was out of it, lost in a miasma of loneliness and despair, and my Japanese wasn't working at all. Even Pei-Pei's English had become incomprehensible.

After a while we were called again into another room where her ashes were presented to the family. Large pieces of dusty, pearly white bone and cartilage were still intact, but most of it was in small chips; chips of my baby.

As per tradition, with special chopsticks, a piece is selected by each person and placed in two jars that are to be kept by the family…lord knows what happens to the rest. I took what looked like a piece of a leg bone, clasped it with my chopsticks and placed it in the jar, sort of in a trance state or like a researcher studying Japanese burial traditions. I just wanted to get this over with. But, part of me, the grieving part of me, seized me again. Watching her family and friends literally picking over her bones was almost too much. It was like a dark metaphor come to life.

Following this, we were led out to the exit. Another family was coming in, following a staff member guiding another casket on an electronic cart. Everything had happened exactly on schedule.

We got back into her father's minivan and headed back to the house where supper awaited us. We all sat in the living room silently for a while, nibbling on sweets and braving a recording of Aiko performing "Honeysuckle Rose," one of the old jazz standards that she loved to sing.

She'd made a mistake in the lyrics, and sang, "Honeysuckle knows!" I thought I was the only one in the room who caught it until Aiko abruptly stopped singing, and told her band she wanted to take it from the top. She explained why for they hadn't noticed (they were all Japanese and spoke very little English). All three of them were sitting there in the living room listening and remembering the day of the recording. I could see on their faces that they were reliving the session, and that Aiko would always live in them. Their love for her burned through the fog in my head like a beacon from a lighthouse, guiding a smile to my face.

In the recording, one of her band mates made a joke about her flub that I didn't understand well...something about *honey*, *sucking* and *noses*. But Aiko did, of course, and let out a cackle of laughter with wings that filled a roomful of mourners with joy, her joy, the way it had in that alley the first night we met.

I asked her brother to make a copy of the recording for me so I could listen to it when I needed to hear her voice, or be reminded to ganbatte – to do my best, and to hang in there.

5

YOUNG, GIFTED, AND RACIST

After Aiko passed, I felt useless. No one could convince me that I wasn't alone in the world. I probably should have left Japan then. But I didn't really have any place to go. I was virtually estranged from most of my friends and family. They were on the other side of the globe, and only had an inkling of what I was going through over here. Every visit home confirmed this. Life was going on without me as I should have expected it would. But, stupidly, I hadn't. I'd lost track of time here in Kawaiiland. Between learning a new language and culture, exploring a new country, and finding, loving, dogging, losing, recovering and then having the woman of my dreams taken away, time had also gotten away from me.

It was about then – when I had finished feeling sorry for myself and for a world depreciated by Aiko's absence – I started trying to write again. At first I was inspired by her memory and the promise I'd made to her, and got a booster shot with President Obama's surprising rise to power. But, eventually my motivation to write was fueled by a convolution of feelings that had been festering within me practically since my arrival in Japan.

A mass that would eventually reveal a foul truth: I was a racist!

Or, rather, I was *still* a racist!

I am the product of a society that has been wrestling with this so-called race question for over 400 years, with many unfortunate failures and some clear successes. So much success that, before coming to Japan, I could not point to an overtly racist act done by an individual aimed directly at me with the purpose of harming me in any way. I'd never been knowingly denied a job for which I was qualified, or entry to any residence or establishment, or even been called a racial slur (by someone outside of my own race, that is). My mother can't say that. I'd wager very few black people from her generation can say that. And if that ain't progress, I don't know what is.

However, I was raised in the same racist cesspool as most people, and I have been scarred, as well.

No child is born a racist, I believe, but racist feelings have been within me since childhood. Or rather, they were uploaded into me and, like some kind of Trojan horse virus, were unleashed as a result of living here in Japan, and being *over*exposed to a people, in my opinion, made up predominantly of *oblivious* racists.

And see what I did? I have gone and drawn conclusions about a people, most of whom I've never met or encountered and never will, based on the behavior of a small segment of their population: those strangers I encounter here in Yokohama and Tokyo on a regular basis. If you're wondering how I could allow something like that to happen to me, then you're probably one of those blessed individuals who have never let racism in… or you're oblivious.

Is there anything I can say that will justify my scapegoating and scrap-heaping an entire race? Of course not. I'll say this much, though: It wasn't one event, or even a handful of events, that brought this about. What I have experienced here is more like the erosive effect the ocean's current has on the shoreline. Little by little, with the appearance of inevitability, the sea encroaches and the beach recedes. Even if you have those tetrapod contraptions set up to dissipate the force of incoming waves, or you've imported sand and mixed sediments to protect the shoreline, the ocean will keep applying the pressure and eventually wash away all remnants of a shore.

This erosion didn't begin in Japan, though. It really began a long time ago in a galaxy far, far away; 14 hours away by plane, to be exact.

It began back when I was child coming of age in the greatest city on Earth: New York.

*****

I was six years old and in the first grade when some white cop shot 10-year old Clifford Glover in the back, in the streets of Jamaica, Queens, killing him in cold blood.

I didn't know Clifford Glover personally, but for the shockwave of anger and despair that swept through my weird little school, and my community, and many other black communities in NY that day, he could have been a fellow classmate. Hell, kin!

"He's dead?" I asked one of my teachers. Dead wasn't a foreign concept to me at the time but the death of a child practically my own age was! Children didn't die. Grandparents died. People who stick heroin needles in their arms, like my uncle Raheem, they die. People who don't run from vampires die…well, kinda die. But kids only get hurt, fall out of trees and get hit by cars, forcing them to wear casts on their legs and arms for weeks. *We don't die*, I thought.

"Ndiyo, ndugu. (yes, little brother) Some honky pig shot him down in the streets like a dog!" my teacher cried bitterly.

I had grown accustomed to hearing slurs of that nature (*honky* and *pig* being synonyms for "white" and "police officer" respectively) for they would echo through the halls of my private school, Uhuru Sasa Shule (Swahili for "Freedom Now School"), and through the streets of Bed-Stuy, on a regular basis. My favorite all-time slur, though, was "crackers"

117

meaning white people. Just always loved the way the world flowed, especially when my father would use it. It had to be his favorite word, too, at the time.

A year after the shooting, that honky pig, who'd actually been put on trial for murder (a first for a NYC police officer), walked away from the courthouse free as a bird, found *not guilty* by a jury of *his* peers (meaning some other honkies, I learned).

Even before the verdict (and possibly in anticipation of the pig being set free; such was the nature of the justice system), me, my classmates, and the entire school, were activated.

In arts & crafts class we made placards with crayons and magic markers; signs that conveyed slogans such as "No Justice! No Peace!" and "Save the Children!" and "Protect Our Kids From The Pigs!" adorned with pink swine that looked somewhat like the *Three Little Pigs* of the honky storybooks I'd be put to sleep with if I'd had a less conscientious mother. Only these pigs were sinister-looking and wore police uniforms, with guns drawn and aimed at black mothers holding black babies. Expertly caricatured by the school's resident artist, and colored in imperfectly by me and my classmates. Somehow our work complimented his and had the desired affect of showing that blacks of all ages were outraged as this travesty, particularly the youth, any of whom could very well be the next Clifford Glover.

We were all Clifford Glover!

*****

Dressed in what became the uniform: bell-bottom Lee Jeans and matching jackets (or dashikis), over red turtlenecks with black combat boots, we'd look like an army of mini-members

118

of the Black Panther Party (which we were in a way). We'd regularly march through the streets of Bed-Stuy in this fashion, singing songs of revolution in unison, showing off the marching drills we'd practice regularly in front of the school, following drill commands given by our teachers in Swahili, the language we studied and used everyday!

I was embarrassed at first, but for a year everywhere we went there was a spotlight on us. A spotlight we hoisted and carried via our voices, style of dress and brazen demeanor. Child soldiers in the ghetto. So, after a while I got used to being the center of attention in a neglected community, and actually grew to like it. My dashiki became a badge of honor, my red, black and green kufi (cap) a crown, while my black boots glowed like the exoskeleton of some exotic Asian beetle, buffed daily without complaint with Kiwi polish (though it was a hassle stringing them up). I used to mumble the songs, ashamed of the spectacle I was being forced to make of myself. But soon my voice grew loud and ostentatious, and I savored the first taste of swagger in my short life.

And, the people of Bed-Stuy had come to know our swagger well. They would hang out of windows, step out of barber shops, pause from their shopping or dice rolling or number-running or drug-peddling or any number of activities observed daily in the ghetto, to gawk in awe or beam with admiration at the promise of the future as it paraded by. Other little kids would run alongside of us to check up-close as if to see if we were really *real*, and would try to mimic our swagger and utter some of the strange African words coming out of our mouths. Some, from seeing us so often, would even learn the catchy English songs we'd regularly sang; adding their voices to ours so that the call and response of over a hundred children would be heard reverberating off of the tenement walls of the brownstone lined streets of Brooklyn from blocks away.

And their parents, seeing the power, charisma and discipline we exuded, and knowing that their children were getting nothing of the sort in those towering brick warehouses of lies and misinformation they called Public Schools, chock full of arrogant honky teachers indoctrinating their kids to passively languish, brood, whine, complain, and die in the great *honkified* world, some would yank their children out of public schools post haste. And bring them kicking and screaming and wetting their pants to the doors of Uhuru Sasa Shule. And, as the years progressed, Uhuru Sasa progressed, and the formation we marched in extended farther and farther and our voices grew louder and prouder.

Songs with lyrics like the school's motto, "Educate, Agitate, Organize," in which we'd proclaim "we are educated, trained and taught to prepare for a war that must be fought!"

Sure, we were part marching singing billboards at those times but people had never seen anything like this before and the possibilities we presented, the vision of a nation within a nation that we evoked, was both captivating and inspiring. *Of course* people wanted to be a part of it.

But, it wasn't all song and swagger. The ghetto is a dangerous place to be militant, both physically and mentally.

*****

There had been a huge demonstration that day, in protest of the not guilty verdict against the cop who'd killed Clifford Glover, and we joined in, carrying the signs that we'd made in school and shouting lines like, "Save the Children!" and "Protect our Babies!" fully aware that we were talking about ourselves.

There had also been rioting that day, but I didn't know anything about that. All I knew was that we were part of something. Something massive. Something important. Big men with big voices were hollering big words through megaphones. My Headmaster, Baba Kasisi Jitu Weusi, our patron and protector, was one of those voices, one of the biggest! Some of the other teachers, as well. And, watching them filled us with such pride. We were part of something special! These men and women were more than just teachers, and more than just our parents, too. They were revolutionaries. Like warriors from the African tribes and nations that our individual classes were named after. Tribes like Zulu, Ashanti, Nubia and Kush!

The honky pigs lined the route we marched, helmets on heads, batons in hand. Some trotted alongside us mounted on horses, leaving mounds of horse droppings in their wake, looking arrogant, anxious and angry all at once. Looking more malicious and unjust than my teachers would depict them in inflammatory words, even more so than the caricatures in the school's newspaper, Black News, portrayed them.

Danger filled the air, but for some reason I couldn't feel it. I felt safe. My whole family, and extended family, was in the immediate vicinity: My mother (who worked for the school), my older brothers and sisters (who my mother had pulled out of public school and placed in Uhuru Sasa), all my teachers, all my friends, everybody I saw everyday was right there with me. So for me, it was all a great adventure.

You'd think, as a child, anger would trouble me. Meh, anger was ubiquitous. It was as common as joy. Someone shouting angrily was just a style of communication. Over the course of the eight years I would spend in Uhuru Sasa, anger would be almost a constant.

There'd always be an innocent child or adult slain by police. Or some young black man mercilessly beat to death by some mob of racist honkies for the crime of catching a flat in their community while black. Or some child found dead with a heroin needle he'd found laying around in his arm. Or even some oil company financing the civil war in Angola. Or a government like South Africa oppressing its black majority, capturing (with the help of our CIA) and imprisoning a revolutionary like Nelson Mandela for coordinating sabotage campaigns against the white racist minority regime prone to terrorist attacks and massacring blacks, like in Sharpsville.

There was always something to be angry about, if you were black, aware and cared. Always some power to fight, some injustice to right.

And my school (and the organization that formed it) stayed in the mix, stayed relevant, and even lead the call for justice in some cases.

The demonstration held on behalf of little Clifford Glover would end without bloodshed and we'd return home safely that day, but it wouldn't always be that way. The times were volatile and the community was a hotbed full of hotheads.

Here was the environment where racism was first introduced to me as an inoculation against racism.

*****

Though they had politicized me into a Black & White world, with very little grey, my school was a blessing I wouldn't fully appreciate until I came to Japan.

Unlike most black children in the U.S. of that time, my

indoctrination was not achieved through the racially biased public school system, where black kids are taught to uphold and honor the white power structure and their cultural superiority, and where precious little was taught about black history, pre-America, pre-slavery, pre-European invasion. Nor were these institutions inclined to present African-American contributions to American history and the American way of life in a way so as to promote the pride and dignity of the young black minds in attendance.

My education was done outside of this paradigm, done privately, by justifiably angry black racists.

I was edified with racial pride and righteous dignity. My education was designed to leave me thinking and feeling if not superior to white people, at least equal. I was trained as if there were a war well underway, in the very streets outside my window, and I was to be a soldier in that war. Not a war fought with arms but with the greatest resource available to us: our minds.

And this enemy was the White Man! A vicious, ruthless, genocidal, enslaving, raping, castrating, lynching, assassinating, evil, evil, EVIL, race of men (and the white women that support and breed them). As for the white folks who weren't actively engaged in these atrocious crimes against black humanity... well, there are always exceptions. Either that or they were clever enough to hide their true nature.

My teachers had the pictures and documents to support their assertions, too. All the proof they felt was needed to twist my mind and heart. 400 years rife with evidence of white wickedness!

I remember being shown as a child a book containing dozens of pictures of blacks who'd been lynched by whites in

123

the South. The methods varied. Some were tied to trees, naked, with throats cut, or were castrated. Some were just hanging from tree limbs by their necks, looking like what Billie Holiday sang of, some kind of *Strange Fruit*. Others had been burned on a bed of wood in large open fires, like some ancient funeral rite, or some cannibalistic Sunday outing with a *nigger on the barbie* as the main course.

As I went through these pictures, I'd give the charred remains of some hardly recognizable human being, or the sign hung around a corpse's neck establishing that it was, indeed, a "nigger," appropriate attention. But, my eyes would zoom in on and adhere to these *people* capable of such crimes: The white people. They were not dressed in white cloaks and white hoods with eyeholes, like the iconic images of white racism in America. There was no towering burning white cross in the backdrop of these photos. Nah. These whites were unmasked, dressed like everyday people of their time which, according to the dates on the photos, was not so long ago. They were smiling, pointing, posing proudly with pointy noses and jutted chins, folded arms, like after a job well done, and swagger in their eyes; having a good old time in the good old days.

These photos were not police records, or from FBI files, but memorabilia; postcards that these *people* would send to friends and family members far and near: *"Nothing says Merry Christmas like niggers roasting on an open fire, Have a happy holiday! Love, Uncle Ned."*

Not the kind of thing you're likely to ever forget, especially in those tender years when your mind is just forming ideas to grow on. These images were chiseled onto my memory, branded on my brain.

And my school complimented this with incontrovertible

proof of black superiority. And not just morally, but spiritually, cognitively, intrinsically, metaphysically, artistically and even physically superior. That despite what them honkies tried to do, all their efforts to exterminate people of African descent, to desecrate and bury our history beneath their own or destroy all traces of it, to ultimately steal our souls and leave soulless black hulls behind, we persevered and even excelled. That our ability to adapt and overcome, our capacity for love and understanding, our soulful connection with Earth and the Heavens, our superior survival instincts, everything about us enabled us to endure and ennobled us to rise someday, and regain our rightful place.

And, I'm forever indebted to these parents and teachers who sacrificed and gave so much of themselves to me and to the *movement*.

But, damn, that's a hell of a thing to teach a child, ain't it?

*****

You know what, though? Despite their well-meaning but misguided efforts, I never really came to hate white people. I never truly believed, in my heart, that they were as bad as my teachers said they were. Even at a young age I was able to intellectualize things a little. Not verbally, but the thought processes were high functioning. Life in New York just presented us New Yorkers with too many contradictions for any generalization, especially racially based ones, to truly stick...unless you *really* wanted them to.

And, I didn't.

The reason I didn't was because a neighbor of mine and a good friend, Chris, just happened to be one of these evil white people my teachers warned me of. But, instead of cracking my head open with a baton, he invited me to his house not weeks after we met, and regularly after that, to play Atari with him. And another neighbor, Benjamin, son of a Hasidic Jew, used to let me ride his bike and read his Marvel Comics. And, their parents never showed me anything but love and respect. In fact, Benjamin's mother showed the *entire* community (a majority black community, mind you) nothing but the depth of her generosity and courage. She even started a community garden and had all of us children planting flowers and beautifying the blight that surrounded and threatened to engulf us.

And, I could go on and on with the contradictions. But, do I need to? Of course not.

So I had to ask myself why did every white person I came into contact with turn out to be an exception? They all couldn't be hiding their true nature, could they? Did they all secretly want to destroy me?

Nope. I decided at that prepubescent age, though I wasn't even fully aware that I had, that my teachers had it half-beautifully right and half-horridly wrong. That they, too, were victims of the same madness they were preparing me to do battle with.

Yep, I love them to death but they were shit kickers and posers.

Nonetheless, the damage was done. The seed of racism had been planted in my soul.

You'd think I'd be pissed now. Here it is, over 30 years later, and I'm still doing battle with this dark seed they implanted in me. But, I ain't mad at them...quite the contrary.

The biggest problem among black people in the U.S., in my opinion, is not hate from without, but hate from within.

My school's agenda was to offset this hate by instilling in each child a sense of cultural longevity, a foothold in history, a foundation, a legacy, and a Motherland: Africa. The primary objective was knowledge of self. The premise being once you know yourself you'll love yourself, and once you've fallen in love with yourself it would be exceedingly difficult to do harm to yourself or to bring harm to your people. These are things that most other cultures and races take for granted, but had been systematically stolen from African-Americans. Self-hate was one of the results.

So, like some kind of rootless, homeless culture whose history began seemingly in chains and cotton fields, African-Americans sort of lunged into the 21st Century. But I did so, not so much in love with black people but certainly without ever holding in contempt, or harboring hate, envy, jealousy or any other dark feelings in my heart for my black brothers and sisters. And, unfortunately, in this day and age, with black-on-black crime numbers as well as the rate of broken black families both still at crisis levels, that's saying something!

So the seed of racism was planted but it didn't sprout. It just lay dormant inside of me. My education thus far just hadn't provided the fertilizer this seed needed to flourish. It lacked an essential ingredient to get me to really embrace it: That all-important why. Why were Chris, and Benjamin, and their parents really evil (despite the façade they put on every time I saw them)? Without the why, it just didn't hold water. So, I was able to navigate my way through much of their propaganda, unknowingly holding on to what was useful and jettisoning the rest.

However, as I got older and headed out into the streets, my well-educated and agitated ass ran head-on into an organization that had some fertilizer that at least attempted to answer the why.

They were an off-shoot of the Black Muslim movement, known as The Five Percent Nation of Islam, or The Nation of Gods and Earths.

Once exposed to their teachings I was well on my way to being a shit kicker in my own right.

6

WORD IS BOND

(for White Boy Chris)

The first time I heard my brother, Sekou, say, "I'm a God!" I laughed my ass off.

I was about 13, and he was in his mid-teens. To me, of course, God was black, but he was an old bearded black guy who hung out in the clouds and did miraculous shit like taught Stevie Wonder how to play a piano and a harmonica at the same time without sight, and gave The Fonz the power to snap his fingers and have chicks appear out of nowhere, ready to get busy. God wouldn't need to drink Joe Weider muscle building protein shakes daily, or pilfer my mother's cigarettes. And, for damn sure, God wouldn't spend his free time using his little brother for a punching bag cause I'd drop dime on him.

But, Sekou... I mean, Raliek Understanding God – Raliek for short – was dead ass serious.

The first major change was the name change. If I called him Sekou the penalty was swift and painful. He favored punches in the chest but sometimes he'd get democratic and land a few in my gut. Though I was perhaps the only person subject to corporal punishment for not acknowledging the name change, by no means was I the only person he impressed it upon. The whole neighborhood began calling him Raliek within a week of his becoming a God.

His cronies would come to the house and be like, "peace young god! Where Raliek at?" And I'd be like "*Ra-* who??" and then my stomach or chest would twinge and I'd remember. "Oh you mean *my brother*, Raliek! One sec."

Another significant change – and this is perhaps more impressive than the blows he dealt me – is that he was always studying what he called *the lessons*! This from a kid who'd gotten the boot from practically every school he'd ever attended, including Uhuru Sasa, and to whom studying was something little geeks like me did. He carried these lessons around in a thick, green, loose-leaf binder with a large "7" within a crescent moon surrounded by a star drawn on the cover in black magic marker. This he called his "Book of Life" and he kept it with him at all times, at home and out in the street.

I just had to know what could turn a total asshole like my brother into this almost ghetto monk-like existence he'd begun to lead since he began studying from it. I mean, he actually had students! Groups of knuckleheads would come to the house on a regular basis just to hear him wax righteously! This happened behind closed doors because my mother wasn't having none of this *the black man is God* bullshit up in her house if she had any say in it (as many times as she'd been fucked over by black men, including my father). These guys damn near worshiped my brother like *he* was Allah! So, I figured there had to be some heavy shit in that book.

Every day I'd lay in wait for an opportunity.

One night he took his girlfriend, Sheryl, out to a movie and I noticed he was empty-handed for a change. I crept in the room he and my other brother shared, picked up his precious book and flipped through it.

My 13-year old mind was not impressed, at first, though. It seemed to me to be a bunch of esoteric nonsense typewritten in horrible grammar, fading photocopies of stories so strangely worded they seemed almost to be in a different language. I got bored after about 10 minutes and put his book back where I'd gotten it.

In the weeks to come though I couldn't help but see how his being God had elevated his status in the community. People spoke of him reverentially. Like if they were speaking of Martin Luther King, or something. He'd erected an image and people respected it. This God, Raliek, carried himself differently. He walked tall with a humble swagger, like a gangster too cool to be ostentatious. He only ate certain dishes, no pork or anything even remotely approaching what he called *swine*. He'd even made Sheryl into the female counterpart to a God, which he called an *Earth*, and she'd gone from wearing jean skirts, tube-tops and Jellies to wearing long dresses, head garments and sandals every day. She even changed her name to True Asia.

These extreme transformations prompted me to re-visit his Book of Life one night, figuring there must be some kind of hidden power in it that I had missed in my first sitting. This time I read it in earnest, cover to cover. I even read some of the stuff *Raliek* had written himself. *Plus Degrees,* he'd called them; basically hardly legible dissertations on such illustrious topics as *how to make an Earth* (that is, get some Chickenhead to peel off her Daisy Duke shorts and adorn herself in refined clothing befitting a Queen) and stuff like that.

It was fascinating! This power to lift yourself and others up, to gain respect and notoriety, what we called "Juice" back in them days; to get girls to do your bidding.

I stored all of this away.

Fast forward a year or two and Raliek and I flipped roles. He returned to being Sekou, again, with a new passion, graffiti. While I transformed into the God known as Master Unique Scientific God Allah.

*****

You might not have heard of *The Nation of Gods and Earths* but if you've heard of Rakim, Big Daddy Kane, Wu-Tang Clan, Queen Latifah, and many other former and current players in the hip-hop game, then you've heard of some of its more famous members. In fact, Rakim was one of the reasons I was most proud to be a part of the Five Percent. So much so that I would spend my entire high school years as a member.

I learned from The Nation that the original man is the black man, the *Asiatic* black man, and that the black man is God. Furthermore, I was taught that the white man is the devil, grafted from the original man, and evil in every way imaginable. And that it was the duty of the original man to teach those who were ignorant knowledge of themselves.

Yet, again, the white man was evil, only this time I was offered explanations for their evil nature that actually made me stop and think, predisposed as I was to do so. You see, this grafting process that created the devil was done by a great scientist with the intention of making an evil entity. And this scientist, being a God, and all wise and civilized, naturally he was successful.

For some reason this made perfect sense to my adolescent mind.

This was in the early 80's. At that time, the Five Percent were EVERYWHERE in New York!

The police were not big fans of the Gods. All they really needed to know was that our doctrines were racist and identified the white man as devils (the NYC police department being white by a vast majority at the time) and the black man as God. That was sufficient to classify us as Public Enemies. The fact that among us were some actual public enemies didn't help matters, either.

I knew a few Gods who were wanna-be gangsters. Some drug dealers and petty criminals, too. Hell, who didn't? Some of the Gods I knew were only poor because they hadn't caught the right victim yet, and righteous only when it was convenient, when it didn't interfere with the acquisition of anything they felt to be a necessity at any given time, whether that be food on the table, a bankroll in the pocket, or even a new pair of sneakers on their feet (often taken from some unfortunate soul's feet as he walked by).

And, even though I was not an active criminal, per se, I was one low-risk ingenious idea from crossing that threshold. I mean, if a crime presented itself to me, and if the risk/reward factor was in a favorable ratio, and if I could actually envision its successful execution, hell, I wasn't above getting my hands filthy. My personal moral code didn't stand in my way. The Poor Righteous Teacher code didn't even deter me any. The only thing that scared me straight was the thought of spending even a second in jail. I knew, from first hand accounts, (my older brothers being regular tenants of the local jails) that the survival rate – at least with your sanity or sphincter intact – for guys like me was low. I always envisioned myself, out of terror and suicidal reasoning, attacking and killing if possible the meanest bastard in there. If I was successful I'd be relatively safe until I had to do it again, or I'd be dead. So, jail, in my mind, was essentially a death sentence and the ultimate deterrent to becoming criminal minded.

One of my good qualities, though seldom used, was that I was honest with myself. When it came to bravado I knew my limitations and usually remained well within them. I knew I wasn't much of a fighter, but I could wrestle, so if I got into a fight, which was rare, I would always turn it into a wrestling match. If I got my hands on my opponent I always had a fighting chance. But, I was what could best be classified as, in the nomenclature of that time, and now: pussy.

I slipped under most radars because of my older brothers' reputations. They didn't take any shit from anyone, and people just refused to accept that *pussy* could come out of that same gene pool and household. Plus, I hung out with guys with whom I could be myself usually and they were so nerdy sometimes they made me look and feel tough by contrast. But, whenever I hung out with actual knuckleheads, I had to work to allay their suspicions. Some suspected that I was soft on the cause, that my heart pumped Kool-Aid. And, they were right, especially when it came to shit like jeopardizing my freedom. You better believe I was pussy as pussy got.

But, occasionally I'd do something unquestionably un-pussy, usually without planning to do so, and postpone judgment against me.

One of those un-pussy acts was joining the Five Percent.

Here was an an act that necessitated the doing of things that most pussies, unless they were insane as well, would never do. For example, as a Five Percent you were required not only to study but to *show and prove*. That is, justify yourself to just about anyone who approached you. You had to prove to *their* satisfaction that indeed you were a member, and engage in a sort of battle of words.

Although the Five Percent tended to attract the more intelligent of youth in the hood, it also attracted more than its fair share of inglorious bastards. My co-members were some of the shadiest characters you're likely to see in the black community. People I would otherwise avoid at all cost.

In preparation for these eventual confrontations – we called *Ciphers* – I studied the lessons thoroughly and practiced daily in the safety of my clique. My clique just happened to contain some rather aggressive geeks and wanna-be thugs I'd known all my life but, I guess to someone on the outside looking in, some of them might have appeared to be as shady of the Gods I didn't know. But, to me, they were just cats in my neighborhood.

Around that time I'd begun to understand something important. You can be as tough as you want to be. A tough image was as useful as actual toughness, but true toughness came from the heart, not from the mouth, or hands, or even from your willingness to use a weapon. Your actual toughness was something less tangible than that, and once you realize you have it you'll never be the same.

I stumbled across this knowledge as I've stumbled across most things in my life: quite by accident.

I was trooping through dangerous territory one harsh wintry day with my boy, Supreme Mathematics Universal Allah (I called him Math, for short), on a mission for weed, which was one of the two things that would raise my courage level. The other was girls, but at the time drugs, by far, was the superior attraction of the two.

So, there we were in Brownsville which, without a doubt, was no man's land in them days. This was the neighborhood that produced Mike Tyson fr'chrissakes. Compared to the tree-lined serenity and relative beauty of the Eastern Parkway where I lived, Brownsville was a virtual wasteland. Empty lots, abandoned buildings, towering and/or sprawling projects filled with just the kind of folk I'd dedicated my life to avoiding. At least that was the stigma with which I, and many people who didn't live there, branded Brownsville. But, there I was, deep in the ebbing and flowing nucleus of it: ground zero at the time. Looking for weed.

Math was one of the shadier cats I hung out with. But, he knew people, so I wasn't overly worried. I was just that side of concerned. I hid it, though, because Math, for some reason that evaded explanation until that day, never thought of me as pussy. It was a helluva compliment that he'd never paid verbally but only by hanging out with me and daring to go places with me where shit could pop off at any moment, showing a confidence in me that I felt wholly undeserving of. So, when he'd mentioned that there was a weed gate in "Da Ville" that was more than worth the trip, I'd said "let's do this!" without any hesitation.

While on this mission, we came across a posse of Gods on a street corner near Tilden. Tilden Projects had a reputation, as most projects did; an ugly one. As we passed by, naturally they noticed us. More specifically they noticed Math's flag.

A flag was a little button worn in a conspicuous location that indicated that the wearer was not only a God but also had achieved a certain level of competency. Though I believed I was at that level of competency, I'd be damned if I was going to walk through Brownsville, or any strange neighborhood for that matter, advertising it. I wouldn't even drive through Brownsville wearing one. It was basically an open invitation to anyone to *try* you, and few things were more tempting to Gods, especially advanced ones, than to *try* another God.

Sometimes, this challenge was just a facade. The challenger would actually be interested in something else on your person other than the flag; like your jewelry, or coat, or even your sneakers could be coveted. If you couldn't *show and prove* to that god's satisfaction, he might find cause to accuse you of perpetrating a fraud, coming among God's Cipher under false pretenses, a snake in the grass, of which it was his sworn duty to expose and destroy. His boys would proceed to give you an ass whipping, a Universal beat-down, or *Just-icing* we called them.

Sometimes it was actually legitimate. There were a lot of gods out there who were perpetrating a fraud, having joined the Five Percent solely for *juice*. Often, Gods like me were thought of that way. I looked like I needed juice. I had a friendly demeanor. I smiled a lot. I talked like a nerd. I was not a typical God. Even though I had brothers who were genuine gangsters, I wasn't a hard case at all.

At least Math looked the part (black as tar, gold teeth, a sinister glare he could brandish at the drop of a hat) and usually played the part in mixed company, but when we were alone he had another personality, vulnerable and sensitive, but, with just enough of an edge to keep even me a little leery. He was perfect. I loved the guy. What he thought of me before this day, I suspected, was simply a guy he employed to keep his balance.

Math hung out with a lot of knuckleheads and they usually peer-pressured him into a lot of shit he'd have rather not gotten into. I never did. With me — though he didn't always — he knew he could let down his ghetto guard and relax, smoke some weed, listen to music and just be light. And with him I could get a feel of what is expected of a typical knucklehead of our age. The shit I'd fortunately been able to avoid by limiting my circle of friends to those whose sense of adventure rarely included hard crime or violence for thrills.

But on this day, things changed.

"Peace God!" one of the gods on the corner shouted at Math and I as we passed.

Math, not one for being out-bellowed, replied in kind, "PEACE GOD!!!!"

It was just a greeting but the way he'd said it felt like a challenge, like he'd cracked his knuckles at us. Math had gold teeth and a sheep skin coat. They weren't about to take his teeth, though I wouldn't put it pass these starving mother fuckers in Brownsville, but his sheep skin was fair game. Math's response was tantamount to shouting: "*And?! We* ain't no suckers, Yo!"

I'd also returned the greeting, but to be honest, I was well-shaken by the subtext of this whole scene. There were about ten of them standing in a circle, seven of whom were wearing Universal Flags.

One of them, a short evil-looking bastard, took an ominous step toward Math and asked, "What's your attribute, God?"

"I come in the divine name of Supreme Mathematics Universal Allah, god," he replied, giving his full name as was customary.

And then, all eyes shifted to me.

I said, "I come in the divine name of Master Unique Scientific God Allah, god," with all the authority of a rookie cop saying, "*stop in the name of the law, or I'll shoot!*"

"*Unique?*" he said suspiciously, looking at me with his head tilted sideways like some niggas tended to do, to make themselves look crazier. It worked like a charm. "What kind of attribute is *that*, God?"

What the fuck??

"*My* kind, god," I retorted, plainly, restraining the offense I'd taken and acknowledging the red flag that had shot straight up my spine at his tone. "*One* of a kind!"

His boys kind of smirked a bit, one even laughed. He caught it and realized that he'd been sassed and he didn't like it.

"Show and prove, God!"

*****

Now, there were certain protocols that were tradition when Gods met for the first time. First there was a greeting, then an introduction, followed, if time allowed, by a discourse on what one has learned from *the lessons*. This process was known as *Building*. The idea is that by sharing your knowledge, wisdom and understanding with the cipher (group), everyone stood to benefit. It also gave other Gods a chance to judge your seriousness, your ability and your commitment to the Nation. And if they were after something aside from a sharing of ideas, like your jewelry or money for example, then they'd be assessing the threat level you represented through how you presented yourself; *reading* you, as it were. At that time, I knew I had ability, and had committed myself to improving and growing in aptitude as a God, but I wasn't zealously committed. I was basically a God when I was at school and in my neighborhood. In strange locales, I only greeted gods if I didn't feel a threat… and I ALWAYS felt a threat, particularly in certain areas of Brooklyn.

Brownsville being at the top of that list.

I did most of my growing up in Crown Heights, and my corner of the neighborhood was more notable for its West Indian population than for its Gods. In fact, most homegrown African-American teens, meaning minimum second generation American, when faced with the choice of joining a clique or crew of some sort, found those choices quite limited in Crown Heights. There were the Five Percent, of course. There was also the Zulu Nation, which had little to no juice (clout) in Crown Heights. There were some athletic endeavors (typically basketball or football), some graffiti crews or break dancing troupes (which required you to steal spray paint, or travel around battling other dance crews – also potentially hazardous), stick-up kids, boosters (shoplifters refining the art) and some West Indian cliques.

There were some nerdy cliques too of course, and many of the people I grew up with wound up in these in order to stay out of trouble. They kept within range of their front doors or traveled away from the neighborhood to other environments where they could be free to pursue their interest in insect research, flight, computer programming, etc...

A good number of these nerds were first generation Americans who, in the 80s, suddenly (with West Indian culture experiencing a surge in popularity) rediscovered the West Indian heritage and accents they'd tried so hard to bury previously- especially a lot of the Jamaican cats- and went Rasta. The Jamaican clique was so popular that even some cats that had no West Indian heritage to draw on became Impostor Rastas or Faking Jamaicans, as we called them. So, in general, Crown Heights was dominated by the West Indians, primarily the Jamaicans, Panamanians and Haitians. In this way, Crown Heights provided a safe incubator for me to grow as a God. In fact, I was known as one of the stronger gods in the neighborhood, as far as knowledge of lessons was concerned.

But, if Crown Heights represented an incubator, then Brownsville was some kind of Darwinian proving ground, the Archipelago of Brooklyn.

When that evil-looking Brownsville God asked me to *show and prove*, I had immediately thought of True God.

True God was one of the Gods from my high school, and was without question the most *righteous* God I'd ever met. For me, he was to the Five Percent what Malcolm X was to the Black Muslims. That is to say, even if you didn't believe a single word of the religion that he touted, after listening to him, you acquired an immense respect for the man and his beliefs. I admired True God even though he scared the shit outta me. His favorite phrase was: *show and prove*. If he became a lawyer I wouldn't be surprised. And from watching him show and listening to him prove on a regular basis, I learned what these words truly meant. He didn't regurgitate quotes and obscure facts from the lessons like many Gods I knew. Like no one else, he was able to truly coincide the Mathematics in the lessons with everyday life in a way that would leave no question in the listener's mind that the foundation of the Five Percent, that being the Mathematics, was *real and alive*.

So, though I never did so in school, for I was too busy smoking blunts and drinking Malt Liquor and other un*god*ly acts, I emulated him this day in Brownsville.

*****

"A master is one who knows and understands himself and his culture. But, knowledge of oneself and one's culture simply isn't sufficient. The devil knows himself and he's aware of the wickedness inherent in his culture. So, he is a master as well, is he not? The duty of a truly civilized man is to teach, to bring civilization to the uncivilized, to raise the mentally dead from their crypt of ignorance with knowledge, and if that man adds his own knowledge to the knowledge *we* provide then he can refine his thinking with wisdom so that he can born his own understanding. His understanding will be similar to the God body, but not at all the same. His understanding will be Unique, god. Thus, we are all unique, god. So, we come together in this cipher and build or destroy; each of us with a unique understanding, a unique style, and a unique outlook.

142

"This would be a very precarious, possibly dangerous situation, if it weren't for the knowledge of self that I presume we all share. Not unlike scientist experimenting with some volatile new chemical compound. Without the knowledge of chemical interactions, of the basic principles of physics, god, well, that experiment could blow up in his face. But, I studied the science, god, and the mathematics involved, and I know myself and my a-like, and so I have every confidence that the result of this experiment will be the creation of a new compound, and if I didn't, then I also have the capacity to create an explosive that will achieve the desired result: Peace within my circumference, for I am a scientist!

"Thus I come in the divine name of Master Unique Scientific God Allah, god. What's your attribute?"

I was mimicking True God's style of presentation. I'd watched him closely, and listened to him carefully. If impersonation is the highest form of flattery, then I was kissing True God's ass something awful. But, the words were mine. I'd filled in the void between True's style and my own with ideas I'd been refining.

I figured these Brownsville's God were unaccustomed to my style of building for they looked surprised and impressed. There was a chorus of "That's peace, god," which was how gods expressed their satisfaction. I managed to suppress a grin, burying it beneath a mien of nonchalance. The message I wanted to send was: *this is how we get down every day in my neck of the 'hood!*

Math also *built* and he too had stepped it up a little. He must've sensed something amiss, as well.

Math was always a higher level than most Gods in our neighborhood but by spending so much time with him I was nearly at his level. I knew if it came to a fight, of course I *would* fight (if taking to our heels together wasn't an option) but our best chance did not reside in our ability to fight off ten motherfuckers. We were "building" in order to save our asses from catching a Just-icing, or having our belongings confiscated, or both.

By the time Math was done breaking down today's Mathematics (he was named appropriately for the mathematics was his strongest suit) half of these Gods seemed to be satisfied that we were *right and exact*: The stamp of approval.

"Where you rest at, God?" (where do you live) asked one of them, looking not quite convinced.

"In Medina." (Brooklyn)

"Whereabouts?" another asked, one of the leeriest of the pack.

This was a dangerous question to answer. So many neighborhoods had beef with so many other neighborhoods; and so many gods had beef with so many other gods. My usual answer to strange gods is Bed-Stuy. A Bed-Stuy address would usually put you in a safety box. Nobody wanted beef with Bed-Stuy. Well, usually, that was the case. But, if Bed-Stuy knuckleheads had recently come this way and done dirt, (something that occurred often, for Bed-Stuy Gods were known for making noise and cracking skulls and leaving corpses wherever they went) then it could have easily backfired. Maybe one of these guys was a relative of someone Bed-Stuy had left for dead. If we answered Crown Heights, with its lack of reputation for being strong in the Five Percent community, then it could send the message that repercussions for robbing us would be light, if at all. If we said some housing project, chances are these guys are familiar with the project and might start dropping names: *do you know so and so?* Oh, you roll with the god, so and so? And if we didn't know *so and so*, then there'd be trouble, especially with that *word is bond* thing floating around.

Word is Bond is short for *"My word is bond and bond is life and I will give my life before my word shall fail."* Which, taken literally, means "if you lie, you should die," and when abused by some thieves or bullies posing as righteous, can be misconstrued to mean, "if you lie then you deserve to be punished!" I wasn't worried about being murdered so much. But, if we were to get caught in a lie about where we reside, that would beg the question: what else have we lied about? And, there would certainly be consequences.

Of course, this was my own ruminating because Math didn't hesitate to say "Ebbet's Field," which was an infamous housing project/cooperative in our neighborhood, but neither of us lived there.

"In the *field*? Word? You roll with Black Supreme?"

"Black's my cousin!" Math shouted, bold as hell, almost proudly.

I knew Black Supreme, and whenever he was with Math I found a reason to make sure I wasn't. I thought he was going to straight up rob me right in front of Math one time, and I had the distinct feeling that Math wasn't about to stand in the way, either. Black Supreme was just that sick. So, the odds of Black having done something egregiously foul in Brownsville were higher than the likeliness of his being feared or respected. But, maybe Math knew something I didn't because the Gods were all love-love after that. Clearly it wasn't fear but respect that Black had garnered in Brownsville. Or, maybe it was fear, who knows? What's the difference? Either way, we were safe, and these Gods just happened to be selling some of the best weed I'd ever puffed. And, after smoking a couple of blunts with us sold us the fattest dime bag I'd seen in a while.

Later, on the train home, Math was quiet. He got quiet sometimes, but rarely when he was zooted. I'm a talker, too, when I'm high but I was feeling really high, like I'd survived a battle in the jungles of Vietnam or something. This was a story I'd tell my kids someday –probably in exaggerated form. Put guns in holsters on the guys, or have them say something like *fuck you two pussies doing in the da ville?*

"Yo, U?"

"What up, Math?"

"Sun, you the fuckin man!"

"What???"

"Yo, I owe you big time, God."

"What you talking about?"

"Them niggas was gonna rob us for sure."

"You think so?"

"Why equal self!" (Yes)

"They *was* on the leery side…"

"The leery side? Sun, they was straight twisted! They'd scoped out my sheep dog from two blocks away and had already fought over who was gonna get it by the time we got to their corner. My money's on that cat with the silver medallion, Intellectual, or whatever the fuck his name was."

"Yeah, he was shady as fuck. I don't even think he was righteous."

"*None* of them niggas was righteous, Sun. Not really. But, I think you reminded them of why they'd joined the nation in the first place. They'd wanted to kick the lyrics like *you* did."

I just looked at him. That was high praise from Math. He

didn't hand out compliments at all. The closest he'd ever come to flattery, that is without something in it for him, was *yeah, you got that one.*

"Word?" I said. I didn't know what else to say.

"Word, Sun. Your shit was potent! Like them gods up in Mecca (Manhattan) at Allah School."

"Fuck outta here. You fuckin' wit me now."

"Yo, Word is Bond, Unique!" he said, looking at me with unflinching adoration. "You took half them niggas hearts!"

I was overwhelmed. He laughed, like I'd said a joke, but I hadn't.

"Man...when you said you got the explosives to bring peace within your circumference, you didn't see them niggas' faces?"

I shook my head. I hadn't really been observing them all that closely. I was in a zone. I'd often get in a zone when I build. I'd get so focused I can't really see straight.

"I thought three of them mofos was gonna shit!" Math added, still cracking up. "And, your words just flowed, Sun. Like math. Like pure fuckin' math, U! You made them niggas think twice about bringing any negativity into the Cipher. You know what I'm saying? You explained the meaning of your name and showed and proved it on the spot, as you were saying it! I've never seen anything like that, sun! Never!"

I was still quiet. He kept on re-hashing my words and breaking down what I'd said all the way back to Crown Heights.

From that day on my status in the neighborhood had changed, especially among the Gods. Math actually told mad people about our little adventure in da ville. I had never really had notoriety before but now I had people walking up to me saying they wanted me to be their Enlightener (teacher). When I had taken on the moniker Unique, there was a segment of the population that refused to call me by that name. My block was made up of mostly West Indians, so a good portion of the people I grew up with had typical British West Indian names like Richard, Lance, Kevin, Adrian and so forth. To these people, the idea of calling me "Unique" was absurd.

"You're God???" they'd laugh. "Well, if you're god, then make it rain, make me rich, shit, make *yourself* rich!"

The Christian image of god was a high hurdle, so I'd actually given up on trying to convince people not to call me Baye. Baye — a Senegalese name I'd chosen for myself when I was in first grade at Uhuru Sasa — was the name everyone knew me by, so it didn't sting as much as it would if they'd called me by my Slave name / Government name. So, it wasn't a big deal. But after our little episode in the *da ville*, and Math telling the tale to mad heads (enhancing it with each telling), little by little, non-gods started calling me Unique, as well. Soon everyone called me by my Five Percenter attribute, my righteous name.

This name business would eventually lead to a serious problem, though.

*****

I began to second guess my affiliation with the Five Percent when it cost me a friend.

My friend, White boy Chris (we called him that sometimes because Chris was a popular name around the way, but there was only one white one), as you might expect, wasn't too keen on my membership in a group that looked on him as a devil. You see, I was leading a double life, a teenage reverse-poser, by my definitions. I was only pretending to wholeheartedly believe that all black men were God and all white people were

148

devils.

And, naturally, it came to a head one day, when Chris walked by while I was building with the Gods down the street from my house.

He was an arrogant dude, Chris, and pretty fearless actually, considering the environment he grew up in. He was the smartest guy I knew, generous and funny as hell. He used to steal weed from his hippy parents (who kept it by the ounce around the house) and share his bounty with our whole posse regularly.

Being one of a handful of white kids in an overwhelmingly black community had toughened him quite a bit, but he never tried to pretend to be "black" or make any overt efforts to fit in. He just did it, while remaining as white as Tom Sawyer. It was I who felt uncomfortable being around him after I'd become "righteous." I was the fraud.

Everyone in my neighborhood knew I was a God and knew that I was supposed to have it in for white devils. But when they'd see White Boy Chris and me together, as they had, consistently, ever since I moved to Eastern Parkway from Bed-Stuy five years earlier, they understood. It was like a Christian having a Jewish friend. Or, a Panamanian hanging out with a Jamaican and a Haitian. Or a black woman married to a white man, their mulatto son playing basketball better than every guy in the community. These were the kinds of anomalies that life in as diverse an environment as my neighborhood inevitably produced. Sure, some found it hard to accept but everyone acknowledged it.

I remember one time I ran into Chris coming home from school, walking up the block wearing a pair of flawless white socks. That chlorine bleach his anal ass used to soak them in before washing was clearly getting the job done. I knew what had happened even before he spoke. It was not exactly a rare occurrence in those days. And Chris had had a pair of burgundy Nike track shoes – fresh from the factory almost – and all the rave at that time.

I'd warned him not to wear them shits on *the Ave* (Franklin Avenue), but he didn't listen.

His face was red, his fist clinched, and there was murder in his eyes. He didn't accept this humiliation as just a Racial Tax due to his being a white boy in a black community. And he hadn't given them up without a fight, as evidenced by the swelling of his face and slight limp in his marching stride. I never respected him more than I did that day.

I had also warned him several times against calling me Baye if he should see me with any of the Gods. I'd told him flat out once that that wouldn't be a good thing, and why it wouldn't.

"*You* think *I'm* gonna call *you* Unique???" he asked, and burst into contemptuous laughter, his voice like Jackie Gleason's without the girth. "Cuz I'm a *devil*? And you're a goddamn *God*???"

He had a way of putting things that made me feel ridiculous. But, I was seriously concerned. I didn't know then that it was my own ass I was more worried about than his but I had a fair amount of worry for his, as well. He *was* my friend.

Unfortunately for our little social anomaly, there were a number of Gods in the vicinity that thought being God meant having it in white people, and felt one of the tasks of being righteous meant depriving white people of their cash and other belongings. I wouldn't have been surprised if the guys who'd stolen Chris' Nikes were Gods. Some Gods were vindictive arch criminals. Made me ashamed to be part of the Nation sometimes, truth be told.

And a guy as perceptive as Chris, and knowing me as well as he did, *knew* I had conflicting thoughts about my membership.

"I don't even know why you hang around with those guys!" he'd said, looking at me with barely disguised pity beneath a bewildered curiosity. "You're smarter than that, Baye."

"It ain't about smart…"

"You don't really believe you're God, do you?"

"I think I have many God-like qualities—"

"Oh, shut the fuck up with that shit!" he said, swatting through my word's flight path. "So only black guys can be Gods?"

"Just do me a favor and don't call me Baye around them, alright? Can you do that? I don't want any trouble."

"Trouble?" he laughed again. "Fuck you…and fuck them!"

There was nothing left to say.

And, sure enough, the day I dreaded came the following year.

Chris was walking by and spied me in front of an apartment building down the block in a cipher, building with Math, Math's crazy ass cousin, Black Supreme, and some other Gods from around the way. He could have passed without incident but that wasn't Chris' way. 'Fuck you and fuck them!' echoed in my ears when I noticed him. He stopped, our eyes locked, and he smiled, devilishly.

Great.

"Hi Baye!" he sang, a heartbeat later. "What's up?"

At that moment, Black Supreme was *building*. The criminal minded bastard was elaborating on how snakes in the Five Percent needed to be weeded out, because the expiration of the devil's un-civilization was rapidly approaching (the following year, 1984, was the year the devil's time to rule over the Original Man was due to expire, according to our lessons) and how we couldn't afford to have fraud perpetrators among us when that time was at hand. So absorbed was he in his sermonizing that he hadn't even heard Chris.

But Math had. He'd known about my unorthodox friendship with Chris but Math and I were friends so he'd never given me any shit about it. The three of us would even puff weed together on occasion.

He glanced at me with concern in his eyes. I'm sure mine registered my misgivings, as well.

My hope that Chris would just keep on walking if I ignored him- which I had- was dashed when he pressed the issue.

"Baye!" he hollered.

I shook my head in exasperation.

Why is this motherfucker doing this?

Black Supreme put his self-righteous spiel on pause and turned around, saw this white boy looking determinedly in our direction, then looked back at the six of us standing in a semi-circle in the *Truth or Square* (which came to be known as the B-Boy Stance), with his mouth open, frozen in surprise. A white person without a badge and gun, or at least the get-up that most undercover cops wore, was a rare sight. One hollering at black people was ever rarer. This aberration wasn't lost on Black Supreme, and for the briefest moment, I could almost smell the tinge of fear his surprise withheld, like if, instead of Chris, his mother had been standing there, or if it were a dog yelling in English.

"Who the *fuck* is this devil talking to?" he snapped, his demeanor having transformed before our eyes from arrogant Poor Righteous Teacher, to teenager busted having sex in his mother's bed, to Vengeful old-testament God eying an idol-worshipper.

Fucking Chris!

"He's talking to me, God," I said after a moment's delay during which I contemplated how to deal with this situation. Several scenarios had run through my mind. Among them: quitting the nation right then and there and walking away with my pigheaded friend. But fear of being labeled a snake by a psychopathic mongoose like Black Supreme chased that thought away and left me with zilch. "He lives in my building!"

"Why the fuck is he calling you Ba — " he said, then scratched his head. "*What* the fuck did he call you???"

"Nothing, God, he was just joking. He's just a—"

"Baye!" Chris shouted again, probably feeling emboldened by the fact that the repercussions I had been so concerned about hadn't come to pass. "Who are your friends?"

The other Gods, aside from Math, taking their cue from Black Supreme, turned on Chris with dark looks on their faces. Chris, to his credit, stood his ground stolidly, braced for whatever may come.

"Who the fuck is Baye?" Supreme shouted at Chris.

"*That's* Baye!" he said pointing at me, unflinching. "You don't even know his *name*?"

"The *God's* name is Unique," Black blasted, though I'm sure he couldn't give a fuck about me or what some white boy called me. He must have just sensed Chris' defiance. He was standing there with a "*What? Am I supposed to be scared cuz you're black and ugly?*" look on his face. God, I loved Chris! But, he was pushing his luck, and mine.

"His mother calls him Baye! So I call him Baye." he retorted. "And as for this *God* business? Puhhhllease!"

Black couldn't believe his fucking ears or eyes if his expression was any indication of what was going through his mind. He turned to the rest of us.

"Did this motherfuckin' devil just —" he couldn't even finish the sentence.

He turned back to Chris, his feet already moving. Chris put up his guards a second late to block the blow that caught him flush in the face. He fell to the ground and actually slid a little. None of the other Gods had budged, though. Black stood over Chris like Ali over Liston, his fist still clinched. Chris lay on the curb, his arm had landed in some dried dog shit. He noticed it, grimaced in disgust, and then glanced up at Black. He was holding his nose as blood began to seep from between his fingers.

"Fuuuuuck!" he screamed nasally when he noticed the blood. Then our eyes met. I was still standing in the same place I was when he'd provoked this incident. In that moment, in the squint of his eyes, I knew I had smoked my last blunt with him. Our friendship was over.

Math went over to Black and pulled him away, cause he looked like he was about to stomp Chris.

"Yo, Black, let him be, Sun. You still on probation!"

Black's eyes never left Chris but he allowed himself to be pulled away.

"You think this makes you Gods?" White Boy Chris yelled at all of us, pinching his nose, sounding like a caricature of a telephone operator from the 50s. "You're not fucking Gods! You're just angry fucking assholes! That's all! Assholes!! All you've proven here is that you can beat up on a white boy. Ooooohh, real tough Gods!!! Well, fuck you!! Fuck ALL of you!!!"

He was looking at me when he said "all."

"You most of all, *BA—YE!!*" he said, rising to his feet, brushing the dog shit off his elbow. "You're supposed to be my friend! And you let these —"

"Chris, man, I tried to —"

"Tried to what? *Warn* me, you piece of shit!" He looked away from me at the rest of the Gods. Then back at me. I could see the pain in his eyes and it broke my heart. He shook his head and sighed, "Fuck you, Baye."

And he walked away.

He never looked back.

Chris never forgave my betrayal, and rightly so. And, if you're reading this, Chris, please know I regret it. You were right. I was an asshole, a dumb kid trying to be something I wasn't. I'm so sorry, dude.

Anyway, in June 1984 I graduated from High School, and the devil's un-civilization still hadn't expired (surprise, surprise, right? The God's had decided to postpone it until a later date). So, after five vainglorious years of rolling with the Gods, I unofficially called it quits. But, *Word is Bond,* I wish I had done so that regrettable day when Chris had so bravely prompted me to, and had come to his defense as a *real* friend would have.

7

BEING ALL I COULD BE

There was no legacy of higher education in my family whatsoever. I was the first in the history of my clan to even finish a traditional High School. I did so mostly because I knew it would make my mother happy after the hell my two older brothers had given her, having dropped out or been kicked out of every school they'd ever attended. I didn't do much better myself. I attended the minimum amount of days to graduate. I had no one urging me towards lofty aspirations like college, and, at the time, few tangible black male role models to look up to.

I was in trouble, vulnerable to all kinds of traps laid out for young, black, direction-free people like me, and I didn't even know it.

It was about then that I became the target audience of a TV commercial campaign I'd been watching for some time. Where as it used to go in one ear and out the other, suddenly, one day, it went in one ear and hung out for a few weeks, kicking it back and forth with my ego, addressing my unacknowledged desires for respect, adventure and escape, not to mention higher education, all in 30 seconds of images, song and carefully chosen narration. It didn't exit my other ear until I had gone to the recruiting station in downtown Brooklyn and signed years of my life away on a dozen dotted lines.

Yep, it was one of those "Be all that you can be" Army commercials.

Next thing I knew, I was standing at attention alongside 50 some-odd boys from 'hoods and ghettos, trailer parks and farms, mountains, plains and prairies all over the United States. Half of us were Black, the other half White, with a dash of Latino, and an Asian on top. We came in all shapes and sizes, prejudices and predispositions, talents and temperaments, Christians and atheist, heteros and homos. We were a snapshot of America's huddled masses all thrown together, in not so much a melting pot as a propaganda pressure cooker, for 10 weeks.

Fort Jackson, South Carolina, in an area known as Tank Hill, is where I did my Basic Training. In World War II barracks we were lodged and on Vietnam War era weapons we were trained. You couldn't help but think- lying there in your bunk in those ancient quarters- that legions of dead soldiers had lodged there and trained there just like you, learning things that would either save their lives or cost them dearly. Here, too, they were proselytized and programmed to put country before themselves and even their families.

The brainwashing took hold easier with some than with others. Seemed a lifetime of watching too many John Wayne movies, singing the National Anthem and pledging allegiance to the flag had laid the groundwork and prepared some recruits to gladly serve, and serve with pride. But, I hated John Wayne, only knew the National Anthem from watching sports (and didn't even know all the words) and the only Pledge of Allegiance I'd ever committed to memory was the one from my elementary school that began: "To the fruition of a Black Power."

Needless to say, I was a much harder sell than most of the other recruits in my unit.

I was there strictly for the college money and a little adventure. Hell, my brain was still in the pressure cooker from the Five Percent, and the residue of my elementary school's race-baiting in the name of love was still stuck to my psyche like dried grits to a plate. The contract I'd entered into with Uncle Sam didn't stipulate that my allegiance was part of the bargain. I'd only signed away my ass, not my soul.

I made that position clear on day 1 to anyone who'd listen.

But, my Drill Sergeant, by the name of James, must have thought I'd said something else- maybe something like "I'm gonna kill you, Mrs. James and both of your little crumbsnatching rugrats first opportunity I get!" because that's pretty much how he treated me from the moment I answered, "You know it!" to his sarcastically asked question, "So, you think you're special cuz you come from *New York?*" Everyone else had wisely answered *Yes, Drill Sergeant* or *No, Drill Sergeant* as per his instructions, and as I should have if I wasn't one of those folks who apparently knew no other way to learn shit than the hard way. For some reason, I'd felt obligated to challenge his authority. The Brooklynite in me screamed: *fight the power, fight the power.*

So, rather than get brainwashed, I just got tortured instead. I was the drill sergeant's whipping boy, my name branded on his shit list.

Further efforts to turn me into GI Loco also met with resistance. I just wasn't built for self-sacrifice. I could march, shoot, toss grenades, salute the flag...hell I could even get with the team spirit. But, I drew the line at dying for any cause I didn't choose, or even pretending to be willing to. That was my relationship with military authority.

As for my relationship with my peers, well...

There are always those characters in our lives that stand out. While most people I meet tend to fade into the subconscious or become part of some elaborate amalgamation in my mind, some retain their singularity and vividness.

Private Frick was such a guy.

He was the first white person I'd ever met without any shred of sophistication. He was so hick he was practically a caricature. But, he was the best soldier in the Company, maybe the Battalion, hands down. Went from Squad leader to damn near Drill Sergeant status in about two weeks. It didn't hurt that he was 25! (Most of us were 18 and 19, wet behind the ears and sticky in the boxers). Plus, though he was only about 5'7 give or take an inch, he was chiseled, cut like some Olympic gymnast who does those ring things without breaking a sweat. And he could do as many push-ups as the Drill Sergeant. (And my Drill Sergeant could knock out 100 without even pausing, 200 before he started to slow down).

Frick's character was just as strong as his body. Most of the white boys in the platoon were a little intimidated by us black folk...in the beginning, anyway. But, Frick? As he would say "Sheeeeet!" He didn't give a fuck about anybody.

I remember the first time he spoke to me directly. A bunch of us were in the shower one evening. Frick assassinated all my ideas about size and race. He was as hairy as an orangutan and hung like a horse.

I... was not.

"Damn, Loco, I thought all you guys had bazookas...sheeeet, you ain't got nothing but a BB Gun!"

"Damn Frick," I fired back, in rhythm...*ranking* is something we did daily back in Brooklyn when I was kid. Usually Mama jokes, though. "Your Moms must get pissed when you use the whole jar of mayonnaise to choke your chicken!"

Everyone, black and white, laughed. Frick and I became real cool from that night on.

Frick specialized in off-color jokes and comments, though I doubt he even knew he was being off-color. He used the "N" word casually, yet somehow he never came off as a racist. In fact you just knew that, though he was chock full of stereotypes and misconceptions, he didn't have it in for people based on color. And whatever preconceptions he'd held (like dick-size, for one) were being addressed on a daily basis right there in South Carolina. (He was from some flyover state, can't recall which).

One time he told me his racial philosophy It went something like this: "Back in my hometown, we all live together, niggas and crackers alike, and it didn't bother me none. Most of my homeboys, dumb rednecks mostly, they don't like niggas... blame everything on niggas. House gets robbed Mustuh been dem niggas! Truck gets hijacked...mustuh been dem niggas! But, sheeeet, I knows for a fact that them redneck bastards was robbing people houses in the next county. And them hijackings, sheeeet, half the time it be the drivers theyselves set the shit up. Knowhutimean? Way I see it, as long as you don't fuck with me or mine, and take care uh your own business, I don't give uh fuck what color you is!"

I never told him that I wasn't comfortable with his use of the "N" word. (This was in the pre- Political Correctness years). I'm not sure why. Thinking back, maybe I was a little scared of him.

It would cause problems later.

There was another standout in my memory. A black cat named Burns. Private Burns was from L.A. But not Los Angeles. On Tank Hill, L.A. meant Lower Alabama, or the black equivalent of a Okie from Muskogee. I think he was actually from Louisiana. He was about 6'3, and with the general disposition and build of some guy who'd been given a choice: finish out the remaining 10 years of your 15 to 25 year sentence here in Lower Alabama State Penitentiary, or join the Army and complete your sentence there, being the best damn soldier Uncle Sam ever squatted and squeezed out.

He'd chosen the latter.

There were three New Yorkers in the platoon, myself and two others. We were the platoon celebrities. NY being a rather famous city, everybody wanted a piece of us. Mostly out of curiosity, but we generated a great deal of resentment and jealousy, too. Burns was seething with it (though that may have been just my arrogance). He had a deep inferiority complex, though, I believed.

And, I wasn't any help.

In addition to my resistance to the authority he'd genuinely sworn allegiance to, and my friendship with the one guy who beat Burns out for most of the leadership positions he'd strive for, I had the nerve to USO the troops with my mediocre Popping, Break-dancing and Rapping skills (these were the glory days of hip-hop, pre-bling-bling gangster rap.) Plus, I'd occasionally feel the necessity to dig into my Five Percent Poor Righteous Teacher bag and pull out some jewels, something impressive. "Dropping Science" we called it. And I'd have a posse of the brothers, mostly a bunch of ignoramuses with country wit, seated around me scratching their heads. Though I'd already "fallen victim" (what the Five Percent say of people who drop out) I had brothers ready to convert and become my students.

I think it's fair to say Burns hated my ass with a dark passion.

*****

When I enlisted in the Army, unlike thousands of black men who enlisted in the Army before 1948 (the year the military was finally desegregated thanks to an Executive Order from President Truman), I did so with little thought for the next generation or the previous. I did, however, share something with those trailblazing warriors: a healthy fear of the South.

This was my first time in the south, actually. To me, the south was this mythic place where unbelievable shit happened. Most of the lynchings that have occurred in the U.S. occurred in the South: Mississippi, Georgia, Alabama, Louisiana, Texas, Kentucky, Tennessee, Florida, and yes, South Carolina – these were notorious lynching states. And though I was there well after the days of roving lynch mobs setting fire to entire black communities, hanging, castrating and burning blacks alive, it was well *before* James Byrd was beaten and dragged behind a pick-up truck until he basically fell into pieces, by some white supremacist in Texas.

In other words, sure there was a legal remedy once the crime was committed, and sure the FBI had the skills and would probably catch the culprits responsible for my lynching, but I'd still be dead as fuck, while some shit kicker would wind up a hero in prison among their supremacist friends, or martyrs on Death Row, soon to be among the honored dead.

Because of the nature of the U.S. military, and its tendency to draw its numbers from among the disenfranchised, it's usually the youngest, poorest and least educated men and women that wind up doing all the serving, and dying. This is the worst aspect of the Army and, ironically, the best thing about the Army.

From my experience, most of the Shit kickers in America are from the disenfranchised class, made up of all races. So, the Army becomes a place where the disenfranchised live, eat, sleep, shit, shower, shop, laugh, cry, sweat, etc., all together in one big open bay, presenting numerous opportunities to find out how much they have in common, if they so choose. They can learn a great deal about one another's thoughts, feelings, and experiences and, if they're lucky, they can learn a lot about themselves, too.

I was one of the lucky ones. Racially, I think the Army was one of the best things that ever happened to me.

White people: these mysterious entities that my elementary school had taught and shown me were prone to shoot unarmed black teens down in the streets of Brooklyn, and assassinate black leaders on motel balconies in Memphis. Now I was living with them, able to ask and have my questions answered directly.

And, these weren't some citified white boys, like Chris, but some real rednecks and hicks, farmers and cowboys, white boys who'd never spoken with black people in their entire lives. Some who'd never even seen black people except in the movies or on TV.

And some of them were the offspring of those lynch mobsters from my mother's generation.

I had an opportunity to really get to know them, to confront my fear and ignorance, and I hoped I had what it took to take advantage of it.

Private Frick was my touchstone, in a way. I learned so much hanging out with him, by watching how he interacted with the other white boys in the platoon, and with the world. His confidence was intimidating, and his temper was certifiable. But his generosity and openness was off the chart. He'd share his last smoke with me, and buy me a carton if I was broke. He'd cover for me when I'd creep away to make unauthorized phone calls to my girl back home, or even help me get my bunk tight enough to bounce quarters off of.

He was an all-around cool ass hick.

One night we were on guard duty together and decided to risk the Drill Sergeant's wrath and make a few phone calls. He had called his wife. I was standing lookout, trying not to listen to their conversation. But, he was a loud one.

"What you mean you don't wanna talk to no strange niggers...didn't I just tell you he's my homeboy?! Now talk to his ass!" And he called me over and handed me the phone. "Here! Say hello!"

"Hello?" I said, and wound up talking to her for a good five minutes. She must've told me her whole life story, talking so fast, accent so strong, I could only catch half of it.

Yeah, Frick and I were tight.

One Sunday morning after services, the brothers were having a powwow; basically sitting around shooting the shit. Burns was there, of course. He wasn't an official leader, like Frick, but he was the acknowledged leader of the black cats, due to his size, his gung-ho-ness and his aggressive attitude. I usually stayed out of his way and watched my back when he was around. I never trusted him — maybe because he looked like a rabid Pit Bull Terrier. Like Mike Tyson would look if he had never come under the fatherly influence of Cus D'Amato: utterly unhinged. And by avoiding him I wound up avoiding most of the black guys in the platoon by default. Not that I missed them much. They were an ignorant lot, to tell you the truth. I was sure I lost IQ points and perspective with every conversation. But, I always attended the powwows. Almost as if attendance was compulsory.

Pretty soon, this powwow got physical and turned into a wrestling competition out in the red clay that was everywhere in Fort Jackson. I'm not really the physical type. More of a thinker, I tell myself, so I just sat on the sidelines making jokes and clever remarks and fucking with people in general.

Burns was tossing people left and right, when suddenly he cut me a glare and called me out.

"Hey Loco! Come get your ass busted!"

Everybody looked at me.

I realized then that it was more than distrust I felt for Burns. I was *really* afraid of him. I had built him up in my mind as the anti-Loco, as only one can do to oneself. And, I knew, in that moment, that I wasn't about to let that motherfucker get his hands on me. I'd been watching him with the others, and though he'd been tossing them around he'd also been holding back. But, I knew that I provoked another side of his nature. He would show everyone, once and for all, that not only weren't New Yorkers so fucking tough without their guns and knives and shit, but that fraternizing with hicks like Frick was a no-go, as well.

He was gonna put a hurting on me, my intuition told me.

Then, outta nowhere, here comes Frick.

This wasn't our first powwow. This was almost a weekly thing. And, somehow it had always worked out that the powwows were segregated. I don't think anyone planned it that way, and we certainly never verbalized it. It just happened like that, consistently, so that it became like an unsung rule.

So, when Frick appeared, a couple of people besides me recognized the peculiarity. Burns was one. He looked at Frick, just for a second, like he was uninvited. And, a second was all Frick needed.

"What? Is this some *niggers only* shit, or can a skinny-ass cracker get in on this action?"

Everybody laughed except Burns. He still wanted a piece of me.

Another Private, I forget his name — some black hick on Burns' dick — shouted out," Burns was about to give Loco some scrapes!"

Frick looked at me. It was just a quick glance, but I could tell he smelled my apprehension, just as surely as a dog would.

"Sheeeeet," Frick laughed. "I put my money on Burns!"

Uproarious laughter.

Great.

I felt like one of those burning black bodies in the photos of lynchings I'd been shown as a child; just as helpless, just as well-done.

"He *barely* pinned down my little white ass the other night when we was just fucking around," Frick added, looking Burns squarely in the face (Burns was squatting, Frick was standing). "If he can't handle *me*, I knows he can't handle a big ass nigger like you!"

I threw on my poker face before anyone could see. Frick had just lied his ass off...*for me!* I could have kissed President Truman for desegregating the Army right about then.

Everyone turned my way, in shock and disbelief, eyes-popping, mouths agape. Frick might have been short but everyone had seen him almost out push-up the Drill Sergeant, and they'd seen his perfect Olympian physique in the shower. They knew this little dynamo was about the toughest white boy alive!

Then everyone looked at Burns.

Some of the fire, the eagerness, in his eyes had died out. It wasn't fear that doused it, though. That wasn't what I saw. It was something, though.

I think he was impressed.

*****

One night, after pulling KP (Kitchen Police duty), I was out behind the mess hall alone, having a quick smoke, just breaking rules and chilling, my usual. Thinking, as I was prone to do, about being back home in New York, hanging with like-minded people, when suddenly out of the shadows stepped Burns.

My guards went up. I'm sure what little hair I had was raised like a cat's when you sneak up on it. I felt like I'd been ambushed.

"Relax, New York," Burns said and copped a squat near me. He called me *New York* sometimes. He had a disarming way of calling people by the place they were from, usually when he wanted something.

I didn't disarm, though.

"What you want!?" I asked, looking around for some of his dick-riding disciples, guys who worshipped the ground Burns marched on; he had quite a few. But they were nowhere to be found. He was alone.

We were alone.

"Damn, nigga, relax," he said, and smiled, proud to inspire fear in a New Yorker. I could probably take him, I told myself. With all the adrenalin that was racing through me at that moment, I probably would've killed him by accident. "Let me get a smoke."

I pulled out my box of Newports, shook one up for him and realized my hand was still shaking after he'd taken it. He must have seen it too, cause he laughed...an ironic yet friendly laugh.

"I know you didn't pin down Frick," he said like Frick had informed him, or something. He lit his cigarette, looking at

168

me over the flame. "Look at you! You're a punk! Frick woulda broke your pussy ass in half."

"*Fuck* you!" I said, instinctively, but I could tell I'd confirmed his suspicion with my defensiveness. My voice had even cracked on "fuck".

He laughed again.

"What I don't get." he began, after a long pull on the cigarette, "is why."

His eyes never left me. He was studying me, truly trying to understand something.

"I mean, that motherfucker. He knew!" and he had to pause because some agitation had seeped out, and I could see that it had been unintentional.

I still couldn't figure out what he was up to, though.

"Why did he get your back like that? What you got on him?"

"Nothing. He's just cool like that," I replied, deciding against living the lie that I had done something I hadn't.

"That motherfucker ain't cool with *me*!" Burns snapped. "Shit, you know what we do with Crackers like that back home!?"

"Probably the same damn thing we do back in New York. But we ain't back home, are we? We're here!"

"So!?" he snapped. "What the fuck? This is still America, ain't it? This ain't fucking South Africa, is it?"

South Africa???

I looked at Burns. I mean, *really* looked at him, the way a person might look at themselves in the mirror before a job interview. And it was like I was seeing him for the first time. And, just like that, I got it! I knew what was bothering Burns.

I mean, I had written Burns off, along with a good number of the other black cats in our platoon, practically from Day

1, as some ignorant, corn-fed, shucking and jiving, country bumpkins, all attitude and muscles, whose life ambitions were to rise up in rank in the Army, buy big cars and small houses, breed a few more of their ilk and retire on military pensions if they were lucky enough not to get all shot up in some war over oil. While I had plans to return home after training to attend University, Burns had no such ambition. I was a Weekend Warrior, which was what they call Army Reservist, but Burns, and the vast majority of our platoon, had enlisted as Regular Army. When I returned home to pursue higher education, he was to be shipped off to some base overseas to complete his minimum four-year stint.

While I had been spoon-fed on all the glories of the black race, most of these other guys had had no such instruction. The only aspirations that had been presented to them, with any foundation in reality attached to it, were sports, entertainment, preaching in a church, the dark arts (drug dealing, pimping, hustling, robbing and stealing and so on) and, of course, the military.

These were the stereotypes I held of many black people, especially those from the South. And it was classism, pure and simple. I was an elitist bastard. Damn near a racist. I was no better than those white folks who did the same.

Which explained, for me, why Burns and some of the others didn't like me much. Nor did they get me. They probably thought I was trying to be white!

I mean, there I was, this fairly intelligent yet elitist bastard from New York, the big city of dreams of all places, who despite his being in the Army was clearly destined for something very different from what they were destined for, possibly even something significant. And there I was running around the woods of South Carolina with a hick who called black folks niggers.

Yep, for a second I saw myself through Burns' eyes, and I didn't like what I saw at all.

But, two words had illuminated my thinking about Burns: South Africa.

That year I had read a book called Kaffir Boy. It was an autobiography of Mark Mathabane, a black man living under Apartheid in South Africa, and how he managed to survive and eventually escape the brutality of his motherland using his intelligence and his tennis skills. *Kaffir* is South African for nigger. It's an amazing book.

In Uhuru Sasa, we had learned about Apartheid, of course, and actively participated in boycotts and protest of corporations that refused to divest and indeed supported the racist South African regime's oppression of its black majority.

Of course this is history now, but when I was a child and even when I was in the Army, Nelson Mandela was still behind bars, and South African storm troopers were still slaughtering people by the hundreds.

But, was this common knowledge like it is now? No. Black folk, overall, had their own fish to fry right in the U.S. Most blacks didn't have the time nor inclination to worry about oppression overseas when oppression was right outside their windows. My elementary school, though, had made time. So, to even hear the words "South Africa" emerge from Burns' mouth spoke to a conscientiousness I never fathomed the man possessed.

Burns had given me a gift that day. He had opened my eyes to my own issues with my own people; the people I had previously thought I loved unconditionally. I learned that

171

day that I had only been lying to myself. That though my elementary school had tried to fill me with deep and abiding love for all things black and beautiful, and though my studies with the Five Percent had tried to impress upon me the godliness and righteousness of all black people, they both had failed miserably. I was just as self-loathing as the next black man who'd had none of these influences under their belt. I was almost as contemptible as any shit kicker, only my contempt wasn't aimed at some external force. It was aimed at niggers.

It was aimed at *me*.

No wonder I let Frick call me a nigger. Hell, if I let him do it, I'd let any white person call me nigger as long as there was no conspicuous malice attached to it, wouldn't I? Needless to say, any black person could do it, too, with or without malice.

"What??" Burns asked, for I had gone silent.

"Nah, you got it right, bruh," I said to Burns, with a genuine affection and respect I'm sure he recognized immediately, for it was the first time I had ever spoken to him in that way. "This isn't South Africa. This is America!"

*****

I mentioned that my drill sergeant hated me. I had challenged his authority that first week and since then he'd taken a personal interest and making me suffer. He couldn't put his hands on me, though. There'd be all kinds of hell to pay if he did. But, he could humiliate me, get all in my face, yell and threaten me all he wanted. He could also make me sweat, run til I collapsed, push-ups til I was a wobbly shaking mass of embarrassment, sit-ups til I threw up, but no physical contact. And though my body was looking better than it ever had, having discovered muscles in places I didn't know they existed, I was indeed suffering. And that's just what Drill Sergeant James (who was black) wanted. Every chance he got he insulted me and punished me. Every minor error was treated like a major infraction. Every misstep was treated like a deliberate attempt to undermine his authority or to be different.

Sergeant James sometimes called me "Brooklyn." At first, I loved the name. It felt like a title. But soon I began to hate it, for every time I heard it I knew it would be followed not much later by aches and pains. "You think you special, *don't you*, Brooklyn?! Get yo ass in the dirt!" was his favorite line.

I couldn't figure out why James had it in for me so intensely. But, after my little talk with Burns, I understood why. I spat in the face of everything he represented.

Basically, James was Burns' future. The Drill Sergeant was from L.A., too. But, he'd dug in and risen to the rank of Staff Sergeant (while still in his late 20s) drove a late model caddy, had a house, a wife, and a couple of kids off post in lovely Columbus, SC, and considered himself admirable; a role model for the soldiers under his command. *Keep your shit wired tight at all times and you could be like me one day.*

I didn't exactly scoff at his lifestyle. I mean, he *was* doing a lot better than many of the people I grew up with. But I wasn't impressed, either. And, now that I knew what it was about me that was rubbing black folks the wrong way, I was on a mission to do something about it.

I was a changed man. At least I was trying to be. I started spending more time with the brothers. And, damn if every swinging dick didn't notice, and find it remarkable.

I'd spent most of my pre-teen years as a poster child for the Pan-African movement, and most of my teens among the

Ghetto Intelligentsia discussing such high-minded themes as the origin of the Devil and the experimentation of high explosives which result in earthquakes. But, somewhere in there I'd also learned how to play Cee-lo, Craps and Spades-the official card game of the black community

We'd be playing Spades and somebody would say something like, "So, you is black, after all!"

"I'm not as black as yo' mama, but I can pass!" I'd say.

"What gave it away, Loco? Cuz I know it wasn't your dick size!"

"Ha-ha very funny! Now, stop stalling, motherfucker, and go ahead and renege like you was about to do."

Even Burns would laugh at my jokes. In fact, most of the animosity between us had vanished after our little talk. We'd found common ground, and sometimes that's all it takes.

Frick, who had gotten accustomed to my hanging out with him, would come looking for me sometimes and, finding me all huddled up with my race, playing dice, would hang around for a few minutes then cut out. He'd gotten the message I was unintentionally sending. I mean, now that I was in the process of letting go all of that self-hatred I'd been carrying around Fort Jackson in the cargo pocket of my BDU fatigues like a weapon, I was really just getting to know these guys. And most of them were pretty cool, for bumpkins. I never meant to diss Frick, though. I just hadn't figured out a way to do the black thing and hang with him simultaneously, as yet. Or, even if I should.

One night, a couple of weeks before graduation, things came to a head.

We were finally starting to congeal as a Platoon. We could run for miles without panting, march in admirable uniformity singing original cadences with gusto, and shoot the shit outta

174

silhouettes a football field away. Our barrack had a gleam it was so clean, and our boots glowed every where we went. I mean, we were a beautiful sight! A Drill Sergeant's wet dream!

But, if Drill Sergeant James woke up with sticky OD Green pajamas over me, he hid it well. He *still* had it in for me.

We were in the barracks getting ready for lights out when Frick shouted out, "Loco, don't forget you gotta pull guard duty tonight!"

Guard duty is on the duty roster and, in rotation, everyone has to pull it. Basically, in two hour intervals, you're a human ADT Alarm System on patrol of the barracks (armed with a flashlight) to make sure everyone is in bed, no one is stealing shit, and no fires break out. But I had pulled it very recently.

"You better check that list again, Yo! I was on the other night!"

"Why the fuck is it always a mistake when lazy ass niggers gotta do what they's supposed to."

Burns had jumped up and, in a flash, snuffed Frick in the face and sent his little ass flying across the room into a wall. A crack raced up and down the wall from the point his head had impacted it, like bolts of lightning.

Drill Sergeant James rushed into the barracks just as Frick was getting to his feet with a little blood on his nose and a look on his face like this was just what he'd been waiting for: a chance to get his shit off! He rushed at Burns quick as a cat, catching Burns, unaccustomed to challenges and surprised at Frick's quick recovery, a little off-guard. Burns fell to the floor with the force of the hit and Frick was on top of him, pounding away. Burns couldn't get a handle on him, Frick was so fast!

I ran over and grabbed Frick, catching his arm just as he was about to bring his fist down on Burns for the fourth or fifth time.

Frick was berserk, though.

"Get the fuck off of me!" He yelled, and with incredible strength almost threw me off of him, which gave Burns the opening he needed. He landed a semi-panicky kick right in Frick's solar plexus.

It was like Frick hadn't felt it at all.

He turned on me, with bloodlust in his eyes, just as the Drill Sergeant arrived between us.

"What the *fuck* is going on here?" He yelled as he pinned Frick against the wall with some slick maneuver that shook him out of his frenzy. It was common knowledge that James was an Army Ranger before becoming a Drill Sergeant, and wasn't to be fucked with, period! Rangers are the Army equivalent of SEALs, some of toughest bastards in the military. "Private Frick, you at-ease, right the fuck now! Loco, get the fuck away from me!"

I backed off but kept my eyes on Frick, who had the good sense not to challenge the Drill Sergeant. He wasn't totally out of his mind.

Sergeant James let Frick go. "You gonna chill out? Or do I have to *chill* you out?"

Frick fumed a little but he didn't move.

"Answer me!" Drill Sergeant snapped.

"I'm gonna chill out!" Frick replied, almost fully back to his senses.

"Good for you, son! Cuz I'd hate to have to put a good trooper like you through that fucking wall!"

Then he turned on Burns.

"What happened!?"

Burns was hesitant to answer.

"What the fuck happened here?" He asked the room. Everyone looked for holes in their socks. The silence was broken by a white guy. I think his name was Van Wie, or something like that.

"Loco didn't want to pull guard duty, and when Frick told him he had to he got all upset. Then, Burns jumps up and punches Frick. That's when you walked in, Drill Sergeant."

"That's some bullshit!" Burns yelled, finally finding his tongue, his lips a little puffy.

James looked at me, hatred in his eyes.

"You got something against following orders, Brooklyn? Still think your shit don't stink, don't you? It's good-for-shit Weekend Warriors like you that..."

"That's not exactly how it happened, Drill Sergeant," Frick said, soberly.

James wheeled on Frick. "Well, what the fuck happened, then? Somebody gonna tell me the truth or do I have to Article 15 all uh y'all asses?"

"I...I made a mistake on the duty roster," Frick said. "I thought it was Loco's turn to pull guard duty, but it wasn't."

"And?" James snarled. "Why the fuck do I have cracked walls and blood on the floor in my barracks?"

Frick looked at Burns, whose eyes had begun to swell from the blows he'd received. Then he looked at me.

"I called them niggers!" he spat out like it was a confession he couldn't hold back anymore. "I didn't mean anything by it... you know I ain't got nothing against y'all. Sheeet, some of my best friends is niggers!"

Drill Sergeant James said, without skipping a beat, like he'd been prepared for this, "you use that word again in my Platoon, for any motherfucking reason, and I mean any of y'all, black, white or what have you, and I guarantee your asses will be on the next bus back to whatever holes you ignorant motherfuckers crawled out of, y'all hear me?"

"Yes, Drill Sergeant!" Everyone bellowed.

"One thing y'all got to learn, and it looks like you stupid fucks gonna have to learn it the hard way. When y'all find your asses in some godforsaken jungle or desert, and the only thing between you and the fucking Jihad is one of these crackers, or one of these spics, or one of these niggers, then you gonna remember: Ain't no color in the Army but Green. O.D. motherfucking Green! Y'all got me?"

"Yes, Drill Sergeant!"

"This ain't America, you stupid motherfuckers! We ain't got no race problems here. None! Only one race here: US! When you go back to America, you're free to go back to being petty racist pukes if you want to. With your nigger friends and your cracker friends, but here we ain't friends and we ain't never gonna be friends: We're *brothers*, goddammit! I hope you assholes understand what I'm saying. Cuz, before you know it, one day, you gonna be knee deep in shit and believe me you won't be thinking about the color of that cavalry coming to save your ass!"

He gave everyone a meaningful look, full of all the experiences he'd accrued in the uniform, and everyone felt the truth of his words.

"Now, police up all this blood and shit before I lose my temper and kill one uh y'all!"

"Yes, Drill Sergeant!"

He strutted out of the barracks and left us all standing there in stunned silence.

I watched him leave, and then turned around to see that

Frick and Burns' had locked eyes. They both looked pained.

"I was out of line." Frick said.

Burns, looking the worst for wear, said, "don't worry about it."

But, from that day until the end of Basic Training I never heard Frick or anyone else (not black, anyway) use the "N" word again. Black guys, well, we're just a tougher nut to crack when it comes to the use of the "N" word. I guess it has too firm a hold in our cultural lexicon.

Then, the door opened again and Drill Sergeant James re-entered.

"Brooklyn! Get your ass in my office. Now, soldier!"

Great.

*****

"Have a seat, Private," Drill Sergeant James ordered, and I obeyed. His office was a tiny airless room which could just as well have been a broom closet, near the front entrance to the barracks. The puke green paint on the walls was chipped and faded, the filthy window was wired and shut, his Drill Sergeant hat hung on a hook on the wall and his Ranger mug, with coffee stains that will never come out, sat precariously on his desk.

There were only a few reasons to be called into the Drill Sergeant's office, and none were good. Of course, there was the off chance that he was going to tell me he was recommending me for promotion to Private E-2 but that didn't seem in the realm of possibilities considering he hated my guts. To formally receive an Article 15 was the most popular reason, so I sat there trying to figure out what I had done that warranted this punishment.

Nothing came to mind.

He sat behind his desk trying to disarm me with a smirk, the closest I'd ever seen him come to a smile. But he said nothing. So I spent that moment trying to decide whether or not I would choose a Court Martial and fight what would be a cooked up charge rather than accept it, as was my prerogative according to the Uniform Code Military Justice.

Then suddenly he spoke.

"Why do you think I ride your ass so hard, Loco?"

"I'm sorry, Drill Sergeant?"

"You think it's cuz you're a hard case?"

"I don't think I'm a hard case, Drill Sergeant."

"You don't, do you?" he asked, like I didn't know myself well at all. Which made me question whether I did or not.

"I don't think I've done anything to deserve an Article 15, Drill Sergeant! That's for sure. And if you Article 15 me I'm not going to accept it. Forget that! I'd rather get Court Martial-ed!"

"Is that a fact?" He sat back in his squeaky, rickety chair and folded his arms, that same smirk on his face. Something about his demeanor made me feel more brazen, like he were inviting it.

"Yeah, that's a fact, Drill Sergeant!" I said, with more edge than I'd intended. "I've been busting my as — my butt around here lately but you just keep riding me and riding me like you're trying to break me."

He chuckled softly to himself, like I'd said a joke.

"I wasn't trying to break you, son," he said warmly. "If I was trying to break you, your ass would be broke!"

His laughter got me a little agitated.

"So, why do you keep fuc — messing with me, when you know I'm doing my best?"

He squinted his eyes dangerously.

"Drill Sergeant," I added quickly. Most every question or statement a trainee makes is supposed to end with "Drill Sergeant." If not, some Drill Sergeants are known to get uptight. James was one of them.

"Since you ask, I'll tell you," he said, leaning back in a chair crying out for oil, and grinning again. "I was doing you a favor."

"A *favor*!!??" I snapped. His tone, and that fucking grin, were starting to irk me. "You call treating me like your bitch a *favor*?? Why don't you do me a *real* favor and—"

Both his feet hit the floor and he sat up sharply, cocking his head to the side the way he does to convey the message *have you lost your natural mind*???

"Private, unless you want to go back to the world minus a whole lotta fucking teeth you better secure that mouth of yours!"

I knew he couldn't hit me. He'd be in deep shit with the brass if he did. But, there were worse things in the Army than getting your ass kicked. Having whole checks disappear legally was one. It was one of the penalties for an Article 15. The other was a bunch of restrictions like no trips to the Post Exchange (general store) and no smoking, perpetual fire guard and Kitchen Police duty. And the kicker, not being able to keep tabs on your lady back home, increasing the likeliness that some cat more accessible was getting the goods. So, yeah, I decided to slow my role and said, "Permission to speak freely, Drill Sergeant?"

He sat back, slowly, like a spring coiling. "Go ahead, Loco."

"Thank you," I said, cordially. "Maybe I don't understand your thinking. How is treating me like shit doing me a favor? Unless you think it's in my best interest to hate your fucking

181

guts!"

Drill Sergeant James nodded his head like he'd come to a private decision. Then he threw me a curve ball.

"Are you a nigger?" he asked. His face was gentle but his eyes were piercing. Apparently this was an earnest question, and he expected an answer.

I thought about it for a second.

Obviously he didn't mean in the same sense that Frick meant nigger, like it's synonymous with black person. And I was pretty sure he didn't mean it the way most black people used it, like it was some kind of cultural term of endearment or fraternity, or as an innocuous put-down. Did he mean it like a shit kicker would use it, to demean or marginalize, establishing their superiority? Did he mean it like my mother used it, when she would say to me and my brothers, "I ain't raising y'all to be some shiftless ass niggas!"? Or did he mean it...

"You're not Army material, Loco," he said, jarring me from my revelry.

"I can handle anything you send my way!" I protested. "And I know you know that. I ain't scared of you!"

"I don't mean it like that, so don't get me wrong," he said, his tone like a shrink speaking to a patient on a psych ward. "I know you can handle the physical tasks. And I know you can shoot and toss grenades and all that shit. I'm even pretty sure with a little training you'd be a damn good leader of men…and they might even respect you if you could get your head outta your ass long enough to lead them. Sho' nuff, you could."

I was dumbstruck. In two months Drill Sergeant James had never said anything to me below the decibel of 20, and here he was, this man I'd come to despise, speaking to me almost man-to-man, unleashing what sounded like *compliments*. He'd shut me up, but good. I just sat there looking at him, dumbly.

"What I mean," he said, "is that you're a thinker. I asked you what most brothers would think is a simple straight forward question: Are you a nigger? If you—"

"I wasn't sure—"

"Don't interrupt me, son," he sighed. "Just listen...alright? Can you do that?"

I nodded, still confused and anxious about this turnaround.

"If you had answered 'yes, I'm a nigger!' sure I'd probably want to break my jump boots off in yo' ass, but I'd know you were Army material. The Army has a place for niggers. And even if you'd said 'no' I still woulda thought you belonged. But, you! You actually sat there and thought about your answer."

He shook his head, his eyes leaving me for the first time since I'd entered the office, glancing away at the Army Ranger coffee mug sitting on his desk. A skull wearing a beret looked back at him. He frowned at the emblem

"The Army ain't no place for people who think as much as you do," he continued, cutting his eyes at me. "Especially not as an enlisted man. You gotta take and follow orders to the letter. The only thinking involved, the only thinking *allowed*, is how best to execute the orders you've been given. You, Loco, you would challenge every order you didn't agree with."

The frown became a sort of anguish and swallowed the Drill Sergeant's face. Deep anguish. Striking emotion from a man that spent 18 hour days yelling in robotic tones, only to go home to a wife and kids he only really saw a couple of days a week.

"I've been in this man's Army for 10 years, son. And, I've served with soldiers like you. I've seen them come and I've seen them go. I've seen them refuse to take orders from someone taking orders from someone taking their orders from someone you'll never see and never meet. And, I've seen these good men, smart men, put other soldier's lives in jeopardy with their failure to blindly obey. Now, I know I'm making thinking sound like a bad thing. But, you know, and believe me *I* know, it isn't. Goddamn it, it's a great thing. An all-too rare thing. And the Army ain't no place for it."

I didn't realize it until I felt a tear land on the back of my hand resting in my lap that I had been crying.

"I hear everything that goes on in here, Loco. Even when you don't think I'm listening, I'm always listening. It's my job to know my men! So, when I see a thinker like you running around with a redneck who calls us niggers, I know why. You're studying him. And when I hear the other brothers in the platoon calling you an Uppity-ass nigga, I know what that's about, too. They can't see you the way I see you. Most of them are *not* thinkers. To them, you're one confused nigga, don't know shit from shinola. But, I heard your stories, about your half-African school and those crazy-ass half-Muslims you used to run with. And, I know you grew up up-north in New York where the white folks are different than these white folks you're with now. To you, this is some kind of educational experience, you're own laboratory of human nature. But, to most of these soldiers, this is their lives! They ain't got nothing else going for them *but* this! I think recently you've realized this and come to respect that fact. That's why I'm talking to you now.

"You got more on the ball than most of the soldiers in here. You're a Weekend Warrior, and one of my orders is to ridicule you for being a reservist and nudge you towards going Regular Army. But, like you, I'm a thinker, too, sometimes. Loco…I rode your ass because I wanted you to know that your type ain't welcomed here. Take your thinking ass back to Brooklyn, and go do something with your life. Do things that thinkers do: Teach, preach, do something useful, but don't waste your life in the Army! You got me, son?"

I sat there looking at Drill Sergeant James, unable to respond, still processing everything he'd said.

"I ain't got all night son!" he said, a little tight. "Do you follow me or not?"

"Yes Drill Sergeant," I whispered. "I follow you."

"Alright, wipe your face and get the fuck outta my office!"

I walked out of his the office into the open bay of the barracks. Most of my fellow soldiers were on their bunks writing letters to loved ones, talking shit and laughing, playing cards, shining boots, soldierly activities. In two weeks I would say good bye to these guys forever. Some of them would rise in rank and some day have platoons, battalions and even brigades of their own. Some of them would be sent into danger's path and return home heroes or at least survivors. Some would meet their makers at the hands of America's enemies, following orders they'd never question descending from places they'll never know. Black and White, Asians and Latinos, all together, united to fight, to kill, and possibly to die for whatever cause came down from on-high.

I didn't feel pity, though. I just felt the awesome humbling power of the world we were living in.

Burns pulled up beside me, looking much the worse for wear from the beating he'd taken from Frick but surprisingly in good spirits.

"What happened, Brooklyn?" he asked. "What the drill say?"

Nothing I didn't need to hear.

8

MAGGIE & ME

With my initial Army Reserve requirements fulfilled (I still had to attend monthly drills and such), a little money, a little direction, and a lot of motivation (thanks to Drill Sergeant James), I returned to New York and enrolled in school!

My choice: Long Island University, Brooklyn Campus.

LIU was basically a black school, with a Nursing college at that, so the student body was made up mostly of black women, and what bodies!

But, the main attraction for me was the Media Arts program. Their brochure boasted of a state of the art television production studio, and it didn't disappoint. I took to studying like it was my life's ambition. I even made the Dean's List those first couple of semesters. Between the girls and the grades I was having the time of my life.

But soon that Army money, and even the student loan refund ran out, and I had to get a job. The easiest part time jobs to get were in fast food and retail. I chose the retail route. I did stints at all the major retailers. If it sold shit you didn't need at prices only a fool would pay I probably worked there at one time or another.

While working as a cosmetic stock clerk at a major retailer on Fifth Avenue, I ran headfirst into my first interracial relationship.

Maybe I attracted the young, attractive counter girl with my brawn, lugging those boxes around that dingy stock cage in the basement. Or maybe it was the way I could always be found studying and doing homework over sandwiches during my break time. Or maybe it was the weed cloud that seemed to follow me everywhere I went I puffed it so regularly. Whatever it was, before I knew it, she was making moves. And I mean literally before I knew it.

I'd had no intention of hooking up with Maggie from Illinois. White chicks weren't even on my radar at the time.

New York, despite its multicultural image, was (and remains in many ways- more due to class and ethnicity than race) a very segregated city. Blacks dwell here, Italians controlled there, Jews congregated there, Latinos lived there, Russians ruled over there, etc. Especially Brooklyn! Find yourself in Bensonhurst you had better not be on foot cuz them Italians over there didn't take kindly to niggas trespassing…uh-uh, not on foot! Find yourself in Brooklyn Heights after dark and it'd be the police stopping and questioning you, maybe even sending you home with a sharp warning.

And in the black and Latino communities…well, I grew up in the NY at the very tail-end of the White Flight from the inner city. And why were they *flying* away? Cause shit had gotten outta control!

Most people think of Los Angeles when they think of street gangs, but gangs used to roam the streets of NY in earnest when I was a little kid. By the time I was a teen they were mostly dissolved replaced by *Posses* and *Crews* which were basically the same thing only usually not as territorial. Even the Five Percenters was considered just a city-wide gang to the press, police, most of the public, and even by some of its members, as well.

Anyway, that mentality stuck with me for a long time. A part of me retained what I felt to be a healthy caution of getting involved with white girls. So, when Maggie cornered me in a cosmetic cage one evening and asked me did I want to hang out with her sometime, I had to give it some serious thought. I had to picture myself walking the streets of the New York *I knew* with this white chick on my arm.

Maggie was attractive, in a girl-next-door who could be a model if she were slimmer and taller kind of way. But, with that ambition shattered, she became a cosmetologist instead and hustled Clinique products, wearing a white lab coat and a brilliant smile. I used to call her a lipstick scientist and she'd laugh so hard. She was really very cute. She had these alluring eyes and she'd turn them on just for me whenever we were in close quarters.

When she'd asked me did I want to hang out, after a pregnant pause for the cause, I had agreed. But, I also told her that between school, work and study, I really didn't have much time for hanging out. She said that was cool, that whenever was alright with her. She was just happy that someday she'd get to know me better.

I don't remember how it began but sometime before our first date, we were getting to know each other *really* well, right there in the stock room. It started with a single kiss, soft and wet and menthol-y (she was a smoker, too). And then it was on!

It was a thrill fooling around during work hours. I mean, literally a thrill! I'd feel this charge of excitement every time I was near her. It felt like we were breaking the law. Like if we had gotten busted we would have been worse than fired, we'd have been executed! It felt like taboo. I was always looking over my shoulder. I'd never experienced this taboo feeling before. But it was like the chocolate syrup on a sundae. She felt it, too.

We didn't talk much. We didn't need to…well, at least I didn't. She'd just come down to the stock room to restock some lipsticks or Skin Clarifying lotion or something, see me, hit me with those sexy peepers of hers, and the passion would overtake us. The next thing you know I'd have her pinned-up

189

against some cage damn near ripping that lab coat off of her. I just had to have her. The contrast of her fair skin and my brown skin was mesmerizing! Her blond hair was intoxicating. She smelled like Kraft Caramels and her skin tasted like Mountain Dew. Her thin lips, her button nose, the odd dirty words (like cock…black folks call it a dick) she whispered, floating on deep passionate breaths. All this combined to make every moment with her fresh and exotic!

It was my first bout with *Jungle Fever*, and it made going to work something I really looked forward to.

After a week or so of carrying on like this, though, Maggie started questioning my intentions.

"So, Loco, when are we gonna hang out?"

"Huh?" I'd forgotten all about it.

"Don't get me wrong," she said. "I love being with you like this, but don't you want more than a fling in a stock room? *I do.*"

"Really?" I said, perplexed. "Well, um, let's see, then, uh."

"Don't you like me?" She asked, looking confused.

"Of course I like you!" I snapped. But, actually, I didn't even know that much about her except that she'd given me a charge like I'd never felt before.

*****

There were two conflicting ideas in my head about white women at that time. Both were racially charged, and neither augured well for Maggie and me.

The first was what I call the Mandingo Syndrome.

The name derived from the book and movie of the same name. The syndrome however dates back much further, to the days of my parents, grandparents and great-grandparents. This taboo feeling I had was derived in part from this syndrome, I believe.

Mandingo is one of the best films I've ever seen about slavery in the U.S. It's totally raw, no moralizing plot and utterly unapologetic! You don't feel any agenda behind it, unlike many other films about slavery. It just paints a picture of life on one plantation and in doing so critiques an entire industry that America was built on; America's so-called *original sin*.

I knew it was kinda ridiculous for me to think of this situation in modern day New York. I mean, that film was about slavery days. Well, I can't say that I consciously focused on this. But, it lingered in my subconscious for sure.

When we kissed I'd remember those pictures of lynchings I was shown as a child by my well-meaning teachers and parents. Shocking paraphernalia they were. And they were not taken during slavery time. Uh-uh. Those lynchings occurred post-slavery, in the 1940's, 50's and 60's! And, can you guess what the number one given excuse was for those *people* (I use the term loosely here) committing those hate crimes? Yep, you guessed it: some white woman had cried rape.

Whether or not the rape occurred is irrelevant (but I suspect that if black men knew that they'd be barbecued or castrated by a white lynch mob for just the accusation they'd keep as far away from white women as possible. I know I would've). The point is, this phenomenon, these homespun widespread acts of terrorism, these crimes against black humanity were part of the black national psyche in the generations previous to mine. And that fear of being killed, maimed or mutilated at any time, for any reason, without any recourse, filtered down to my generation by various means; mostly word of mouth. It was the stuff soap boxes were made of and put a reverberation of righteous indignation in every black racist's voice. It was a platform for politicians looking to advance their careers. Numerous institutions were founded and prospered on this energy.

The other idea bouncing around my head was what I call the Iceberg Slim Syndrome.

Iceberg Slim was a former pimp who became the writer of such classics as "Pimp: The Story of my life" and "Trick Baby." His influence cannot be overstated.

A couple of the by-products of the Iceberg Slim Syndrome persist even to this day. One, is that white women who craved black men were looked upon as depraved sluts or victims of their own racial stereotyping, or, for whatever reason, weren't getting the loving they needed at home so they lured black men (unintentionally more often than intentionally) to their detriment, and sometimes their deaths, with sex.

The other by-product is, by virtue of the white man's insane reaction to a biracial union (hence the lynching and other atrocities; basically just terrorist warnings to keep away), black men came to think of white women as the most prized possession of white men and so procurement of a white woman was akin to achieving revenge for the debasement of black people and, in effect, spitting in the white man's face.

And, in the eyes of other black men, it spoke to your courage and *power*. The audacity to diss the white man in what was essentially his land (America). Kudos was in order. The first time "You da man!" was used was probably when some black guy saw another black guy with one or two white chicks on his arms. "The Man" originally meant "White Man" or "White Power" as in "The man sent me to prison for 10 years when they caught me with some white bitch!"

Yep, interracial dating taps into some shit most people, black or white, would rather not deal with.

But, my temperature was running high at the time, and despite my apprehension I wanted to really experience Maggie badly! At least part of me did; a very influential member of my crew that tends to take the helm at times like these.

*****

New York City is made up of five boroughs: Brooklyn, Queens, The Bronx, Staten Island, and of course Manhattan. When most people (except New Yorkers) picture New York, they picture Manhattan, big city of dreams and what not. When visitors say they've been to New York, they've only been to Manhattan, usually, did some shopping on 5th Avenue, caught a Broadway play or two, ate at a few eateries, slept in a nice hotel with a view of Times Square, climbed the Statue of Liberty, and went home feeling they've had the NY experience.

I submit that if you've only been to lower and midtown Manhattan you haven't experienced real New York at all, and probably only met a handful of real New Yorkers, at that. Most real New Yorkers live outside of this area of Manhattan and only venture there to work, shop or hang out. There are people who actually live in Manhattan and don't qualify, in my book, as New Yorkers.

Maggie was one of them.

She'd moved to New York a couple of years before I met her, lived in Chelsea (a rapidly gentrifying area at the time) in a share with a roommate, and had only, to date, ventured as far north as North Central Park (below 110th Street-the beginning of Harlem) and as far south as Battery Park. She hadn't even left Manhattan but a few times and most of those were to go to JFK (in Queens) to catch a flight home to visit her folks.

On our first date, while I was counting the seconds until I could get her back to her apartment and get my first taste of extra-racial loving, she'd explained, over hot dogs and papaya drink at Gray's Papaya (all my budget would provide) that in two years in NY she'd had two boyfriends, and the most recent had been a black guy (which dashed all my thoughts of being her first experience).

"He was such a dud!"

"Oh really?"

I don't remember his name but from how she'd described him he sounded like a real herb. No wonder she'd lost interest in him.

"I mean, he had a great job and a lot of money. But, he didn't like hip-hop, he didn't smoke grass, he didn't do coke, he didn't like to go clubbing, he didn't live up to my image at all."

"Your image?"

"Yeah," she said. "Black guys are supposed be cool, like you!"

I guess I was supposed to be flattered, to be typical, and I didn't want anything to come between me and what the evening promised, so I said, "Wow, thanks! You really think I'm cool?"

"Oh yeah! Definitely!"

"I don't know what to say."

She smiled, thinking she'd scored some cool points or something.

"I had a black boyfriend back in Normal. Normal, Illinois, is where I'm from. He was from Chicago, and he was sooooo cool!"

"How so?" I asked. I'd met one guy from Chicago. He claimed

he was a member of the Black Disciples and had a tattoo of a trident on his arm. At the time I knew very little about street gangs outside of NY, and the way he bragged about it I figured he was pulling my leg a little. The way he'd described them I figured wherever they were had to be 10 times as ill a place to live as Brooklyn. And, in my mind, no place on Earth was *iller* than Brooklyn. This was just prior to the NWA (Niggaz With Attitudes) era when the world (meaning New Yorkers, meaning me) would find out just how *ill* the rest of the country really was.

"He was a DJ at a club on the South Side near the Lake, and he used to get me and my girlfriends in on the guest list. We all had black boyfriends...except my friend Beth. She thought black guys, you know, your cocks, were too big. Ha! She doesn't know what she missed (smile- wink-wink). Anyway, I really miss them. We used to have so much fun!"

I felt it was a good chance for a segue away from what I didn't need to hear into what I really wanted to know, so I asked, "Why did you move to New York?"

"Well," she began, and her face turned sour.

Great.

Leave it to Loco to open Pandora's Box with his intuitive and persistent thirst for knowledge through asking the most pernicious of questions: why.

"My father...he...he didn't like black people. No, to be honest, he HATES black people. He's a real racist."

"Uh huh."

"So, when I brought Malik...he was the DJ... I brought him to my house so we could...well he was my boyfriend...anyway, I thought my parents were going to be out of town, but they came home early. And, I was...I mean, they caught us, well, you know."

"Damnnnnnn! That must have been rough," I said, knowing I'd never have to go through that cause I'd be damned if I'd ever go to Normal, Illinois for any reason.

Maggie started crying, right into her papaya drink.

"Well, look on the bright side," I said, to cheer her up. Time was a-wasting. "At least he didn't make *you* into a racist, right? I mean, look at you...you've had, to my count, two black boyfriends already, and working on a third. Just because your father is a racist bastard doesn't mean —"

"My mother, too!" She cried out. "When my father was acting all crazy and saying all those awful things to Malik, she just stood there, nodding her head."

"I'm sorry to hear that," I said. Sorry, but not surprised.

"Anyway, after that they kinda threw me out. Told me if I wanted to...to sleep with black people that I wasn't going to do it under his roof. I loved Malik, and I wasn't going to let them break us up. So, I moved in with Beth. She had her own place. Then, Malik told me he got a job as a DJ here in NY. I told him that I would come here to be with him as soon as he got settled. That was over two years ago. But, I never heard from him. I came here and stayed with my friend Karen. You'll meet her. And, I went to look for him at that club. He'd told me the name: The Garage."

"Really?" *The Garage* was getting pretty famous in New York. And the DJ, Larry Levan, probably could have been interested in a DJ from Chicago, since House music originated there. But the look on her face told me her tale wasn't going that way.

"Oh, you know it?" she asked.

"Yeah, I've heard of it. I believe it's not far from here."

"I know. I went there, but they told me they'd never heard of

Malik," she said glumly. "I couldn't find him anywhere."

"Maybe your father scared him off."

"I guess so, but it's not like he'd never seen a gun before."

"Huh?? What??"

"What? Oh, I didn't say. My father had a shot gun, you see, and he...he didn't shoot Malik or anything like that, but he did cock it and aim it at him, though."

"Geezus!" I could hear her father's words in my head. *"You fucking my daughter in my house, nigger! I oughta put both of these barrels in your drawers and blow your big nigger dick off! You too, you nigger loving bitch! I should kill both of you! I could tell the cops around here anything!"*

"Are you alright?" she asked, concerned by the expression on my face, I assumed. *"Listen, let's change the subject."*

"Good idea." I said.

"I got some good skunk at my apartment. Let's go get in the mood!"

"Great idea!"

Few of my friends had actually ever been with a white girl. That didn't stop them from saying that they had, though, and offering up their thoughts on the matter. I had friends telling me all kinds of shit, like: "white girls are mad freaky...they do anything you want 'em to do! *Anything!*" and "better take her to a hotel. Go to her crib you might not leave alive!" and "Watch your ass, yo. All them white bitches is hoes and she's bound to give you the clap, or something!" *"Something"* meaning crab lice or herpes. This was pre-AIDS era, before sex became lethal.

I was a mess on the walk to her apartment building. That Jungle Fever had me delirious with lust, while the Mandingo and Iceberg Slim syndromes had me jumping at shadows all along the tree and brownstone lined streets of Chelsea.

197

Nevertheless, I managed to lug all this mental, racial luggage up the four-floor walk-up to her apartment.

I was spent by the time we arrived.

"I guess Karen's not here," she said as she opened the door and turned on the light to reveal a very cozy and clean one-bedroom apartment. "Have a seat. Would you like something to drink? Sorry about all the steps, this building needs an elevator."

"Nah, I'm good," I said, huffing a bit.

"I'm gonna have some wine. You sure? I got some cheese, too, somewhere."

Wine and cheese? "What, no *crackers*?" I said, and laughed. She didn't get it.

"I might have some. I'll be right back!" And she scuffled away and left me sitting there. I looked around her place like a black anthropologist studying the living habits of white folks. I imagined myself whispering into a little mini-recorder, "The domesticated Caucasian tends to decorate their dwellings with an abundance of ornaments, doodads and doohickeys that speak to its current or aspirational class or status."

I remembered my former friend Chris' apartment back in the days. His family wasn't rich but they were very comfortable. Had a baby-grand piano and a dining room table that could seat eight comfortably, though there were only 5 of them. They'd also had all kinds of homey doodads and doohickeys that I couldn't rightly name but had seen on various TV commercials and shows like the *Brady Bunch, Leave it to Beaver* and *the Partridge Family* and what not. So did Maggie and Karen. Doodads galore. She came back a couple of minutes later holding a tray with glasses, cheese and, yep, crackers.

"I found some!" she said like she'd found a missing piece to the puzzle that was me.

"Cool."

She walked over to a doodad, slid it open and pulled out a couple of bottles. "Red or white?"

I'd never drunk wine from a glass in my life 'til that point. The only wine I'd ever drunk, as a matter of fact, was *Night Train* and *Thunderbird*...from the bottle of course, after pouring a little out for the brothers who couldn't be there, for whatever reason: jail, dead, MIA from fucking some white girl, whatever. I was so ghetto.

"Whatever you're drinking is fine."

"Okaaaaay..." she said like I'd answered incorrectly. "I think you'll like the red. It's Cabernet Sauvignon, actually. From Chile."

"Is it chilled?" I asked.

She froze, and stared at me.

"Something wrong?" I asked. "I was just joking, you know, *chile* and *chill*, get it?"

"No, not that." she said and smiled. "I just can't believe I finally got you here, in my apartment. You don't know how long I've been waiting for this moment. I mean, we're *alone*, now. We've never been alone like this before and...I don't know...I just want to remember this moment. I wanted it to be special, you know. I had so many things I wanted to say, so many things I wanted to show you."

"Like what?"

"To tell you the truth, I can't even remember now." she laughed, blushing. "Oh, wait!!"

She put down the bottles on the coffee table, reached under the table and pulled from a compartment what looked like a chemistry set with test tubes and pipes.

"What's that?" I asked, just as I noticed the clear plastic Baggie- large enough to hold a couple of peanut butter and jelly sandwiches- half-full of weed! "Oh shit!"

"What???" She said.

"What the fuck, Maggie? Are you a *dealer*?"

"A dealer?" She looked aghast. "Are you *kidding*?"

"Well, damn, it looks like you got a whole laboratory over there!"

"What are you talking about?"

"What's with the chemistry set and shit?"

"What? This? "She held up the test tube and I could see that it was all one-piece. "This is a bong!"

"A *what*?"

"I thought you said you smoked —"

"I do, but..."

She started laughing, then. "What, do you smoke *joints* or something?"

"No...well, I used to when I was a kid. Now I smoke Els."

"*Els*?" She asked.

"Yeah! you know, Phillies, El Producto, White Owls, even Optimos!"

"You mean blunts?"

"Yeah, blunts!"

"You black guys, and your blunts, hrmph," she smirked, while she loaded up her bong. "Malik got me to try a blunt this one time and it was like my whole chest was on fire! Here, try this!"

My first bong blast...of hydroponic skunk! It hit me like a wave of discombobulation, followed by a carefree-ness I've seldom felt since.

We sat there just chatting and laughing, smoking hydro

and drinking Cabernet. Sometimes when I smoked weed I'd get paranoid or hypersensitive. Other times I'd get deep and thoughtful and start dissecting the meaning of life or the origin of the Universe, and fun bullshit like that.

But, this time...

I was a huge Richard Pryor fan, like most black people (Eddie Murphy was just arriving on the scene). I still think Richard Pryor was the most ingenious and courageous comic that ever lived, and that's pretty much the general consensus. Richard Pryor loved to compare black people and white people. It was one of the staples of his comedy routines.

I sat there trying to write Richard Pryor routines in my mind. But I think I must have said them aloud cause Maggie was responding. I was so high I felt like we had telekinetically bonded and she was responding to my thoughts.

"Blacks and Whites do the same shit. White folks just do shit a little different. While niggas stand around on the corners drinking quarts of Olde English and Ballantine, wasting half the damn bottle on ghetto rogations for niggas doing bids in prison or done got shot by some cop, white folks drinking Cabernet Sauvignon, ain't wasting a drop, watering it down with tears over their racist daddies and some nappy-headed nigga he drove off with a shotgun."

"He wasn't a nigger. He was a nice guy," Maggie giggled. "And he had a flat top fade."

"Five brothers all put in a buck to get a nickle bag of dirt with stems and seeds in it, and shit, roll two Els and sit around bitching about how many tokes the next man took: '*three* pulls and pass, motherfucker! *Three!*'"

Maggie burst out laughing, and fell on the floor.

"Need a damn roach clip by the time it goes around once!"

201

I laughed to myself. "While white folks buy hydroponic skunk by the fucking bushel and smoke it for a month."

"A week or two maybe," Maggie gasped in laughter from the floor. "And it isn't a bushel, you fool, it's an ounce."

"In a device what looks like something Einstein would get high with!"

"I can't believe you've never seen a bong before, that's hilarious!"

This went on for a couple of hours or so. We had a blast!

I came to call it the H-factor.

That Hydro put the H in H-factor, and made me forget all about all that baggage I'd brought to the table. It eradicated all the racial bullshit, syndromes and fevers, all the barriers my society had insisted I erect. And, all that it left behind were two people digging each other, feeling each other, and making the most uninhibited sex two people ever made.

The H-factor rules!

At least for a while it did.

One night, a few weeks later, while we lying in her futon, in the afterglow, Maggie turned to me and asked:

"So, is there a reason why you haven't introduced me to your friends, yet?"

"My *friends*?" I laughed, buzzing from the hydro we'd smoked pre-session.

"You *do* have friends, don't you?"

"Everybody has friends, I hope."

"And a mother and father? You do have parents, right?"

"Yeaaaaaah..." I slurred, as it dawned on me that we were having a conversation with ramifications.

"So, what is it?" she asked, eyes welling up. She rolled over to hide her face. "Are you ashamed of me?"

"Of course, not." I placed my hand on her shoulder. She shrugged it off. "Hey! Come on, now."

"What is it, then? Are your parents like my parents?"

"You mean, *racists*?" I said, aghast, like black people were incapable of such depravity. "My father is nowhere to be found, and my mother, well, hell, she loves everybody."

I didn't mention that my mother, to my knowledge, didn't know any white people so her love for everybody hadn't actually been confirmed. Nor had she, to my knowledge, ever considered white in-laws or bi-racial grand children before. As far as she was concerned that was as far from a possibility as a black president of these United States. Pulling up to her door with Maggie on my arm would be a hell of a litmus test to hit her with.

"And, your friends?" She rolled back over to face me, a little optimism in her eyes.

"They vary," I said truthfully. To most of the guys I knew, white girls were kind of at a premium, especially in New York at the time, so the only negative feeling I might generate is a little jealousy.

Black *women*, however, were a different story. And three of my closest friends were actually black women. My life was filled with strong, intelligent, progressive black women; teachers and administrators, nurses and lawyers, community activist and entrepreneurs. Many were heavily into the Pan-African Movement, especially the women who were involved with or parents of children at Uhuru Sasa. While the guys were subject to fall victim to all kinds of calamities: drugs and jail being the most popular, the women were always the most consistent and stable part of the community I grew up in and remained a part of.

In fact, it was black women that filled me with the most apprehension and misgivings about being with Maggie. While I knew that most black men would applaud me, attaboys and kudos were almost assured, black women's reactions would be decidedly different. Opposite, in many cases.

The Mandingo and the Iceberg Slim syndromes are exclusive to black men. Black women have a whole slew of other complexes and syndromes, some legitimate, others irrational, all painful, sometimes to the point of bitterness. I hadn't even breathed a word about Maggie to the black women I cared about, which essentially meant that Maggie was a great big secret I'd been keeping from most of my loved ones.

You see, historically, while Mandingo was being beaten, burned, hung and castrated, it was the black bride of Mandingo who had to watch in horror as her husband, lover, provider and father of her children was humiliated and mutilated like an animal.

And, while the Iceberg Slims were hellbent on exacting revenge upon their former masters, it was the black women who were, at best, ignored in favor of these white female conquest, or, at worst, forced to endure the savagery of black men whose minds had been warped by this syndrome. The abuse, both physical and emotional, the neglect, the abandonment, and betrayal after betrayal as their men pursued the Great White Poo-tang that promised, in their warped minds, redemption and reparation, had taken an agonizing toll on black women.

Like Zora Neale Hurston said, "de nigger woman is de mule uh de world."

And, just as remnants of the Mandingo and Iceberg Slim syndromes persists among men, so do remnants of the trauma of having endured these things persist for black women to this day.

So, even in Manhattan, essentially the only borough of the five in New York City (at the time), where a black-white coupling wouldn't automatically draw undesirable attention, I was nervous as hell walking around with Maggie. I wasn't worried about white people. I couldn't care less what they thought; not in Manhattan, anyway. Most of them were originally from out of town so their fear of me inclined them to stay in their lane, or they were too rich or self-consumed to give a fuck about what a couple, of any color, do in the privacy of their bedroom.

No, I was nervous about running into black women. Maggie was right: I did feel a little ashamed.

Maybe if I had been in love with Maggie it would've been easier. Upon running into a black woman, I would have been able to keep my head held righteously high and say with a pious yet sympathetic expression, *"My sister, don't let your hate and misery consume you and make you so bitter that you can't even accept and appreciate true love when you see it. You have my prayers that you too may find the love you desperately need and have it save your soul, as it has saved mine, before it's too late."*

Yeah, that would've been nice.

But, I wasn't in love. I was just having fun and enjoying my bonanza. I had remained distant from Maggie, emotionally. Some kind of self-defense / self-preservation mechanism had kicked in.

And, I'm pretty sure Maggie had picked up on it, for after our little pillow talk, she'd started pushing for us to spend more time out in public. And, while out, I could feel her observing me. And, I could feel myself trying to behave naturally, trying to act normal. And, it worked because in Manhattan it used to be pretty easy to avoid black scrutiny if you knew where to go.

And, I did.

Then, one night, Maggie pulled a fast one on me.

She'd invited me to go to a party with her and, assuming the party would be in Manhattan, I'd agreed to go. She didn't know anyone in any of the other boroughs...I thought.

"In Brooklyn?!" I'd snapped, caught off guard when Maggie had finally told me — the night of — where the party was to be held. "*Where* in Brooklyn?"

"On Lafayette Avenue, I think. I got a map," she said, looking very excited about her first expedition to the outer boroughs. "She said it's not far from the A-train."

"The A-train?!!" I was still reeling from the 'In Brooklyn' sucker punch, as well.

"Yeah...why? Is it dangerous?"

I wasn't sure how to answer that so I didn't.

"You said she. *She* who?"

"Kim...you know Kim, that pretty black girl in Flori Roberts. She didn't tell **you** about the party?"

"Must have slipped her mind," I replied, a very bad feeling creeping up my gullet.

*****

I knew Kim, of course. I had very few black co-workers in those days. And, as Kim would put it, "We gotta stick together, knowhutumsayin', my brother?"

Yeah, she was one of those *Spooks who sat by the door* black people who just rubbed me the wrong fucking way sometimes. They have a habit of speaking to me like we're co-conspirators in some elaborate plot to pull the wool over *da man's* eyes, and the key to *our* success was to hide our true identity in order to

206

kill the beast from within, or some delusional shit like that. It was actually kind of creepy, especially since, when we'd met, she didn't know me from a can of paint. And to assume that I would automatically agree because I was a "brother" from her neck of the woods was kind of offensive, too.

Kim was a full-time Flori Roberts make-up girl at a semi-ritzy department store with a predominantly white clientele, so she essentially spent most of her life in the white world. Thus, she had developed what I call a "floor" personality, which was totally separate from her "real" personality.

She'd come down to the stock area where I worked, walking like she had a stick stuck up her ass and a $500 bottle of Cristal balanced on her head; that is, until she saw me. Then she'd conspicuously look around to see if the coast was clear...of white people. Once she confirmed that it was safe, she'd turn into her *real* self, super ghetto-fied chick, as if to prove to me, or to herself, that despite the Pollyanna Sunburned Barbie role she played on the sales floor, she was nobody's Oreo cookie. And for exhibit A, she'd start working her hips and bodacious ass like a $50 dollar a pop lap dancer. Exhibit B, she'd open her mouth and start spewing some inane shit like: "What's up, Loco, my favorite studious nigga! Damn, is it just me, or do white folks make your skin crawl, too?"

So, why would Kim invite dewy-eyed Maggie to a party, in Brooklyn no less?

Hmmm.

Maggie and I had not made the fact that we were involved known at the job. Not that there was any policy against employee dating. There wasn't to my knowledge. And we'd never discussed it, either, so it wasn't a conscious decision. It had started as a secret rendezvous on top of boxes and against cages, and it just continued that way. But, I often wondered if anyone knew. It became an issue the night of the party.

*****

"Did you tell Kim about us?"

I must have let slip some panic in my voice because she answered, "Maybe I did, maybe I didn't. What difference does it make? You didn't want her to know?"

"Makes me no never mind." I said, with a wave off, figuring she must have told her. *Fuck it.* "Let me see that."

She handed me the map. The party was in Fort Green, a couple of blocks from my school, LIU, actually.

Great.

I took a deep breath and told myself that there was nothing to be so anxious about. *So what, the party was in a black neighborhood* (at least Fort Greene was until gentrification got its hands on it) I told myself. *So what you gotta take the A-train to get there, one of the blackest train lines in the city. So what there was bound to be a shitload of sisters there! You knew it was going to happen sooner or later. You knew you could only hide your betrayal from your people but for so long in a city like NY, and that at some point you were going to have to face up to it. So just brace yourself and take it like a man!*

"Let's take a cab." I suggested, sticking out my hand to flag one down "The subway is too crowded."

The thought of being on the A-train with Maggie was not a pleasant one.

Three yellow taxis — without passengers and with the off-duty lights off — passed me by, one even stopped for a white couple a few feet ahead. I was about to tell Maggie to flag one down for us, but that would have just exacerbated the humiliation.

"Fuck a cab, they're too expensive anyway. Let's take the train."

The A-train runs through three boroughs, from upper Manhattan to lower Manhattan, crosses into and through Brooklyn, and out to Queens. In those days, while in Manhattan, the passengers tended to be a mix of black, white and Latino. But, the closer you got to Brooklyn, the blacker the passengers got, and by the time you reached *Jay Street-Borough Hall,* the last transfer point for trains heading to the white neighborhoods of Brooklyn, it became 99% black. There might be some brave white souls headed out to Howard Beach (notoriously Italian and violently territorial), one of the few remaining white neighborhoods along the A-train, but that was rare. Those folks took shuttle buses home from the city.

On this night, Maggie represented the 1% not-black, sitting beside me, clutching my hand, feeling the tension of the attention we drew. A lot of head shaking and tooth-sucking was aimed at us. But, if that was the worst of it, I was cool with that.

The doors to the next car slid open and a crew of boisterous black teens entered the car. I could see from the opposite end that two of them were wearing Universal flags!

Geezus, they were Gods!

Great.

If I had been alone I wouldn't have felt any anxiety. Even if I had been with a black woman I would have been cool. But, sitting there holding hands with a blue-eyed, blond haired devil, in one of my preppy get-ups I'd taken to wearing since starting University and acquiring a 20% employee discount, I felt tense as hell.

As they came closer I could see one of them had noticed us and alerted the others. Their banter ceased, laughter filled eyes turned curious, in an unfriendly way. When they were damn near on top of us I gave one of them some eye contact. And I recognized him! He was from around the way. He recognized me, too. I nodded and he nodded back.

He knew I was Five Percent! Or, rather, had been.

Maggie was crushing my hand.

I heard him tell the others in a stage whisper, "Yo, that's the God, Unique!"

Another said, "Fuck outta here!"

"Word is bond! He live around the corner from me!"

"Damn." another sighed. "He fell *hard*!"

"Yeah, but that Devil is banging! Man, I'd fall victim for that shit, too."

"God, we should give yo' ass a Universal Beat-down just for saying some shit like that!"

They all laughed, looking back, but continued walking, their playful banter restored.

The train pulled into Lafayette Avenue station.

"You knew them?" Maggie asked in disbelief as we got off the train.

"One of them," I said, trying to seem at ease but adrenalin was racing through my system like mercury. That incident could have gone a bad way easily.

The party was in a Brownstone just off of Fulton Street, minutes from the subway, on a tree-lined shadowy street. The music poured out of the open parlor windows and front door, decorated with balloons.

As we approached the door, Kim came rushing out of it into the yard.

"Maggie! You came! Thank you so much," she hollered, slurring a bit, hostess Barbie-style. Then she air kissed and hugged Maggie. "And, who's your..."

Her eyes bulged, genuinely surprised.

"Loco!"

Then, Kim looked down at Maggie's hand still clutching mine, then up at Maggie's face. Glossy eyes, plastic smile. Then, back to mine. And, her eyes changed. Just that quick. The smile remained, but her eyes became arch and deadly. And, then, quick-fast, they changed, again. Back to her Flori Roberts product peddling eyes.

I almost felt sorry for her. I'd rarely seen one face make so many emotional jumps to light speed in such a short span of time.

"Loco, Loco, LOCO! What a surprise." She gave me a hug, but no air kisses. "Well, don't just stand there. Come on in!"

Yeah, I'd have bet my next paycheck I fucked up her high.

*****

It wasn't a typical Brooklyn house party. I knew that as soon as I walked in the door and spotted a white couple sitting on the steps chatting and sipping wine, from real glasses! And, when the female of the two said, "Hey Loco!" I realized who she was. It was one of the Estee Lauder counter girls, looking even sexier than she did at work!

"Hey you!" I said, cause I couldn't remember her name.

"Erica!" Maggie shrieked as she ran over to her, hugging and kissing her on the cheek.

"I see y'all already know Erica ," Kim said. "Come on. Let me introduce you guys around."

211

She was moving quickly introducing Maggie and me, as a couple, to her party attendees. A good number of them were people I recognized from the store's various departments, and of course they recognized me, as well. I was practically a token black person (one of about 4 or 5 out of a couple hundred staff people).

There was Susan from Human Resources, and Ted from Men's wear. Claudette from Chanel and Pauline from Juniors. Barbara was an Assistant Buyer of accessories, I think, and Alex was this flamboyant gay guy who did the fashion coordinating for the mannequins and also helped design the world famous Christmas window display, for which people lined up around the block to see every year.

And he was smoking a joint.

"Ah, Loco, you handsome stud you! I had high hopes for you, yes I did," he sang, with what smelled like sensimilia smoke streaming out of his nostrils. "But, here you are, a mere hetero, with Maggie on your arm, a dagger in my heart!"

He laughed loudly, and tried to hand his joint to me.

"Partake of some of Jamaica's finest with me darling and I'll forgive your frailties."

I almost reached for it, but thought twice. While Alex- or Alexandra, as he liked to be called- was indispensable, responsible for thousands of Christmas dollars pouring into the store every year, I was decidedly not. And with representatives from some vital departments standing around excusing Alexandra's drug use as some artistic dalliance or gay eccentricity, I was sure they would not extend to me the same lenience.

"Sorry," I said, liking him and his *fuck all* personality. "But, I'm as drug-free as Nancy Reagan!"

He had a good laugh. "Suit your succulent self, sweetheart," he said, and passed it to a friend he had come with.

I realized something, as Maggie and I were introduced to person after person: The majority of the people at the party were white. And the few that were black, sprinkled here and there, made me feel downright nigga-ish they were so racially neutral.

One guy, his name was Nathaniel, was Kim's neighbor. He was an actor, Shakespearean I think, and I could swear he had powdered his face to make it lighter for it had a kind of pasty film on it. He had a deep voice, James Earl Jones deep, and enunciated words with a clarity that gave them enhanced meaning, like a great orator. I could see him playing Frederick Douglass or Othello in a play.

"You have a beautiful voice," Maggie said, looking enthralled.

"Why, thank you!" he said. "I do radio commercials and some voice over work for films and such."

I stepped off and left them chatting, exploring the rest of Kim's digs.

The whiteness of the party didn't stop at the guest. I mentioned the real wine glasses I'd noticed at the door. All the house parties I knew used paper and plastic cups, as a rule cause they won't get broken, or stolen. But, aside from that, there was also a strong white influence on the menu. I mean, the contrast was stunning. Instead of trays of fried chicken, potato salad, macaroni salad and assorted other staples, she had laid out trays of hors d'œuvres and fancy appetizers I'd never seen before. All kinds of pate, pigs in a blanket, cheese, tiny sandwiches and shit you'd see at a party on "The Jeffersons," when George was trying to impress some "honky" to help him keep *moving on up.*

I looked up from the spread to find Kim checking me out, arms folded.

"Looks good," I said. "Did you make it, or did you hire a caterer?"

She glanced at Maggie who was chatting it up with Nathaniel, the Shakespearean. Then back at me.

"Fuck I look like? Betty Crocker? Of course I hired a caterer!" she snapped. "And it cost a fucking arm and a leg!"

"Well, I'm sure your guests are impressed, so I'd say it was money well spent."

I must have had some irony in my voice cause she made a face that would have sent her other guest running scared into the street. A face I'd seen a million times on a million black women, so it didn't faze me.

"You roll up in here with Miss Mid-Western Barbie on your arm and got the nerve to try and judge *me*?!"

"Fuck you talking about," I said a little loudly. "I was just complimenting your vittles. Why are you buggin'?"

"Keep your voice down, motherfucker," She whispered through the teeth of her plastic smile as she looked around. The coast was clear. She indicated with her index finger, on the down low, to follow her. I glanced over at Maggie. She caught my glance, smiled and winked and continued chatting.

Kim led me through the kitchen into a doorway with a narrow rickety wooden staircase leading down to the basement.

Kim was a beautiful woman. I mean, seriously beautiful, model beautiful. Had long real (I think) hair, permed and straight. Had bedroom eyes and kissable lips. White teeth, high cheek bones…just exciting to look at! She was short, though, about 5'4, with tits and hips and ass disproportionate to her size but definitely has caused many a traffic accident. She was wearing the fuck out of a mini-party dress, that night. I mean, she was, without a doubt, the hottest hottie at her own party.

She wheeled on me.

"Let's get something straight, Mr. Loco!" she said with sass through her pouty lips. "I didn't invite *you* here! I invited Maggie, and I told her she could bring a friend, assuming she'd bring her boyfriend or something. And, she walks up in here with yo' ass! If I had known you two had dealings I wouldn't have invited her, either."

"Why not?" I asked. "I mean, I can see you up to something, but—"

"That ain't none of *your* goddamn business!" She said, jabbing her finger at my nose. I could see she hadn't sobered up entirely. She was still slurring a bit, and her eyes were red like she'd been sneaking puffs on Alexandra's spliff. "All you need to know is I don't need no *niggers* up in here niggering shit up! You follow?"

I had never liked Kim...not until that moment. I didn't agree with her assertion but the sincerity with which she'd declared her position was, I don't know, moving. She was ready to fight any comers to achieve her goals. I respected that kind of self-reliance and determination. It was the same quality I saw in most of the women who'd raised and nurtured me into the person I was becoming.

"First off, Ms. Kim!" I said, with a razor's edge. "If you want to keep that finger you best get it out my face! Second, the only one up in here niggering shit up, as you put it, is you! I don't know who you take me for, but I ain't that nigger, and I ain't never been that nigger, so niggering shit up ain't my thing! I wouldn't even know how."

215

She lowered her finger like it was a pistol and I was some criminal she was trying to decide whether she could trust or not.

"So, before we make ourselves into enemies, which you seem determined to do, why don't we try being civilized first? And, if that don't work, you can throw me the fuck out. It's your party, and your crib, and I totally respect that."

I saw her eyes give first, followed by her dynamic smile.

"Are my eyes red?" she asked, apropos of nothing, like she'd come to the conclusion that our little altercation never occurred.

"Yep!" I said and reached into my pocket and pulled out a bottle of Visine I kept on me. She took it from me, held it up and smiled at it, acknowledging it for the peace offering that it was. She started dropping it into her eyes with practiced skill. Once done she looked at me like she'd just opened her world to me, and handed it back with a wink of thanks.

"This ain't my house," she said. "Actually it's my grandmother's house. She's on a cruise in the Caribbean somewhere. "

"Nice house," I said.

"Ain't it?" She smiled amorously as she looked around at the unfurnished dank basement. It was plain to see she coveted the house. "Anyway, Loco, you better get back to your Maggie. I'm sure she misses her big black stud."

"She's upstairs shooting the breeze with Darth Vader," I said. "So, you gonna tell me what you're up to?"

"What do you mean?" she asked innocently.

"You know what I mean," I said. "Why you throwing a Jim Crow jamboree in your grandmother's crib, of all places?"

"*Jim Crow Jamboree*," she sang, laughing. "I love the way you put shit sometimes."

"I'm serious, Kim." I wanted to know if she was on some *"black people suck so I wanna be white"* shit, or was there some strategic thinking involved in her invitational, cause her behavior at the job left much to be desired. "What's your story?"

"My *story?*" she almost yelled. "My *story?* Loco, you *know* my story! Ain't that why you rolling with a white chick? This is *their* world, that's why. *They* run shit! And if you want a piece you gotta go through them! Niggers can't help you. They ain't gonna do nothing but drag your ass back down with them, am I right? If you want help, if you wanna learn something useful, if you wanna grow, if you wanna be somebody in this world, then you gotta accept that fact and deal with it. And the fact is: all the power, all the influence and, yes, all the money is in *their* hands! All I'm doing is networking. Networking my beautiful ass off, positioning myself for success!"

She looked at me, both tenderness and wariness in her whitening eyes.

"Tell me you're not doing the same thing. I know you're in college now, trying to learn something so you can make a better life for you and yours. I see you studying in the stockroom, reading textbooks and writing reports. Tell me Maggie ain't just another textbook in your knapsack. Some research for your own personal report. Tell me she ain't something you're studying so you can take that knowledge and use it to your advantage."

I was about to object, but held my tongue. I wanted to hear her out.

"I know I'm right, so don't ask me what my story is. *My* story is *your* story, is any black person's story; any black person who wants to do more than survive in a white world; the ones that wanna thrive, that is. And I'm thriving, baby!"

I studied Kim for a moment as she spoke. I wasn't sure why but she reminded me of Burns, back in the Army, just then.

"Or am I wrong about you?" she said, looking at me, her eyes filled with an enormous sympathy. "Are you just one of these tired niggers running around thinking with their dicks and trying to get it wet in any piece of ass they can? And if it's white pussy it's all the better? I get these motherfuckers running up on me all day! Trying to shoot some game to me, get my number, thinking they gonna get some, so they can feel more like a man. Tell me that ain't you, Loco. Tell me you ain't no pathetic ass brother like that! Cuz, if you are, then you certainly are *niggering shit up in here*, and you can get the fuck outta my grandmother's house right now!"

The door to the basement opened just then. We both looked up the staircase and watched Maggie peek her head in.

"Loco?"

"Yeah, I'll be up in a sec, Mags."

"Sorry I kept him Maggie," Kim cried, Barbie-style. "He was helping me out."

Kim turned and looked at me meaningfully, back to her thriving social climbing face."*Well?*"

"Nah, you got it right," I said, though I wasn't 100% sure if I was lying to her or lying to myself. All I knew was that I was lying to somebody. "Our stories are the same."

"I thought so," she said, winked, and gestured towards the stairs. "After you, Mr. Loco. I don't want you looking up my dress at all my goodies."

I laughed, cause she'd read my mind.

*****

218

In the weeks after the party, Maggie and I grew further and further apart.

Kim had planted a seed in my mind the night of the party and it had grown into an entire crop. It began by my asking myself why I was really with Maggie. Was she special to me? Was I falling in love? Did I see a future for us? Would I even be bothered with her if it weren't for the H-Factor?

I kept coming up with the same answer: No.

And, I think she felt the same.

While, in the beginning, she used to piss and moan if I were too busy to meet her, after a while she just started rolling with it. And, whenever we did meet, outside of work, it had become routine: hydro, sex, hydro, sex, hydro. She used to wonder what my intentions were, but I guess she'd gotten her answer for they'd become plain to see.

Of course, we still worked together and had to deal with the "shitting where you eat" mistake (my first time, but would certainly not be my last). But, there was no more sexual tension, only awkwardness.

*****

One day, I arrived to work early and went down into the basement. On my way to my stock area I had to pass other stock areas. All stock areas were secured by cages. Most of the crime that occurred at the store- as is the case with most retailers I suspect- was from employee theft, so the cages were a necessary precaution against this.

As I passed the high-end fragrance cage I glimpsed one of my co-workers, a black guy named Theo, behaving kind of suspiciously. Then, I watched as he had slipped some small fragrance boxes into his jacket pockets, looking around as he did so. When he spotted me he froze. I turned my head quickly trying to pretend like I hadn't seen anything, and kept walking. But, before I knew it Theo had pulled up behind me.

"What's up Loco, Honey?" he said.

"Hey Theo, how's it going?"

"Lovin' the skin I'm in," he laughed, with a wink, a poke at my interracial relationship, no doubt. "You're in early, baby."

I turned away. But I could feel his gaze. He was scorching the side of my head with his laser beams that passed for eyes.

"Yeah, just gonna get in a little studying before my shift starts," I said, looking around for nothing in particular, trying to dodge his beams.

"Uh huh," he said, like he didn't believe a word of it. Theo had a way about him. Like Alex, he was also gay. Working in retail, in a fashionable store, there are always tons of women and gay men. Comes with the territory. But, unlike Alex, who was working in a creative area, Theo was not. At least not yet. He did have talent, though. He was a cartoonist, attending an art school in Manhattan, and could draw like a madman. But, like me, he was working part-time just to make ends meet.

The thing about Theo that made him special, in my estimation, was that he was a fully liberated individual. He was free. Free in a way most people will never know. So free, in fact, that he scared the shit out of most people. His freedom allowed him to see things. The cage of lies and pretense most of us have erected around ourselves and voluntarily live within, whether we're aware of it or not, he had escaped from, and could see our cages as clearly as if the wire mesh and barbed wire were solid matter. "So, the question is, are you gonna drop dime on me or what?"

"What?" I turned to face him. He'd asked the question in a tone of voice different than I'd ever heard him use. A "Straight outta Brooklyn" tone. It was like suddenly hearing Pee Wee Herman speak in his natural voice, totally out of character.

I knew that Theo was from my neck of the woods, in Brooklyn, but to see him decked out in sequins shirts and tight jeans, with shoulder-length permed hair, he seemed so natural you'd think he'd always been that way. This new voice, however, spoke to me of the life he'd led before he became openly gay, when he had to pretend to comport with a community that would have marginalized him, if not assaulted him, and never would have accepted him in his full glory (at the time, violent acts against gays, called Gay-Bashing, were rampant in New York).

I didn't know which voice sounded more interesting, his gay voice or his "pre-gay" one.

"I know you saw me, Loco. Don't try and front, my brother," he said.

This was so weird.

"Ain't none of my business what you do in your area," I said. "No one would believe me any way."

"You got that shit right," he laughed.

I started to walk away.

"Listen Loco," he said, looking around to see if anyone were near enough to hear. But, we were alone. Just that buzzing sound of machines. "Because I like you, I'm uh let you in on my scheme. Between me and you , you understand?"

Part of me wanted to hear and part of me didn't. But Theo had this kind of magnetism when he talked that you find it hard to walk away from him. He was a charming bastard with enough charisma to turn an angry lynch mob into an applauding audience. That's why I knew no one would believe me if I had squealed on him. Most people could never imagine someone as open and flagrant as Theo as a thief.

I stopped walking. "Let's hear it."

For the next few minutes he told me of how he'd been clipping fragrances for months, by the shitload. He explained that he had customers lined up to take the product off his hand, but with the growing influx of impostor fragrances, the demand for the expensive *real* stuff he sold was going down.

"But, beauty products? I got clients screaming for that stuff! Clinique, Estee Lauder, Chanel, all that shit you have access to. I'd make a killing!"

"Uh huh." I could smell the rain coming.

"Or rather, *we'd* make a killing, unless you've found your joy busting your ass for peanuts, here's a chance to make it worth your while."

"Are you serious?"

"If I could get in your cage without arousing suspicion, I wouldn't need you and this conversation wouldn't be happening."

"OK. Let me see if I got this right: I steal the stuff, give it to you. You sell the stuff to your clients and give me a cut, what? 75-25?"

"I was thinking 50-50, but that's negotiable if you're in—."

"Since I'd be taking all the risk, I should get the lion share, no?" I asked. "Cause the trail would lead to me first, wouldn't it? Which makes me wonder how you've managed to do this so long without arousing suspicion. And how many other *partners* you have running around here getting jerked outta percentage points by your suave ass."

He looked at me queerly for a sec. Then looked around like he'd heard someone creeping. But there was nothing to see. He probably just wanted to think without me seeing his thought process written on his face, I figured. He hadn't planned this, and he was hesitating, realizing that it wasn't going to be easy to draw me into his scheme. I decided then I didn't want any parts of it.

"Listen, Theo, I'm not gonna yank your chain," I said, as his face contorted into disappointment. "I'm not really interested in getting into this shit. To tell you the truth, I'm a horrible criminal, and I hate looking over my shoulder. I can't even lie worth a shit. So, you go ahead and do your thing. You don't have to worry. Your secret's safe with me. I'll get by on peanuts until I can get some cashews and pistachios in my own right."

"Fine, Loco," he said, nodding. "I can respect that."

Then his eyes turned gay again. This, however, *was* kind of creepy to watch, especially with all this talk about nuts. "Well, darling, I'm off. Love that shirt, by the way! Perry Ellis, right? It suits you in a *sexy* way."

He winked and walked off.

Not two weeks later I found myself sitting in the security office submitting to questioning before the green-eyed scrutiny of the head of security, Tom. He was looking at me like he'd finally earned his keep and bagged the elephant.

"You should have stuck to fragrances, Mr. Loco," he said like he'd figured out my scheme. "So many hands in that cage it was impossible to finger who was doing the lifting."

I was about to protest my innocence, yet again, but I knew it was a waste of breath.

"Your mistake, if you really wanna know, was dipping into the beauty stock. We still don't know how you managed to get the fragrances, though. But, we'll figure it out. That's all we do here. Figure out how *you guys* do it, and put you where you

223

belong!"

Again, I was about to say something. The way he'd said *you guys* felt a little dodgy. But, I was held in check by the look in his eyes. I could see something reminiscent of what I saw in the eyes of those *people* in those pictures of lynchings, though not as severe: A zero-calorie sugar-free shit kicker. But, still, it was so ugly it was scary, for it didn't seem aimed at my assumed proclivity to steal, the way a cop might hate criminals, but it seemed to be aimed at *you guys*.

"Of course, if you wrote down on that paper there how you did it, and who your partners were, I'm sure I could get some of my buddies on the *Force* to cut you some slack. A slap on the wrist." He handed me a pen like I'd asked for one.

This Motherfucker…

"I told you I didn't do anything," I shouted, taking the pen and using it as a pointer. "And, *you* know I didn't! The only reason you got me in here is you think I know who's making you look stupid. Imagine how stupider you're gonna feel when you have to apologize and kiss my ass when I walk out of here."

He smiled, like he knew something I didn't know he knew. Like there had been hidden cameras and mics recording the conversation Theo and I had had a couple of weeks earlier; a thought that shook me to the core. Not that I couldn't find another part time job lifting boxes in a basement…but it would have been embarrassing, to say the least.

"You really think we're gonna let your ass anywhere near that stock room again?" he asked as he stood up, walked over to the door to his office peeked out (like he was gonna lock it and whip my ass or something) then opened it halfway.

Out in the waiting area I could see Theo, sitting there crying, looking broken.

He closed the door before Theo could see me.

"We caught your faggot-ass partner! And that little bitch already 'fessd up!"

"So, you *do* know I didn't do anything!" I shouted.

"That's not what *it* said," Tom said, jerking his thumb towards the door with a devious smirk on his face.

"You're lying!"

"Am I, now," he said, dubiously. "We also have some statements from the counter girls. Though they've never seen you steal anything, they all say that sometimes when they come down to the stock room you look like you're up to something."

"What? That's bullshit!"

"Well, except *Maggie*," he said, with a snare. I didn't like the way he'd said her name, either. "She says you'd never do anything like that. *Never, ever, never*...she says. And, I guess she would know, wouldn't she? Seeing that she's your piece of ass I hear."

He paused for effect, and shot me a glance that only a great actor or a true to life bloodthirsty shit kicker could muster, full of icy indifference. If he could have his way, he'd snuff out my life light as quickly and with as much regret as a lifelong hunter would a deer. Then the glance vanished like it had never been there. But, I'd sure as hell seen it, and I knew what it meant.

"But, her judgment is questionable, obviously," he sneered. "Anyway, we'll see what her urinalysis reveals, won't we?"

And, it hit me, like a fucking brick — though I could never prove it — what this charade was really all about. I'd wondered what, if any, fallout would result from Maggie and I going to Kim's party together, and it becoming common knowledge that we were a couple.

I knew now, from the satisfied look on Tom's face, that

though I could not be arrested, and that I could not rightfully be associated with any crime, that my days employed there were, indeed, coming to an end.

As was my relationship with Maggie.

I'd told her as much the next time I saw her. I said that we weren't going to work out. I lied and said our relationship had become too much of a strain and that I needed to focus more on my studies.

She was beside herself and blamed me for everything. Even though she was the one who had stupidly taken a hit off of Alex's joint at the party (I hadn't even known she had) she insisted her being fired was my fault. She'd tried all kinds of things to flush years of Hydro use out of system, but her urinalysis had still come back positive enough to put her in violation of the company's drug policy.

Somehow she'd made the leap of reason that if I had dropped dime on Theo then she wouldn't have been tested. She insisted that I had sacrificed her to uphold some kind of *black code* among "the brothers." I told her that was absurd, that her testing was directly related to someone at the party squealing on her, and that racist ass Tom's disapproval of mixed couples.

"So, you're a fucking coward! Just like Malik!" she'd screamed, her last words to me as I walked out her door and left her and her H-factor behind, unsure which I would miss more.

As I made my way to the train station, to head home, back to black Brooklyn, I reckoned she had been half right with that *black code* business. Race *had* taken a more prominent role in my assessment of our relationship. That incident with Tom had shaken me up something terrible. That look in his eyes was a look I never wanted to be on the business end of ever again.

And if dumping her was all it took to keep myself off the shit kicker radar, then that was a small price to pay.

At least I thought so at the time.

She was right on that account, as well, it seemed. I was a coward!

That there were Toms walking around a city as diverse as New York — some of them in positions of authority — was enough to make me wary of all white people. I'd see Tom almost every day. He worked the doors at the employee exits, and used to play chummy with me; all high fives and dirty jokes when our paths would cross. All of that ended the day he learned that I had a white "piece of ass" as he'd put it. Just that quickly, I'd become road kill on his people's path to Aryan supremacy, or a victim of, as Public Enemy had so astutely put it, the *fear of a Black Planet!*

I realized that I no longer truly trusted white people. I didn't hate them. I didn't want to bring harm to them. I just wasn't inclined to extend the benefit of the doubt or to unnecessarily be around them.

It was actually my altercation with Cheryl that was the clincher.

9

A LIAR, A THIEF, AND A TALENTED WRITER

Cheryl was my boss and, like most of the management in the store, was a white woman. She was an assistant buyer and managed the entire Clinique counter, so she was actually my and Maggie's boss.

And, she was cool as hell!

If I wanted overtime, for instance, she was the one to ask and more often than not would hook me up. If I needed a day off to cram for a test or write a paper, she would help me out, no questions asked. She never riffed at me when I studied at work, or caught up on some much need ZZZs, and if she knew that Maggie and I were a couple, she kept it to herself.

She answered to the cosmetics buyer, a white woman who had, after taking one look at me, actually hired me. I'm not sure why she'd taken such a liking to me, being that she didn't really know anything about me. But she loved me the way rich WASP love endangered species. She was always hugs and cheese whenever our paths crossed, asking me did I need anything and what not. But, for Cheryl, she was always strictly business and a bit demeaning, as well. So Cheryl wore a distressed look as a matter of course, the way most people wear underwear. She lived under duress. But, she never took it out on me or the other staff.

I really liked Cheryl. We had developed a very good relationship. She was cold and professional with the other staff people but with me she would share parts of her personality that she would never share with the others. No one else would have ever guessed she liked to go to night clubs and pick up guys, or that she drank Tequila like a Mexican fish. I wasn't sure why she'd confided in me, though. Maybe I came off as empathetic and discreet.

I never shared her secrets with anyone, though. When co-workers would say, "How can you work for that woman? She's like Nurse Ratched," I'd just smile and shrug with the secret knowledge that she was nothing like that, really. She just looked it.

After the Theo-the-Thief scandal there was a major overhaul of the security procedures at the job. And the rumor mill had it that hidden security cameras had been strategically installed. Every single piece of stock was inventoried so regularly that it would now take mere hours instead of days to notice shortages. The atmosphere had become suffocating in there. But, I rolled with it cause I needed the job.

That is, until I noticed that along with the security changes, Cheryl's behavior towards me had changed, as well. No more chats. No more smiles. No more flexibility. I figured that the head of security, that bastard Tom, had told her something to the effect that I was a suspect or that she should be extra vigilant with the cosmetic stocks for whatever reason.

For extra vigilant is what she'd become! Damn near paranoid. And the behavior seemed to be directed at me, and me alone.

One day, I spoke to her about it because it had kind of hurt my feelings.

"Cheryl," I said to her. "Why do I have to come to you every time I need the key to the stock cage?"

"It's the new procedure. You know that."

"*No,*" I sang, softly, trying to handle this situation delicately. A good relationship hang in the balance. "The new procedure calls for the keys to be signed in and out. You don't need to be in the middle. Besides, every time I interrupt you for the keys it distracts you from other important matters, doesn't it?"

"That's not your concern, Mr. Loco," she said coldly and

dismissively. *Mr. Loco???* She hadn't called me that since my first week working there, we'd hit it of so well. "I've got it under control. I can chew bubble gum and walk at the same time! You just do your job and let me do mine. If that's not too much trouble."

I was shocked. So much for delicacy. She'd never taken such a curt tone with me before. The kid gloves came off.

"Ok, Cheryl," I said, sharply. "Let me put it this way: I feel like the reason you require me to come to you in order to get the keys is because you don't trust me. And I don't like it."

"That's too bad!" She snapped. "Someone was stealing from our cage. MY cage! Was it you? I don't know. All I know for sure is that it wasn't me!"

"It wasn't me, either!" I yelped. "Are you sure it wasn't one of the counter girls?"

She looked at me like I'd said *"are you sure Elvis Presley didn't come back from the dead and rob the stockroom?"*

"Listen, I'm pretty busy, so if that's all."

"No! That's *not* all. We've been working together for over a year now, without incident. We've built up trust...mutual trust—"

"This isn't about trust, *Mr.* Loco," she said. Some of the edge in her voice had been replaced by sadness. "This is a business. This is my career! And this incident reflects poorly on me! Now, everybody knows that you and Theo were thick as thie — Anyway, he was your friend, wasn't he? And he was stealing right under your nose. Did you know?"

"He wasn't my friend," I said. "And we weren't thick as thieves!"

"I *asked* you did you know."

"No," I lied, and not well. I felt so guilty, and at the same time defensive. "I don't work for security. It's not my job to spy on my co-workers. If security were doing their job properly then Theo wouldn't have been able to do what he did, right?"

Cheryl was shaking her head. This was a closed matter to her. Either I was a thief, a co-conspirator, or in possession of guilty knowledge. All were detestable in her book because all constituted acts of betrayal and deceit.

"I'm so disappointed in you, Loco," she said like I'd confessed to something. Maybe I had with my eyes. "You were given a golden opportunity here and you just threw it away… for nothing."

"Huh?" She'd thrown me with that one. Personal disappointment was one thing, but professional disappointment? "What do you mean?"

"This was an opportunity for you to prove the popular consensus wrong. You know what they think here, don't you? Tom in Security, for example. He thinks *all* black people are liars and thieves! He wants you fired just as a precaution! He said, 'sooner or later, he's gonna steal something. I guarantee it!' I don't like him. So I defended you. I *vouched* for you! I told him that he was wrong about you, that you'd never stoop so low. That's why you still have a job here, by the way. I threatened him, told him if he tried to implicate you in any of this without any evidence to speak of, he'd regret it! I practically called him a racist."

I still didn't get her meaning, and was about to say so, but I was so moved by her support that I got a lump in my throat.

"You know, Loco, I grew up in Indiana, and in my hometown, the people feel pretty much the same way Tom does. They say such horrible things about black people…you wouldn't believe. But, I decided I wouldn't listen to their hearsay. Unlike Tom, most of the people back home have never met a black person before so what did they know? I decided I would see for myself.

"At my university, there were some black people, mostly jocks, and they lived up to everything that I'd ever heard about black men. They were like mad dogs! I never met a black guy who didn't try to, you know, sleep with me. One of them even...well, I'm not gonna say rape cause my friend, Susan, she *did* invite him to her room and they had done it several times before, but...anyway, she'll never be the same. She even dropped out of school, and since he was some hotshot on the football team..."

She paused and looked at me like her anecdote had told me much more than it had about why she was so disappointed in me.

It hadn't.

"Anyway, after college I came to New York, and started working here. And then you came into my life. I never told you this but you are the first black person I've ever, well, liked. You're smart, and you study hard, you work hard, you're funny. I know as your boss I should have kept my distance from you, Loco, but I wanted to prove those narrow-minded folks back in Indiana wrong. I wanted to believe that all black men weren't like those animals at my university...you know, I wanted us to be real *friends*. That was my mistake—"

Mistake??

"I'm sorry, Cheryl," I said. "But, did I miss something? I'm still waiting to hear about this opportunity I squandered. Which opportunity are you talking about, specifically? The opportunity to count your lipsticks and skin clarifying lotion? To lug your boxes around this dusty-ass basement? Were you planning to promote me to counter *boy*, or assistant manager of

233

box lifters, or something? Or do you mean that rare opportunity – especially for us black guys – of being persecuted for a crime I didn't commit? Or the opportunity to prove to racist pricks like Tom that black people *can* be trusted? Huh?? Cuz I'd kill for the chance to do that!"

She looked stumped and reflective for a moment. Like maybe I'd given her food for thought.

"Or did you mean something personal, like the opportunity to prove to you, and those ignorant crackers back in Indiana, that all black men are not trying to rape white chicks?"

"I didn't mean it like that, and you know it, Loco. Please, *please*, don't purposely misconstrue my words," she pleaded.

"Then stop patronizing me and make it plain," I said. "Cuz, right now I'm having a hard time telling the difference between you and Tom."

Suddenly, she stood up to her full 5'6 height and looked up at me, huffing. I thought for sure she was going to slap me.

"You *knew* Theo was a thief! I know you knew!" she fired, her index finger a pistol aimed at my chest.

"Even if I did, so what! I ain't *mister* Theo. I'm *mister* Loco, right?" I fired back.

"If you knew and said nothing, that's the same as stealing."

"So you think I'm a liar *and* a thief!" I said, righteously furious.

"Well, *aren't* you? Tell me I'm wrong!" she said, her voice almost cracking. *Please*, she didn't need to add. It was all over her face.

We stood there silently face to face for a few heartbeats, during which, I believe, we both saw the door on our friendship slowly, pneumatically, swinging closed. Either of us had the chance to run and catch it before it did. I could have lied and said, "Cheryl, I swear on a stack of bibles, cross my heart and hope to never sleep with white women without written invitation, I had no idea..." and she would have smiled and allowed herself to believe me. Maybe. And she could have said, "Loco, you know how much I care about you, but I've got to go through the motions because they're watching me. Personally I could care less if you knew about Theo or not. I *know* you didn't do it. And, by the way, my friend, Susan, was black." And I *probably* would have laughed and accepted that as ample apology for insinuating I was a lying thief from a breed of rapists. But neither of us budged. And, that door shut, with a vacuum, sucking the love out of the room.

"I think you and Tom would make an adorable couple!" I said, sarcastically. "I think they're showing *Birth of a Nation* over at the Angelika! And, it's Friday, so there's sure to be a nice romantic cross burning in Bensonhurst tonight. You should ask him out."

"Get outta my office, Loco!"

"You know something, Cheryl? *You're* the one who missed an opportunity!" I said, turning to leave. "You could have been the first white person from Lynchville, or wherever the hell you're from, to see what the world outside of their own assholes looks like."

"I said, *get out!*"

"Fuck this," I said. "I quit!"

Then, I stormed out, went upstairs to Human Resources and told them the same — effective immediately!

I have a flair for dramatics, I discovered long ago. And the chance to tell my white boss off, followed by a march into HR and subsequently into unemployment, was the kind of occasion to flex dramatic muscle that was hard to pass up.

The drama carried on for a couple of weeks. I wanted, hell, I *needed* to hear ringing endorsements of my tirade against tyranny in the workplace. So I milked my friends dry, riffing to anyone who'd listen, about them "motherfucking racist fucks!" And how I'd told them motherfuckers what they could do with their "oppo-fuckin-tunity! Them crackers ain't gonna never forget a nigga like me, you can beleeee dat!"

Yeah, I rode that wave of bullshit until the day I reached in my pocket and came up with lint.

Then, reality and regret set in.

I could have handled that differently, I scolded myself. *Cheryl wasn't so bad for a Cracker. At least she was trying not to be a racist piece of shit. I could've given her some credit and cut her some slack! But, nooooo, I had to mount my self-righteous high horse and condemn the woman. Great. Now I gotta hit up Moms for carfare and food money.*

I entertained these kinds of thoughts as I dusted off and updated my retail-heavy résumé, and prepared myself for another fun-filled round of job interviews.

*****

Meanwhile, there was still school to deal with.

The student body at LIU was mostly black, but the faculty was almost entirely white. A fact I didn't find especially troubling before the events at my former place of employment had taken place. But, after, it began to rub me the wrong way.

I became something of a militant on campus, images of Public Enemy dancing in my head. Imagine a cross between Bobby Seale and Flavor-Flav, or like Huey Newton after he'd had a makeover done to him by some late 80's Ghetto Fabologist or New Jack Swinger. Certainly he would've been advised to fade the sides of that Afro and flatten the top, right? And undoubtedly he would've traded in those heavy-ass combat boots for a pair of Gucci sneakers or some Timberlands, wouldn't you think? And, let's face it, black leather jackets may have said *"militant"* in the 70's, but in the 80's they were more Gangsta than militant, so he wouldn't have been able to resist a denim Ralph Lauren Polo jacket, jeans to match, and a Public Enemy T-shirt, I bet. And no accessories say militant like a Clock necklace and a 14k two-finger ring with diamonds, Right?

Looking back, I guess I must've looked pretty... nah, fuck that, I was cool! I had attitude, and I had style. What I didn't have was love for higher education as it was presented to me by a bunch of tenured crackers.

Naturally my attitude affected my grades. I went from the Dean's list to damn near non-matriculating.

And, I believe it would have continued that way until I'd totally given up the ghost if I hadn't met yet another white woman.

Her name was Barbara.

She was a professor at LIU; taught English Literature and Creative Writing. I'd had a couple of English courses before I'd taken hers. Can't remember the courses nor the teachers. The courses had been mandatory so I'd taken them. But, in my junior year I'd taken hers. And, from the start, I knew that it would be different.

I'd sit in her class and listen to her hold forth on the great European poets of the past like Wordsworth, Coleridge, and the likes, and find myself oddly intrigued.

I think it was Samuel Coleridge who first caught my attention. One of his more famous poems, in particular, called,

"Kubla Khan," rocked my world a little. I think what I fancied about him the most was that he was an 18th century junkie (Opium addict) and, while high, dreamt a poem. Upon waking he jotted down as much of it as he could remember. And, now, centuries later, here we were studying it. There was something about that scenario, and the poem, that spoke to me in a very personal way.

Especially this part:

> **And from this chasm, with ceaseless turmoil seething,**
> **As if this earth in fast thick pants were breathing,**
> **A mighty fountain momently was forced:**
> **Amid whose swift half-intermitted burst**
> **Huge fragments vaulted like rebounding hail,**
> **Or chaffygrain beneath the thresher's flail:**
> **And 'mid these dancing rocks at once and ever**
> **It flung up momently the sacred river.**
> **Five miles meandering with a mazy motion**
> **Through wood and dale the sacred river ran,**
> **Then reached the caverns measureless to man,**
> **And sank in tumult to a lifeless ocean**

" *the caverns measureless to man,*" Coleridge had dreamt. *He's got a helluva way with words*, I thought.

Sitting there in Barbara's class, I remembered that when I was a kid I used to write poetry and occasionally I'd work up enough confidence to give my little poems to girls that I liked. Most of the time they'd ridicule me into opium-free reclusion, so I'd given up my poetry penchant for my ego's sake.

But, *Kubla Khan* reminded me of the anticipatory thrill I felt putting pen to page and creating. Also of the exhilaration I'd feel on the rare occasion when some girl would read the poem I'd given her, come over to me afterward and say, "Thank you, Loco. It's beautiful."

One of my first assignments was to write an essay about this experience, and this I did, with gusto. Only, I'd done it the night before it was due. I sat at my kitchen table, my opiate of choice close at hand, and wrote out all my romantic ideas about drug-influenced creativity and so on.

When Barbara returned our papers to us, I was prepared for a "C" or worse. But, she'd given me an "A-!"

"You are a talented writer," she told me. "You should think seriously about writing as a career."

"Uh huh."

I was still predisposed not to trust white people, still flirting with racism. Here she was praising a work I'd barely finished, un-typed, handwritten on loose leaf paper in my chicken-scratch cursive, as "talented." I glanced around at my mostly black classmate's papers to see what the going grade was. There were a lot of Cs.

But, still, I didn't trust her.

This went on for the entire semester, during which I'd written a number of essays and received high marks and compliments for each of them. By semester's end Barbara called me to her office and gave me the "talk."

"Loco," she said. "Your writing is terrific and I think you ought to consider becoming an English Major."

"Uh huh."

"I'm giving you an "A" for the course, " she added. Now she had my undivided attention! It was the first "A" I'd received since the Dean's list days of my freshmen year.

239

"But, I'm a Media Arts major. I don't want to change."

"You could take on a double major," she said. And explained to me what that entailed. To summarize, it meant I'd have to take a whole lot of English courses (on top of my Media Arts course load) between then and graduation. Not to mention all the money. My job was gone. That Army loot was loooooong gone. And, I was digging a trench of debt with student loans that it would take decades to climb out of.

"I don't know, Barbara. I'll think about it," I said, which is the softest "no" I know.

"Next semester, there's going to be a Creative Writing course. Do me a favor, and take it!"

I agreed.

The professor, Lewis, was white, too, but I decided to give his course my best effort, regardless. My *rebel without a pause* routine had worn thin, anyway, so I decided to be just another student, again, from then until graduation. I could fight the power all I wanted once I'd completed my requirements. As a junior, I was looking *the first in my family's history to finish University* right in the face, and it started meaning more to me than a piece of parchment. It felt like I was saying goodbye to the legacy of underachievement I'd inherited and hello to the beginning of a new legacy.

And, Barbara was right. Lewis' course changed everything.

Like most Creative Writing workshops, he'd give us a theme and we'd write about it. Every week a new theme, and every week, for almost the entire semester, I was the star; and not only by Lewis' reckoning. All my classmates had copies of my work on their desks before them, and agreed with him!

My god! I have a talent! I remember thinking, excitedly.

It was an extraordinary experience for me. All my life, to

240

that point, though I had intelligence, I could never do anything above average. I couldn't play sports all that well. I wasn't especially deft at any musical instruments. Couldn't sing, couldn't dance. I couldn't even distinguish myself rolling an El — God knows I practiced enough.

Moreover, during my teens (once I'd left Uhuru Sasa and gone to public school), I never had anyone really go out of their way to encourage me to pursue anything beyond the basic requirements, not scholastically anyway. I was written off as a bad seed, especially once I'd joined the Five Percent.

So, to find myself in University catching kudos from my peers and receiving praise and encouragement from professionals was a phenomenal feeling; a wave of euphoria unlike drugs, sex, or anything else had ever given me.

So, after that first semester of Creative Writing I took on English as my second major, and got "A"s and "B+"s in almost every class whether it was writing, literature, or poetry…didn't matter. I was all over it! Even my media arts grades paled in comparison.

In my final year at LIU, I was taking an Independent Studies course with Barbara. I'd meet her sometimes at her apartment in Park Slope and we'd discuss a writing assignment she'd given me. I loved these meetings for she'd help me recognize my strengths and weaknesses as a writer, based on my work. And being in a professor's home made me feel as if she'd taken a very personal interest in my prosperity.

I had my own apartment by then so in addition to going to school full time I was also working full time. I was always pretty tired and pressed for time. So, for one assignment she'd given me, I used an essay I had already written for myself some time ago. I had written it in third-person, but the assignment had called for first-person. Thinking I was slick, I went and changed the piece I'd written from third-person to first and handed it in to her. Of course she realized what I'd done almost immediately, but she let it go and used the work to teach me about the powerful emphasis and personal nature of the 1st person use of pronouns like "I" "We" "and "Us." I'd missed a lot of them in the essay, leaving them in their original 3rd person form, and this was her way of letting me know that not only was she on to me but that she had also moved on to more consequential matters.

Or was that Lewis who taught me about that?

I confuse the two of them sometimes, for in my mind Barbara and Lewis are like this tag-team of serendipity I've amalgamated into this one awesome entity, this force for creativity, this perpetual muse that serves as both engine and caboose for a lot of my writing. As I endeavor to succeed as a writer, I am also honoring their effort. And when I feel my confidence waning, as I so often do, I can hear Lewis saying "hmmmm" in that way he does, and his incisive questioning as to the "why" of my work in order to allow me to find for myself the piece's rudder, its strengths or weaknesses. And I can see his remarks on my papers, where he'd recommend I read writers like Jim Thompson, Dashell Hammett, James Ellroy, and Raymond Chandler because he sensed that these writers would stir something in me, and help me to see the possibilities and find my own voice. And, damn, was he on the money! And I can feel Barbara's deep empathy and insightful critique of the mind that chooses print as its medium for expression, and the experience that makes that expression a necessity.

Sure, they were simply professors doing what professors do, and if they should come across a student whom they believe has potential it's essentially their duty to do what they can to set that student on the path.

This they did admirably.

I've drifted off of the path more times than I'd like to count, but they were the first to actually tell me that, like James Baldwin, Zora Neale Hurston, Langston Hughes, Chester Himes, Toni Morrison and many of the writers I read, adore and admire, I too could do something magnificent with the written word if I so choose and apply myself accordingly.

And, unbeknownst to them, they did so much more than that.

I still carried those mental postcards of menacing and merciless white faces smiling and posing as black bodies burned- charred corpses in frozen poses of agony, or as castrated cadavers swung from the limbs of trees painted with their blood and feces, in a scrapbook in my mind. I could whip them out any time I needed them. I'd come to believe that these postcards served an integral purpose; a graphic reminder that I must never forget who I am, and where I come from. That I must keep the indignities that my ancestors endured, the sacrifices that they made, and the culprit responsible for their torment, close to me at all times, lest I forget. This is my trauma.

But Barbara and Lewis provided me with some other postcards to put in my mental scrapbook. And, these images were just as powerful, just as indelible; even more so because the people in these photos are not strangers in some dark forest clearing in American dis-remembrance, road kill on the freeway to a more perfect union. These new additions to my racial portfolio are of three people. All three are smiling. All three are writers, endowed with the capacity to create postcards that inspire change and growth, and challenge the depravity displayed in those others postcards.

And all three are, undeniably, human beings: Barbara, Lewis and Loco.

Barbara and Lewis furnished me with weapons to banish the burgeoning hate from my heart. They actually made it a feat requiring a conspicuous leap of logic and loss of rational thought to hate, disparage or even class off white people simply because they were white. I loathed to even entertain the notion of doing so (though I have been guilty of it since, relapses here and there). I willfully refrained, and was intolerant of people who didn't make the same effort in my presence, avoiding them whenever possible, confronting them whenever necessary.

How do you thank people for such a gift? *Thank you* just doesn't cut it, does it?

Well, I thank them by writing. Writing my ass off. And by trying to live my life according to the lessons they taught me simply by being themselves.

And, when I feel myself growing vulnerable to these kinds of thoughts, condoning hate-speak and cordoning off the language of tolerance and equality, I dig in and I engage!

I actually believed that I had it licked, that I had totally eliminated my capacity to harbor racist thoughts about any group, particularly white people, for I hadn't done so for quite some time. I was *on the wagon*, as it were, seated comfortably, singing jubilant songs of freedom and redemption.

Then, I came to Japan, and, before I knew it, the ground was rushing up at me, and that wagon I'd ridden for years had left me in the dust with a mouthful of sushi.

10

NOT FOR THE FAINT OF HEART

(Slice of life stories from Japan)

Coffee with my beloved

Purposely arriving an hour early for a private lesson at a Starbuck's in Yokohama, I sat at the only available table in the crowded cafe, placed my tall sized cup of Sumatra coffee on the tabletop and whipped out the reason for my over-punctuality: A book I've read four times since it was first published about 30 years ago. I'd been savoring it for the past few days. I was three quarters through its 320 some-odd pages and thinking I might unfortunately finish it in a day or so. I hoped for some miracle- like maybe I might have forgotten huge blocks of the story, prolonging the payoff a bit.

I took a sip of the elixir of life, took a deep breath (trust me, the story requires it), and dove back in.

An abrupt movement distracted me. The couple seated at the table to my right, who had been comfortably smiling, making eyes and making love with their hands across the table when I arrived and had, subsequent to my taking the table beside theirs, lost all semblances of joy, replaced by a discomfort you'd expect from a couple being instructed at gun point — muzzle pressed against their noggins — to pretend convincingly to be in love, or die!…Well, they'd decided, halfway through their lattes, that death was preferable and it was time to go.

Part of me wanted to shout, *"What the fuck do I have to do to make you motherfuckers comfortable enough to be the decent people I know you have the capacity to be??? Cuz apparently spending my day off sitting silently and unobtrusively reading a Pulitzer & Nobel Prize winning novel while sipping a cup of over-priced coffee in a trendy cafe aint e-fucking-nough!"* And, man do I hate that part of me. But, I groaned, inside, instead.

246

Another part of me wanted to forgive them for they know not what they do, nor do they know of the creature they are stirring in the doing!

When I felt them smearing their fear over me one last time before departure, I turned to them and said, "Sayonara," with a smile and a wink, and returned to my beloved.

I felt an itch on my neck, a tingling almost burning sensation. I rubbed it and caught a shadow in my periphery. I turned about. Another couple had arrived. The guy was standing stark still behind me, holding the tray, his girl teetering on pumps beside him, holding his arm. I'd just caught the edge of his eyes turning away from the hole they'd been boring into my neck. She was still staring. But, making eye contact with me must have broken the spell for her eyes kind of rolled from me up to the ceiling.

He was scanning the room for available tables. I did so, as well. There were none aside for the one beside my own. There was, however, a short line of people extending a few feet from the staircase landing, blocking the bathrooms, waiting patiently for tables to become open. There were also two anxious staff people looking to accommodate them, apologizing profusely for the inconvenience. I turned back to the couple. They were making eyes at one another, communicating with nods and awkward expressions, obviously discussing, in this muted lingo, whether or not to sit beside me.

I turned away and looked at the page without reading, because the scene playing out behind me was turning my stomach, as it usually does.

I told myself, "ignore it, ignore it, just ignore it" over and over.

After a solid 45 seconds of this nonsense, apparently they'd come to a decision. The guy placed the tray on the table, ever so gingerly, as if the table were a part of something dark and demented and that merely placing the tray upon it might awaken the evil that lurked within it. They sat, eyes on me, thinking I was reading, then back at each other, silently reassuring one another that they'd made the right call. *"He looks alright..."*

I took another deep breath and adjusted my focus from the page to its words.

A chair near me turning to the side with a screech drew my attention. I knew what it was before I turned to look but, like watching a nature show, you just gotta see these chimpanzees eat their feces or throw shit at one another. The guy, seated on my side of the table, had turned his chair so that his back was partially to me and the only way he could see me is if he were to look over his shoulder.

"Ignore, ignore...assault...ignore..."

After I kicked their table and sent it, and their lattes, and cell phones, flying across the café — in my mind — I returned to my beloved. She whispered to me:

"...the more they used themselves up to persuade whites of something Negroes believed could not be questioned, the deeper and more tangled the jungle grew inside."

The guy sitting on the other side of me packed up his stuff and left, and as he did the next people in the queue, two girls, came over, giggling and chatting with one another. They placed their coats and pocketbooks in either chair, totally carefree, talking about what some guy at the office had said to one of them the other day. They turned to go back to the counter downstairs to get their drinks. They had taken a few steps that way when one of them suddenly turned and came back to the table. She slid open her pocketbook and pulled out her purse. Then, she looked up and in doing so, saw me for the first time. She stumbled on her pumps a bit, like she'd been jostled.

I was looking at my beloved…but I could see her at the same time no problem. Eight years of observing things without people knowing, while living in an environment where everyone is trying and failing miserably to do the same to you, and one can develop a knack for such a thing. Most Japanese I've come across do it poorly. Unaccustomed to the need to do it — in a country where most people avoid being worthy of a stare, and those who don't usually want to be stared at and are unperturbed by it — the result is a city of people who, at best, do so like rejects from the counter surveillance unit of the Japanese Secret Service; trained but unable to successfully pull it off in the field so they've been restricted to desk work. Nevertheless, they still feel this compulsion to relive their failure over and over with me as the subject of surveillance.

After a 10-second scan around the room, where the only thing she is really scanning for is right in front of her – a free table – she grabbed both pocketbooks and trotted to the staircase, glancing back at me one last time, just in case there was any doubt in my mind the reason for her sudden and otherwise unnecessary safety measure, or maybe wondering if she should go back for the coats, as well.

The coats I was setting a-flame in my mind.

I wish I could really read at these times, instead of just looking at the pages. But, not only can't I read, I can't do much of anything aside from process. It's like I'm trapped in a quagmire, where ignorance is not an option. Nor is action, really. I feel, nonetheless, obliged to acknowledge it, record and analyze it. I *must* process it. I must experience it. It feels like I'll die if I become the kind of person who can be unaffected by it. No, worse than that. That I was never alive in the first place. That I was never really human.

Somehow, I was everything they were afraid of. A lusty, bloodthirsty, unintelligible savage from the darkest jungles of the soul, trying to hide the truth about myself in plain sight, outfitted in respectability and civilization, in a cafe, behind a book – of all things – and an expensive cup of coffee. How ridiculous and terrifying I must look to them!

Read! Don't think! Just read…

But, I kept thinking. I couldn't stop. *A man didn't come to Japan*, I thought. *Something sub-human did, and I was just the disguise it wore. But these people can see through my disguise, easily, and that is why they react the way they do…*

The girls returned with their drinks, pocketbooks in their clutches, smiles gone, joy vanquished by apprehension and suspicion. They scanned the room as they approached the table. The line had thinned. A table on the other side of the room opened just as they were slowly, warily, planting their asses in the chairs. They sprung into action as a unit, both spotting the opening at the same time, and telling the other at the same time of its existence. It was really silly and horrible at the same time, to witness the ease, the thoughtlessness, the innocent savagery with which this was done.

My stomach bubbled and gurgled, like diarrhea was a-brewing. I took deep breaths through my nose. Watching them cross the room, drinks and bags and coats in hand, I tasted bile in my mouth. I lifted the coffee mug. It was shaking in my hand…just a little, just enough to confirm my humanity. I actually felt better watching it shake. I took a sip. It tasted like shit. I looked down at my beloved. I had spilled a few drops of coffee on page 235.

I read between the drops.

*****

You know, after each of my first four readings of Toni Morrison's Pulitzer and Nobel Prize winning novel, *Beloved*, either immediately or within a few days, I would look in the mirror and say something to the effect of, "See, that's what writers do, Loco! You're not a fucking writer! She's a writer! You're, at best, a hack! You don't have any idea what life is about, what people are about, what's going on in the world, or even in your own heart and mind. You're a liar, and a piss poor one at that! You don't even have the capacity to deal with the kind of truths that Toni illustrates so poetically and astutely."

These are not the kind of thoughts a writer likes to have after reading a book, I gotta tell you.

I used to wonder, who the hell had Toni written this book for, anyway. Who was her target audience? Black people? Black women? White people? Educated people? I mean, this book defies demographic marginalization. But, I just knew *I* wasn't the target.

I felt that she knew that I, and people like me, wouldn't get it. That she had created a challenge. I imagined she said, "I'm not gonna bring the story to you. You gotta come to it. You gotta go brush up on life, have it embrace you and kiss you, have it take care of you when you're sick and listen to you when you need an ear, hold you up when you need support, have it kick you around a little, spit on you and shit on you, you gotta love it, set it free, watch it come back and let it die in your arms. You

251

gotta live a little, Loco, and *then* read my work."

I accepted her challenge. Went out and lived a little; came back to my beloved, time after time only to find that I hadn't lived quite enough. *Get back out there,* my beloved told me, *and live some more.*

So, I did.

I moved to another world called Japan. I lived in it for eight years.

Then, I came back to my *Beloved.*

Beloved had changed and grown in that time. And, something so transcendental happened that even those silly fucks in Starbucks couldn't sully it with their foolishness. In fact, they've helped me more than I could ever thank them for. I finished *Beloved* for the fifth time today, and after eight years of living, and loving, and changing, and growing, I have finally done it!

It's official: I am Toni Morrison's target audience now.

I feel like a better man, like I've just gotten a promotion and a corner office with a breathtaking view... from God.

I used to ask my beloved, "How does one go about winning both a Pulitzer and the Nobel Prize for literature?" I'd asked her about four or five times, but she'd never answer me. She'd just give me one of those sage smiles that made me feel like even if she'd answered me I wouldn't get it.

But, now I think I do:

First of all you gotta live, love, change and grow. Then, you gotta write something that lives, loves, changes, and grows. And, if that ain't enough, it has to inspire others to live, love, change and grow into the kind of humans that can fully appreciate life, love, change and growth.

Throw in a little luck, a few key influencers in your corner, and a lot of political nonsense, and you might find yourself with a few awards.

"But none of that stuff matters, ultimately," my beloved said. "The only thing that you need to focus on is the work."

I will.

Iiwake, the game

The 2nd floor of Doutor cafe is the smoking section. There were a few available seats, but most were stuck between or opposite people, I noticed. Most eyes spotted me instantly and then checked their vicinity for free seats. The people with empty seats beside them started to shift and fidget. I had four to choose from. I selected a free table for two not too far from the staircase, and copped a squat. The woman sitting at the table beside mine hadn't looked up when I arrived, but did as I sat down. She gave me a double take and her totally relaxed posture became erect as a cat with a growling dog nearby.

I wasn't intending to play but she started the game with a bang by moving her bag from the seat across from her which was near me to her lap, but...she was probably expecting a phone call from her boyfriend and I reminded her of him. He's a handsome but insecure black soldier stationed at Yokosuka Navy base, who kicks her ass twice a week for letting the phone ring as many as three times before answering. The cell phone was in her handbag and she didn't want to miss the call or have any delays answering it. That would also explain why she turned her chair away from mine. When she catches a glimpse of me she can psychosomatically feel it in her recently cracked ribs currently on the mend.

10 Points

Usually I go out of my way to ignore the show the Japanese put on whenever I'm in their midst but occasionally, when I can't think of anything else to write about, or it's just too damn intriguing to ignore, I check it out surreptitiously as possible. And occasionally I play a game in my head (and on paper sometimes). I call it: Iiwake.

Iiwake is the Japanese word for excuse.

I started playing it a while back without realizing it. It hadn't been a game when I first began. Far from it. What I was doing was trying to find alternative reasons for the bizarre behavior of the Japanese people around me. What I do is I endeavor to detach myself emotionally and examine everything going on around me from as objective a state of mind as I can manage.

The point system works out this way: 20 points if I make myself laugh (reduced to 15 points if I laugh out loud), 10 points for merely creative Iiwake, 5 points for mediocre, -10 points if I fail to come up with an Iiwake and -50 if I think a negative thought about my fellow Japanese customers. My high score is 175.

My low score is too embarrassing to mention.

Why do I play Iiwake?

Well, it helps me rule out paranoia.

When I first began to feel the atmosphere of spaces changing upon my entrance, I thought I was becoming paranoid. It's awful thinking that all the discomfort and anxiety going on around me is somehow being caused by me or is as a direct result of my presence.

So, initially Iiwake served three purposes: one was to get out of my head for a bit (never a bad thing) and see life through another's eyes, so to speak. The second was my secret hope that by doing so I would be able to gather ammo in my ongoing internal war against the part of me that finds too many Japanese people irretrievable cowards and unconscionable xenophobes, thus repulsive. If that side of me wins I would be forced to leave this land that I have grown to adore, with a bitter resentment. If I could find other reasons and rationalizations for their behavior – something that paranoia had until now blinded me to – then I'd score points and so would they. It's a Win-Win kind of game.

The third reason was simply for entertainment. If I could laugh at them or at myself then I would feel so much better.

Take this woman that was sitting beside me, for instance…

Half-way through her cup of coffee she stood and decided that…umm…that she was going to leave her soldier boy with the penchant for using her as a punching bag, leaving him for good this time. She would go home immediately, pack her stuff, and go stay with the grandmother in Nakano he'd never met…

10 Points

As she was leaving to start her new life, another customer came up the stairs and was scouting for a seat. He spotted the one she'd just vacated beside me and was on a beeline for it when he noticed me and suddenly remembered…that his girlfriend was coming to meet him but wouldn't know he was upstairs in the smoking section because he hadn't told her he smoked. He had been keeping it a secret because she'd expressed on several occasions that if he were a smoker that would be a deal breaker. So, he diverted and sped for the window seat across the room which was also available and from which he could see his girlfriend's arrival and pop those mints in his pocket before he spoke to her.

10 Points

Another woman, middle-aged, well-to do, arrived at the stairway landing. She sees me and decided...that now is the opportune moment she'd been waiting for to quit smoking. "It's a nasty, stinking dirty habit and I must quit now," she mumbled under her breath and returned downstairs so as not to be tempted by the death sticks being consumed so gratuitously on the 2nd floor.

15 Points

Another woman appears at the landing, younger this time, maybe late 20s. She spots me and the available table beside mine. Then she surveys the rest of the room looking for...ummm... looking for her friend. *Right*, she's looking for her friend that she's supposed to meet here, but her friend's not here and all the other seats appear occupied, so she gingerly, painfully slow, takes the seat beside me, her whole body turned away from me. She's giving the room a twice over...for her friend. She actually didn't want to sit down as not to put too much pressure on her buttocks because of her explosive hemorrhoids that have been inflamed for days now, and that medicine the doctor had given her only alleviated the pain temporarily...and the doctor had also prescribed plenty of, ummm, ultraviolet light, right. For an unrelated condition...her skin, which was actually kind of lackluster. Which would explain why she can't take her eyes off the seats in the rear by the windows. And, suddenly, when someone at one of the window seats rose to leave she darted that way, almost spilling her mocha from her tray in her haste to follow her doctor's orders.

20 Points

A couple arrive at the landing now...the girl spots the table beside mine and heads directly for it, but before she could sit down her boyfriend actually grabs her arm and with a penetrating gaze conveys the message, "did you forget?" (ummm...god, this is a difficult one...Iiwake is not for the faint of heart)... "We sat over there on our first date? Over there!" He points at a currently occupied table for two over yonder, and almost on cue the man who was sitting there stood up and began packing his things to depart. Lucky them.

5 Points

Another woman comes upstairs, spots the table beside me, and sees that I'm writing the words you're reading now, and decides that...that the absolute last thing she would ever want to do in life is disturb my composition with her presence, and upon seeing no other free seats, replaces her ashtray and heads back downstairs. God she was thoughtful, because if she couldn't sit by me without sucking her teeth and jumping every time I made a move like most people do, she would have, indeed, disturbed the fuck out of me!
Fuck!

-50 Points

Another man had come upstairs while I was writing so

257

I barely caught him noticing me and the empty table beside mine. He walks to the middle of the room and does kind of a slow pirouette scanning the room for a seat, as his eyes pass by the seat beside me they actually make a detour up and over the area I'm seated in, looking for a seat on the ceiling or something... because he had a...umm....fuck! He had a mental blind spot. Yeah, a mental blind spot, and he...ah, fuck it, he's probably just crazy!

-5 points

Then, he comes and sits beside me. I try not to notice anything about him in my peripherals. I mean, the really crazy ones... they make me feel homicidal. But, he's just a-flinching and a-fidgeting and scratching his head like he's having an actual allergic reaction to... something. Ah, got it...He's allergic to my tobacco smoke. It's not a brand typically smoked by Japanese so his polluted lungs aren't able to... Another seat opens up and he jumps up and heads for it because...oh fuck him...I'll take the point loss!

-50 Points

Soapland

I used to have a private student- let's call him Hiroki- who was a *really* cool guy! Hiroki confessed (more like stated) to me at our first meeting that he had chosen me from a number of available teachers in the area because I was black, and he liked hip-hop. Lucky for me, I liked hip-hop, too. He was a pretty high level English speaker from the get go, so instead of studying English, on Saturday afternoons we'd sit around Starbucks for an hour talking about hip-hop; me schooling him on the old school and he bringing me up to date on the new. *Easy* Money!

Sometimes our conversations would wander into the area of girls. He fantasized about getting his hands on some big-booty black chick like the ones he saw in the hip-hop videos, and I told him I felt the same about the Japanese girls walking past us every couple of seconds, sipping on Frappacinos. "Japanese girls are mendokusai (too much trouble)," he'd say, and I'd tell him you ain't seen trouble until you've crossed one of those big-booty video chicks you're fantasizing about. "Just stick to your fantasies, yo!"

Yeah, we hit it off.

One day while I was admiring some of the abundant eye-candy strolling by, he told me that the girls at the Hostess clubs looked much better and were much less trouble. Just pay and have fun and go home.

"Really?" I said, like I hadn't been hoping he'd take the conversation in that direction one day. I wouldn't have dared do it myself. Sometimes it's hard to tell where that line between acceptable and unacceptable is with private students, so I often follow their lead.

"Soaplands are even better! Have you ever been to one?"

"Why, no...what's that?" I asked, thinking, *'YES! Now we're cooking with Crisco!*

He explained that a Soapland was a sort of sex-free sex shop where customers can have good, clean fun with beautiful Japanese girls...with a guaranteed happy ending within the loopholes in Japanese laws regarding prostitution.

259

"There's no intercourse, sorry, but I've *never* left a Soapland disappointed," he said, grinning broadly, like I needed a little arm-twisting.

I'd seen the Soapland process in several porno movies and it looked intriguing to say the least. And there was little chance of catching anything funky if there was no intercourse taking place, so it sounded great to me; something to write about one day, or one of those *quirky Japan* stories to tell my friends back home.

We met up the following Friday night and he took me to a spot in Ikebukuro he frequented, where he said the girls were top-notch.

We got to the door and I followed him into the vestibule where a bouncer – earphone in one ear, secret service style, and an *I'm a LOT tougher than you think* posture – was waiting. As we passed him, the man stopped Hiroki.

At the time, my Japanese was much more limited than it is now (which is why I had never braved one of these places alone and was waiting for a Japanese guy to offer to escort me). But, I'd been fluent in body language for decades. And, what I heard from the Bouncer's finger, aimed derogatorily at my face like I was a photograph or standing across the street, was, "this guy's with *you*??"

"Yes, he's my friend," Hiroki said, smiling proudly. He had been giddy up til that point, just thrilled to death that he was going to introduce me – his new foreign friend – to one of the aspects of his world that made his world the envy of the world, at least as far as many men are concerned.

The bouncer gave me another disapproving look. "I see…"

I was beginning to see, too. But, Hiroki…he'd probably never been stopped at the door before.

"Is there a problem?" he asked the doorman.

"Well, the thing is....you see," the bouncer began, with a pantomime mask of deep regret on his face, which failed miserably to melt the ice in his eyes. They were frozen to Hiroki as if I were merely the topic of discussion, not standing before them. "We don't usually serve foreigners here! None of the girls can speak English and...well, they are really afraid of foreign guys."

Between his gestures and the few words I could pick out of his explanation (*gaikokujin, Eigo, syaberarenai, kowai...*) I got the gist.

"I see," Hiroki nodded. "Well, I've already explained all the club rules to him. And he's a very nice guy. And he can speak Japanese a little. So, there won't be any problems."

"Yeah, but, you see, the club has special rules, and...you understand, no?"

Hiroki didn't get it, actually. But, after three minutes standing in a doorway of a sex shop open for business, I fully comprehended the situation, and started feeling bad for Hiroki; especially when he turned and gave me a look that would break Hitler's heart.

"Come on, man, let's go!" I said, reaching for his arm. "Fuck this place! Let's go get some brews!"

Hiroki turned once more to the bouncer and said, "I'm never coming here again!"

We went to a bar down the street, and ordered some beers. Hiroki was depressed as hell. I kept trying to cheer him up, trying to change the subject from "That fucking place!" which is what he kept repeating. I felt responsible for putting him in that position. If it weren't for me he'd be on an inflatable mattress with some soaped-up hottie sliding all over him by then.

If it weren't for me…

And that's when I realized that, remarkably, *for the first time in my life* I had been the victim of *outright, Jim Crow style* racial discrimination, not so much because I was black (actually I'll never know if my color was a factor) but because I *wasn't* Japanese (or Asian).

And, ironically, instead of feeling a victimized rage in the pit of my stomach, and an irrepressible urge to do harm to someone (which up til that point I imagined would be my reaction whenever this dark day came to be) there I was consoling a friend.

I learned something important about myself that night, thanks in part to this first. Something it would take me some time to process.

You see, I didn't feel victimized because at that point I had been living in Japan long enough to believe that it was only a matter of time before something like that happened. I mean, it was simple to surmise that in a country where the natives routinely avoid standing, sitting or even walking near you whenever possible, that they just might have a problem "cleaning" you which would require actual physical contact. The irreverence of daily life in Japan had groomed me to look indignity in the face and say, "Fuck these people! Let's go get a brew!" I could just roll with the blows because I was already punch drunk, and one more punch wasn't going to kill me.

Hiroki however took the blow right in the solar plexus of his pride and national self-image, and it left him reeling center ring. You could have performed the coup de grace with a pillow after that.

The rude awakening he'd suffered for some

reason overshadowed whatever humiliation I felt. He knew that his people were "shy" around foreigners, but it's a good bet he didn't know that that "shyness" clause in Japan's contract with humanity had a loophole in it wide enough for blatant discrimination to slip through. Or, maybe he did, but hadn't really considered how those consequences might play out in the real world because he would never be at the business end of them.

But I'm no mind reader and that night Hiroki couldn't really put into words why he felt the need to repeatedly curse the establishment, but I imagined that considering how he felt about his country, it must have felt like he'd gone to a Soapland with his Japanese co-workers (as he did often) only to find out, in the worst possible way, that his sister was Mermaid of the Month there.

Poor guy...

Teachers Teach and Do the world good

There's a stigma attached to what I do here in Japan.

That stigma is: Loser!

The people who tout this slur are generally doing something other than teaching English, a profession that presumably required more than a University degree, a passport from an English speaking country and a heartbeat to achieve. Or, they are among the professional educators living here who, in addition to the above basic requirements, are also in possession of a manifest love and abiding respect for the profession of teaching, evidenced by the sacrifices they've made to obtain various advanced degrees and teaching certifications.

I'd counter it's all a matter of perspective, though. Where I come from, a University degree and the wherewithal to leave your family, friends and presumably some semblance of a life behind to begin another in a *very* foreign land, are rarely found in a "loser's" portfolio. I could also argue that a portfolio that contains outrageous student loans that take years (and tears) to repay for an overrated University education that says little more about who you really are than that you subscribe in part to the meritocracy, and that you have the capacity to take on somewhat challenging tasks and complete them, certainly doesn't scream "winner."

I prefer to think of myself as neither a loser nor a winner. I'm just a man on a path, and that path has led me to Asia. And if I can manage to stay on it and keep grinding, it will, without a doubt, take me wherever I need to go.

Without a doubt!

However, while I'm here in Japan with my degree, my visa, and my heartbeat intact, I've got things to learn…

And, apparently, to *teach,* as well.

I didn't always feel this way, though.

I came here with my mind open and my hand out, ready to receive what Japan had to offer or, if necessary, take what I needed and disregard the rest. They'd have my body, time and energy in exchange, which I felt to be a decent bargain. But, like those European pirates of old, I had my eyes on the prize. I came here seeking riches.

Not money or precious metals and stones, though. Nor was the booty of my ambition on some Japanese girl's backside. My booty was ethereal. I came for inspiration, for experience, for knowledge, for rich material and colorful characters to paint the pages of the books I intend to write. I didn't want to enslave the natives. I just wanted to use them as my muse. I was on a mission to find seeds of intangibility to take back to my own world and nurture into something uncommonly useful, something that could inspire real change.

My initial job, that English teaching gig with NEON? It was just a means to finance my expedition. I did what was required, sometimes more and sometimes less. But, always with my needs and goals in the forefront of my mind. Never the students'.

Then, I came to work at a junior high school, and everything changed.

You see, while I was teaching with NEON, the majority of my students were adults, chock full of misinformation and preconceptions I had little hope of impacting significantly, and little desire to make the effort it would take to do so. My motivation to be around them was more research oriented. And, truth be told, for the most part, so was theirs. I'd venture half of the students were there to simply meet and chat with foreigners in a controlled environment. But me, I was like one of the crew of the USS Enterprise, with my own personal Prime Directive: interact but avoid interfering; rules I would bend but rarely broke.

But this was not the case when I came to work at a junior high school. The entire dynamic changed, and that change impacted me in ways I had no way of foreseeing. My prime directive flew right out the portal. My new clientele wouldn't have it any other way.

In public schools, as much as parents, teachers and administrators like to make out like they run the show, the kids-some consciously while others instinctively- know it's *their* show.

I'd never been a big fan of kids. To be honest, they scared me. I was always pretty good with other people's kids, for I'm practically (at least until I came here) a big kid myself. Any of my friends will tell you the same. But, I remain childless for a reason. I never wanted the responsibility of teaching a child to do something I was still struggling to do myself. That is, make its way in this crazy ass world. With all the stuff going through my heart and head at any given time, I really felt like I would fuck a child's mind up, and how!

*****

One day, after I had been teaching for a couple of years in the public school system, I was riding the train to work, enduring the usual obscenities from my fellow strap-hangers. It was a particularly rough morning, one where I had "chased" away a man with my "foreignness."

I was standing there trying to regain my composure when someone tapped me on the shoulder. I spun around with hate in my heart only to find myself face to face with a very cute girl. It took me a moment or two to pull myself together. I must have been a bizarre sight but she showed no sign of recognizing this transformation from a man angry enough to put his fist through a wall to a person curious about why he'd been tapped.

"Loco-sensei?"

"Yes?" I said, searching her face for something familiar. She was about 20 or so, dressed like a college student, kawaii-ness (cuteness) laced with a burgeoning sexuality; think a fashion cross between Minnie Mouse and Miss Piggy. But, no identifying features jumped out at me.

She noticed and was taken aback a bit, but not much.

"You don't remember me, maybe," she said kindly. "I was your student at NEON three years ago. I am Mika Tanaka!"

I was about to pretend to remember her by name, I felt so bad, but I didn't.

"Sorry, I don't...?"

"No, no, no...I know you must have many students. Please don't worry about that..."

"Well, still, I..." and then I realized we were speaking in English. She sounded like she'd lived abroad. "Mika, huh? It's nice to see you again."

We smiled at each other awkwardly. More than half the eyes in the vicinity were on her, I noticed with a glance. She seemed either unaware or totally comfortable with being the center of attention.

"Your English is pretty good!" I said, using one of the Japanese icebreakers I've unconsciously picked up over the years: Say something complimentary.

"No, no, it's still poor," she said, blushing. "I am studying English in University, now."

"That's great...I'm happy for you," I said. "You must have some great teachers, cuz —"

"You were the best one!"

"Thanks," I said. Just as I've picked up the custom of flattery, I've also learned to take all Japanese flattery with a grain of salt. They're *literally* just being nice most of the time. "Just doing my job."

"I remember you told me that to speak in English well, grammar is important but not most top important. You said confidence is equal important. You said that if I want to be great speaker I should not be afraid to speak."

"Wow, you have a good memory!"

"Oh yes, I remember everything you taught me! And I do what you said...everything!"

That's when I started feeling nervous. Someone listening to me is one thing. Someone taking my advice is another thing. But, people remembering everything I said, word for word, and following my instructions to a "T" when I *know* I'm prone to go off on tangents, especially back in my NEON days when I really didn't care much whether students learned that nonsense NEON used to have us teach? And where sometimes I used to just run off at the mouth just to pass the time? This is *quite* another thing!

"You told me to make foreign friends. My boyfriend is very nice black guy from California. I met him when I was student in America...I didn't hang out with Japanese people only in California, just like you told me. I hang out with *only* foreigners and speak...spoke only in English. My boyfriend will move to Japan next year..."

She went on to list several things I'd told her that had helped her to not only become a better English speaker but, as she explained it, "....you help to give me a happy life! I always want to see you and to say thank you. I went back to NEON when I come back from the U.S. but they said you quitted."

"I teach at a junior high school in Yokohama now," I said, still a little overwhelmed by Mika, and disappointed that I couldn't remember her at all. Maybe because she wasn't the same person she was when I'd taught her, I told myself.

"Your students are very lucky! They have the *best* teacher!"

"Thank you," I said, feeling like some popular retiring educator receiving accolades from the student body; a verbal gold watch.

"Oh, this is my station!" She gave me a curious smile, and

then rushed at me, embracing me in a hug that could only come from the heart, and planted a kiss on my cheek. When she released me she looked like she wanted to say more. But, instead she just got off the train and stood waving at me from the platform, almost in tears.

While I waved back I noticed how many people in the area were observing this exchange with utter fascination.

The guy who'd run to the next car would have benefited, I thought.

I did.

I learned from that brief exchange with a former student that *I had the power to do something impactful here.* And, like the great KRS-1 once said, *"Teachers teach and do the world good..."*

Still think I'm a loser? Well, you're entitled.

But, I beg to differ.

Bonding, Bullying and Betrayal: A Day in the life of an English Teacher in Japan

My eye caught the hand movement and spotted the projectile as soon as it left its source: Matsui-kun.

Takahashi-sensei, the other half of my teaching team, was writing something on the board, her back to the class, so she didn't know she was a target. She probably couldn't imagine being the target of anything thrown by a student. I, along with most of the class, watched this object sail across the room in slow motion on a beeline for Takahashi, only to fall short of its target, somewhere between the first row and the teacher's desk, and roll towards Takahashi's feet.

She never saw it.

But I did. And, immediately, I saw red.

269

It was the first time I'd felt rage directed at a student. I mean, as far as I was concerned what Matsui did, even if done playfully, amounted to attempted assault and battery. And to make it worse, it was done practically in my face as if to say, "you don't even matter in my world, Loco-sensei," confirming my suspicions about how many people here consider my feelings, and dislodging some other deep-seated insecurities as well, I suspect. On top of that, I have about as much tolerance for that kind of shit as my teachers in Uhuru Sasa would have had for it: Zero!

...And, before I knew it, before I could consider the ramifications of such an act, I had hurled the piece of chalk in my hand across the room and hit Matsui square in the chest. If I had been holding a coffee mug then that too would have been sent flying his way. Perhaps anything as big as a dictionary would have grown wings in my hand.

Why? A little background:

First about Takahashi-sensei. She was still relatively new at this teaching thing. She had been at it for only a year so basically she was still an apprentice. She's very nice, smart, and her English is not awful. But, unfortunately for her, something about her rubbed her co-workers the wrong way. At least that's what I thought. I mean. I couldn't imagine that the stern treatment, the accusatory tones and harsh criticism she received was simply hazing. Hell, I had been working with these same people almost two years when she arrived and they had (with a few exceptions) from the start shown me a great deal of patience and consideration...even after my Gaijin Honeymoon (the special treatment and allowances granted because I was a foreigner) was over.

Even my closest friend in the school, Kawaguchi-sensei,

who I'd never heard and therefore couldn't imagine doing as much as even raising her voice, treated Takahashi worse than a Burakumin 部落民 (Japanese outcast). Every conversation any teacher had with Takahashi — in particular the other female teachers — they seemed to be at the brink of exasperation, like at any point they might either storm away, spit in her face or drop-kick her.

At first, I thought it was simply jealousy. After all, all of the teachers aside from Takahashi are well over 40 and some over 50, while Takahashi was early twenties, fresh from university, bright-eyed and bushy-tailed, cute, fashionable, and to kick them all while they were down, she's been blessed /cursed with bountiful breast; and she favors tight-fitting cleavage-accentuating sweaters. At least she used to. But, I couldn't believe it was that simple. Whenever an answer seems to be arrived at without much thought I question it. It's my habit.

So, I asked my buddy Kawaguchi-san (who seemed quite beside herself sometimes when she interacted with Takahashi) what the deal was. She told me, in no uncertain terms, that Tahakashi was a fuck-up and lies to cover up her fuck-ups. I was shocked. Not at the prospect of Takahashi fucking up. She was a new jack. There were bound to be fuck-ups. Not even about her lying about it. Hell, there are approximately two ways to deal with having fucked something up: face the music or duck blame. Most people, in my experience, duck blame if possible.

No, what surprised me was Kawaguchi's venom and total loss of decorum. She'd usually hedge around harsh declarations. With her, nothing was ever *absolutely* wrong. It was always chotto chigau to omoimasu (a little wrong /different to my thinking). Nothing tasted like shit to her. It was always aji ga chottoooooo (The taste is a little ummm....) She even uses fairly formal Japanese when she is addressing students, something very few teachers do. So, who the hell was this woman, I wondered.

She told me about how, on several occasions, Takahashi would screw up such and such a report and lie about it or she'd be late for meetings pretending not to have been informed about such and such and blah, blah, blah... While she was talking I just kept searching her face for some sign of the women that was there before Takahashi had joined the staff. The woman I knew wasn't petty or malicious at all. Then again we had only worked and sat side by side for a year or two. How well does anybody know anybody anyway? Not to downplay the seriousness of these misdemeanors Takahashi was accused of (and being punished for) but Kawaguchi was going off the deep end over them.

In her first year, Takahashi was the home room teacher of a third-year class, but this year, she was given a class of first-year students. I actually thought it was a great break for her. The third year students know all the ropes and I figured they'd drive her crazy. Just last year, one of the crazier third year students hauled off and slapped the shit out of the home room teacher, but that student, Senri was her name, was certifiable... an actual future mental patient, and by no means represented the student body. The first year students last year had been soooo sweet. You could just eat them. They spent half the year shy and obedient and the second half obedient, fun and eager to learn.

This year's deposit of first-year students, however, was another fucking story. It was like there was some kind of rotation, equally dispersing the worst of the worst from the worst elementary school in the area among all the junior high schools in Yokohama, and it was our school's turn to take on this lot from *that* elementary school...

Poor Takahashi. It was bad enough she was being bullied by her colleagues, but now she had to figure out how to get a class of future nine-fingered Yakuza, hostesses and Pachinko parlor employees to appreciate studying anything, especially something as utterly useless as English. I started feeling sorry for her, despite my buddy Dr. Jekyll and Mrs. Kawaguchi's admonitions about her. I hadn't even realized at first that I had become her ally. Maybe I commiserated because I saw some parallels between our predicaments. Like me, here she was in an environment where the natives treat her with hostility for reasons beyond her control. Or, maybe I was just a sucker for a pretty face and bodacious assets.

Sometimes she came to school looking like she was one harsh word away from losing it. What she would do then, who knew. In America, emptying a 45. automatic into your boss or several magazines of M-16 rounds into everyone in the office, or simply quitting might be option A, but here in Japan, people in her situation — disliked, and treated like shit, even due to the standard hazing at a job — have been known to off themselves; suicide seems to be option A and B. I became really concerned about her. I really didn't want anything like that to go down on my watch, knowing I could have done something about it.

Sometimes Takahashi and I would have private moments together. Like in the recording studio when we were preparing tests for the students and we needed to record English conversations...we'd be alone in the booth behind closed doors and she'd give me some deep eye contact and say,

"Tsukarechatta." (I'm tired)

I'd heard that word used that way several times before. Like when I broke-up with my ex-girl. She'd begun using that phrase in reference to our relationship months before, as our relationship slowly deteriorated. The nuance being more at "I've exhausted all options," than simply "I'm tired." At those times I'd share little anecdotes about my experiences with Takahashi. Stories from my first year at the school and how trying it was, and continued to be, to fit in but how, little by little, it had gotten more bearable. I'd end these stories with a "Gambarimasyou" (let's hang in there) so she'd feel less alone.

Whenever I spoke to Kawaguchi about Takahashi, I never failed to mention how well she was coming along and gave her examples of how she'd handled a particular problem or resolved an issue in the class. Kawaguchi was beyond appeasement though. She'd listen to me, not knowing where I was coming from, not realizing that I had taken on the task of Takahashi advocate, and counter every kudo I offered with some slander.

I couldn't really argue with Kawaguchi, though. I too noticed that though Takahashi was clearly qualified to teach English, she lacked certain other skills necessary to manage a classroom. She was at the bottom of the totem pole in the office, and scolded constantly, and it seemed the students (these worst of the worst students) sensed her feeling of powerlessness and instability and instead of seeing someone they should handle with kid gloves, they saw easy pickings. Walking into her class was like walking on the set of a new TV series called: "Kids Gone Loco." Whenever I joined the class and once they saw my face — a face they didn't see everyday due to my schedule — but every two weeks or so, a ripple of uncertainty would course through the room. "Should we continue to act like we ain't got no sense in our heads or comport ourselves in a respectful manner?" Most would go with the latter...but there were two kids who opted, unfailingly, for the former.

One was Satou-kun, a 13-year old future henchman / Yes man for some Yakuza boss. He didn't have a bone of leadership in his body. He took his cues from another student, the leader: Matsui-kun...

*****

A little about Matsui-kun...

I remember the first time I met him. I came to the class prepared to do my usual introduction lesson, where I talk about myself, in the simplest English possible, while showing pictures of my family back home in the U.S. In most cases this is their first interaction with a foreigner so I try to make it a pleasant experience and as entertaining as possible by hamming it up a bit. I always intend to withhold that I know Japanese because once they know that, well, what's the sense of trying to speak English some of them always conclude...that is, those who hadn't come to that conclusion before they even walked in the door.

But, inevitably, I slip up by responding to something said in Japanese unwittingly or saying something in Japanese only someone fluent in Japanese would say, or even behaving the way speaking Japanese modifies one's behavior. Kids pick up on the slightest things.

Matsui picked up on it first.

Matsui is the smallest kid and has the happiest disposition of anyone in the class, maybe any student I've ever met;

genki (energetic) to the Nth degree. At first glance you get the impression that he's trying to compensate for his stature with his character, like some Japanese-version of the Napoleonic complex. Only he does it with a great deal of charm. And, you almost root for him, want him to be successful. He laughs and jokes non-stop and only speaks with the volume on max. One of those kids you're more likely to use gentler terms like rascal or mischief-maker than menace or delinquent. Everything except his size reminded me of someone I knew.

It was clear from that first day who the leader of this class was going to be. Most of the students knew each other already having mostly come from *that* elementary school, and Matsui had probably been the leader back there, too. I didn't think about any of this that first day, though. I was too busy trying to make a good first impression and to seriously assess the students. But, Matsui ...he was assessing *me*...aloud.

"LOCO-SENSEI! YOU CAN SPEAK JAPANESE CAN'T YOU," he yelled in Japanese with the kind of joviality that is hard to resist, joy in every word.

"A little," I said, giving my pat answer.

"YOU'RE LYING!" he snapped with a raucous giggle. Then he jumped out his seat and started addressing the class. "HEY EVERYBODY, THIS GUY CAN SPEAK JAPANESE...BETTER WATCH WHAT YOU SAY!"

Takasashi-sensei was there beside me. This was her home room but I could see in her demeanor that she had already relinquished control of this class. Somehow, in the week before this first lesson with me, Matsui had pulled a coup d'état and while she remained the figurehead lame duck Empress, he was Shogun. But, this kind of thing is not unusual. In Japanese schools, the teachers pretty much let the kids do as they please and because of the respect elements in the culture generally that means study hard and behave accordingly. But, maybe 10% of the time, at least in my experience, there are classes who decide that they'd rather run amok.

"LOCO-SENSEI, HOW DID YOU LEARN JAPANESE?"

Since the cat was out of the bag, I said, "I've been living here for several years so —"

"YOU GOT A JAPANESE GIRLFRIEND, RIGHT?"

"What?? That's none of your business. Listen, sit down and let's —"

"LOCO-SENSEI SUKEBE! (horny / lecher) HA HA HA HA HA HA!"

Everybody laughed. I glanced at Takahashi sensei, again. She turned bright red and started scolding Matsui. Her scolding fell on deaf ears, though. Half the class was held enthralled by Matsui's audacity while the other half seemed embarrassed or too scared not to laugh. Matsui scanned the room while he held forth from his throne. He apparently siphoned energy from his audience. Then, he turned to me.

"LOCO-SENSEI, GOMEN NE" (I'm sorry), Matsui cried at the top of his voice. He jumped up out of his seat again and ran towards me and jumped in my arms. I caught him instinctively, and he gave me the warmest most affectionate hug I'd ever gotten from a student, even warmer than some of the girlfriends I've had in Japan. I was dumbfounded. Here was this little rascal in my arms, hugging me about the neck like it was the most natural thing in the world; I actually thought he was going to kiss me on the cheek. He was light as a toddler and I didn't let him down immediately. It was a moment. We had bonded, somehow. At least I felt something.

And, I realized just then who he reminded me of:

He reminded me of me...when I'm drunk.

*****

From our first meeting on, this had become our routine: I'd come to the class a little early and catch him rattling windows with his vociferous screeching and menacing other students... upon seeing me, he'd stop whatever he was doing, holler, "LOCO-SENSEI!" and run-jump into my arms, all hugs and an irresistible quality.

Having routines with students was not unusual. I have about a couple dozen students with which I have a greeting routine, many consisting of some variation of the pound or the pound hug. They've seen in umpteen movies that black people have some of the coolest handshakes and most of the students had memorized their favorites and were dying to try them on the real thing: me. Some of these handshakes I recognized, and remember the movie, video or TV show that gave them international fame, but some of them were obscure. Some of them, when produced by a sixteen year old Japanese boy, surprise the hell out of me.

But, Matsui simply liked leaping into my embrace, like a loving son might do upon his beloved father's return from a prolonged business trip abroad, or a chimpanzee might do when his favorite trainer shows up with a tasty treat. I think that's the feeling he might have tapped into...something paternal and protective, because when I saw him I was all cheesy grins and open arms.

Yep, he'd found my weak point and charmed the hell out of me.

His charms didn't work on Takahashi, though. She saw

right through him for the terrorist that he was. He was a non-conformist, something I found admirable but Takahashi called, "trouble" almost from the start. It took me a little while to see through my rose-tinted lenses, though. I was still seeing Spanky, not Damien.

But it wasn't long before I saw the "666" birthmark behind his ear.

One day, a couple of weeks into the semester, he decided that English class was recess, the classroom was the playground, his classmates were his flock, and Takahashi was the Jungle Jim, the see-saw and the swings...almost metaphorically speaking. I mean, he didn't actually ride Takahashi, not physically anyway, and his classmates weren't exactly overly willing participants, but the rest is a non-metaphorical description. All learning or even pretense at learning basically ceased to happen.

I'd been at this for a few years now but until this year I'd never had a class like this. My co-workers would tell me horror stories and I'd be like, "that happened in Japan!?" "You're exaggerating!" "C'mon...that's bullshit! Ain't no student spit on a teacher...get outta here with that!'

At this point, I should mention that I don't work for the school, but for a contractor the Board of Education hires to provide English teachers for the schools in their district. And, the company I work for has handed down certain guidelines on reprimanding and disciplining students. And, to put it simply, the rule is: Don't! Don't touch them. Don't scold them. Don't even think about touching them or scolding them. It's not your job. Leave it to the Japanese teachers.

My first year at the school, there was an isolated incident where one student who was being bullied by another finally had had enough and went after him, in the middle of the class, with a pair of scissors. As I approached the student with the scissors stealthily from behind, the Japanese teacher practically dived in front of the damn thing to stop him from slicing the other. The way he had thrown himself into the fray led me to believe that maybe the Japanese teacher's guidelines say something to the effect of: in the event of an altercation, if there is blood spilt it had better be yours, or heads will roll.

So, when I walk into Ringling Brothers Barnum and Bailey, and see Takahashi trying to go through the motions of teaching a class, almost on the brink of tears or collapse, while the class is going…well, berserk, according to my guidelines that came down from on-high, I should allow this. But, fortunately, I didn't have to, at first, because most of the students were a little intimidated by me. Either by my maleness, my height and girth, or perhaps even my blackness was a factor. All these factors conspired to keep these rascals in check. But, one day, it didn't matter anymore. It only took me a moment to realize how I'd been neutralized.

Yep, you guessed it: it was Matsui, with all his running and leaping and hugging he'd shown all who'd been intimidated that Loco-sensei ain't nothing but a great big teddy bear. Like Pooh-San (Winnie the Pooh), only SUKEBE!

You gotta give him credit, though. He's a bright kid. I watch him, sometimes. I watch how he manipulated the other students. One of the advantages of not being afraid to be in the limelight and having a very big mouth and no reservations about saying anything that comes to your head to anyone – students and teachers alike – is you're un-common- in Japan anyway. Damn near a working-class hero. Add to that he's naturally charismatic with a joie de vivre, daring, funny… Yep, half the class was wrapped around his little finger and the rest kept their mouths shut.

And, if challenged, he was merciless- before, during and after classes.

Last week, in the middle of my lesson, while I was getting the students to repeat some English phrases, Matsui kept taunting another student, twice his size, sitting clear across the room. Telling jokes and making insults. Most of the class was laughing and the rest wanted to. At one point, the target of his derision said something I couldn't understand. To be honest I can't understand much of what they say- maybe 50% at best- because the kids speak in code and slang and sometimes the Japanese equivalent of Pig Latin, so it's virtually impossible to catch everything unless you're a thirteen year old Japanese student. But, whatever he said must have rubbed Matsui the wrong way because at that point he got up, stood on his chair (he's really short) and threw his pencil-case, with a little mustard on it, at the other student, who took the blow upside the head like he'd had it coming, his comeuppance for challenging Matsui. Then Matsui asked politely, at volume 10, for the student to return the case. And don't you know...he got up and brought it back to him. Matsui accepted it and thanked him with a nod/bow, like this was just the way it is and there was nothing either of them could do about it.

Then he looked at me. I'll never forget his eyes that day. He was smiling that same 1000 watts of love smile he always shines on me, but his eyes...There was something there, like wisdom. Not like an adult's wisdom, but definitely wiser than I feel comfortable with any child around me being. That precocious snare broke the bond between us, I think. At least for me it did.

The next day when he saw me in the hallway and came running, I side-stepped his leap. He landed on his feet like a cat, turned on me, and the smile was gone, replaced by something that was always there but somehow I'd missed it before; something dark, unforgiving and calculating. It was only there for a moment, just a flash of the real Matsui, I think.

Then he turned away and ran down the hallway like the incident had never occurred.

The next day he threw something at Takahashi-Sensei…and I threw a piece of chalk at him.

"OOOOOOOOOHHHHHHH!" the entire class exhaled aloud. As shocking as it was for me to see something being thrown at the teacher, it was even more so for the reverse. Students looked like I had taken a dump on him. Their looks were so shell-shocked I actually got scared and thought, "Oh fuck, what have I done now."

Takahashi turned around from the board at the sound of the students and asked, "What? What happened?"

None of the students said anything, not even Matsui, So I said, "…I'll tell you later."

*****

Life here in Japan has slowly but surely re-wired my sensibilities as well as my expectations of people; in particular, kids. So that now, what wouldn't have even been picked up on my radar a few years ago, sets off all kinds of bells and whistles: people dropping trash in the street, talking loud or talking on cell phones on the train, my roommates playing loud music at night, etc, etc… According to my old sensibilities, these were all misdemeanors, but with my re-wired sensibilities, they are definitely punishable felonies.

As was Matsui's throwing stuff at Takahashi…

Looking out at the crestfallen faces of my students, I regretted my overreaction and wondered how it could have come to be. Yes, I was in defensive mode- practically on suicide watch- when it came to Takahashi. I didn't know if having things thrown at her by students would push her over the edge but it couldn't have helped that's for damn sure. Besides, I knew it was important for us to present a united front against the unruly masses, show that we had each other's backs. Especially now because, to me, the object tossing represented an unacceptable escalation in bad behavior, and needed to be put down and deterred. He had to be made aware that that kind of thing was not going to be tolerated…and Takahashi certainly wasn't going to do a damn thing. Someone had to do something.

But, aside from the power struggle going on, to be honest, I was a little hurt. I mean, he had really won me over. The bond we had was short-lived, but it lived. It was real. I liked his hugs the way my mother likes my hugs. I really like physical affection and I loved the way he ran and jumped in my arms when he saw me. It made me feel more human, and in a really dehumanizing society like Japan has been for me, I had, without really noticing it, looked forward to it every time. I didn't care that he was a knucklehead and liked power. I like knuckleheads, and I like power, too. Some of my best friends were knuckleheads at some point but either grew out of it or learned how to put it to good use.

So, I guess you could say I kind of missed him already.

Matsui stared at me for a long time after that, his face frozen in an odd expression somewhere between befuddled and despondent. He was really starting to worry me. Maybe the shock had been too much for him. Or, maybe he was simply thinking, plotting his revenge. After all, he'd lost face big time and he knew that the class was waiting to see how he would handle this situation. Perhaps he'd never been challenged before by a teacher. His henchman, Satou, watched Matsui with an open-mouthed gape. Occasionally he would look over at me with darkness in his eyes. I made a mental note to watch my back around that one.

Takahashi was walking around the class checking notebooks while I stayed up front trying to look relaxed and pretend like everything was normal, hoping this whole situation would just blow over and be forgotten. Pretending that all the tension I felt and the drama playing out in my head was just that: imagination. I do that sometimes.

However, when Takahashi reached Matsui, she must've realized that he, and in fact the entire class, had been silent for going on 2 minutes or so which was unprecedented. She looked around the room at the various students then at Matsui's frozen stare at me and asked him what was wrong.

"Loco-sensei pss pss pss pss pss pss..." he whispered, another first.

Takahashi-sensei face dropped. She turned to look at me, then back at Matsui, then down at the floor where the yellow piece of chalk lay, now crushed- no doubt beneath Matsui's slipper. Then, back at me. Then a light in her face went out...and I knew that whatever ideas I had about a united front were dashed.

When she rejoined me at the head of the class she whispered, "Loco-sensei? Matsui says you threw chalk at him?"

Her tone was incredulous. Not like she didn't believe him but like she couldn't believe what I'd done. She was as shocked as the students. Though it was hardly a question I almost denied it. She probably still would have believed him.

"Yeah..." I said, after a moment's hesitation. Then added, "but only after he threw something at you!"

I'd said this in English and hoped she understood it was done in her defense. But her tone was all, *Say it isn't so, Loco,* laden with shock and disgust and laced with guilt. It was like she hadn't even heard what I said.

I peeped over at Matsui as the bell sounded for the end of class. He was still sullen and looked on the brink of tears. I felt pangs of panic-tinged regret coursing through me. What the hell have I done?

I collected my unused teaching materials, lost in the contemplation of going and apologizing to him. I had been out of line, after all. Then, I caught a glimpse of movement in front of me and looked up.

It was him.

"Loco-sensei, I'm very sorry I made you angry!" he cried, at a barely audible volume.

"Eeee!" I snapped. "What?"

"I made you angry, right?" he said a little louder, his Japanese like a toddler's Japanese. "And...I'm sorry. It's my fault."

"Uhhh..." Just then I caught a movement behind me in my peripheral and I wheeled around ready for a surprise attack. Satou was back there, but he also wore a mask of shame. He didn't say anything. He just stood there with his head downcast.

"Kochira koso," (I'm the one who should apologize) I said, turning back to face Matsui. " I'm sorry."

"No, no," He bowed and gave me a hug without looking up, his head against my stomach. Then he turned and marched out of the class into the hallway- Satou in tow- without even a glance back. I stood there trying to figure out if this was a ploy or had his apology been genuine. Had I neutralized him with a piece of chalk? Was a brief flash of my anger enough to make him re-think his position?

As I made my way downstairs to the teacher's office, I felt like a heavy burden had been lifted off me.

When I got to the office I noticed that Takahashi was already there. And, as was becoming a common sight, she was being chewed out by Kawaguchi-sensei. I wondered what the matter was but I had learned to keep my distance from my buddy when she's getting in Takahashi's ass about something. She's like a different person. It's kind of spooky. I felt sorry for Takahashi, as usual. She looked like she was being bitch-slapped by a pimp. The other teachers in the office were pretending not to notice this, but it was like not noticing a total solar eclipse. It was the Tyrannosaurus Rex in the room.

From what I could gather from hush tones that rose and fell, Takahashi-Sensei had handed in some report late causing blah blah blah to be blah blah blah-ed. More of the same shit. Kawaguchi-sensei ended her harangue with an awful funky, malicious "Ne!?" and walked away from her. Takahashi-sensei took her leave of the office, probably to run to the bathroom and cry. Poor thing.

My desk is next to Kawaguchi -sensei's. As she passed by I put my head into a text-book and tried to act like I didn't even know she was there.

"Loco-sensei," she whispered. "Chotto kite ne." (Come here for a sec)

I followed her out of the office and into the conference room across the hall. Kawaguchi-sensei usually does this when she has something important to tell me that she doesn't want the rest of the staff to know about.

She sat me down. "You know...Takahashi-sensei, she told

me about what happened with the student in her class."

"She did!?"

"Yeah, she told me that you threw a piece of chalk, and it hit Matsui ...is that what happened?"

"Yeah, basically...he threw something at her and I kinda lost my..."

"He threw something at Takahashi-sensei?"

"Yeah..."

"She didn't tell me that part..."

"It's not important anyway...I was wrong. I shouldn't have done it."

"Yes, please be more careful..."

"I will..."

"Yoku Wakatta!" (I get it now!) She snapped, and laughed. "Ne, ne..." she whispered in the echoing conference room we were in, looking around like she was about to let me in on a great secret. "She told me about that when I brought up her latest fuck up. I tell you she is a sneak and a liar but I know you never believed me, deshou? (right?)! Hora! (See!) She was trying to get me off her back using you, deshou?"

"You really think so?" I asked.

Kawaguchi just smiled...

I'd like to think that I was the kind of person who wouldn't be fazed by shit like this. I mean, I shouldn't have expected her not to tell anyone, right? Hell, I might have been a danger to the students, having taken to throwing things at them. Of course she would feel it was her responsibility — in the name of student safety — to report it. But, I have to admit: I was fazed. I did feel betrayed.

And next time my little buddy Matsui gets into one of his tyrannical states, and even if he starts to launch larger objects, whatshername: the dime-dropping fuck-up with the tits, a hazing episode or two from a suicidal date with fate via the front of some speeding commuter train...well... that Bitch is on her own!

CONVERSATION #3

ANYTHING

This conversation took place with a private student in an AC-free pavilion in Yokohama. I was eating an ice cream to cool down.

Me: This is good!

Student: Is it sweet enough?

Me: Yeah, it's fine. Why, is this diet ice cream or something?

Student: (laughs) No, but American ice cream is sweeter than Japanese ice cream, so I thought—

Me: Is that a fact? I hadn't noticed. Tastes the same to me.

Student: I see. And it's much smaller than American ice cream, too, I think.

Me: Have you gone to America recently, or something?

Student: Not recently. I went to Hawaii five years ago. But, everybody knows—

Me: I have an idea: Let's try something different for today's lesson.

Student: What do you want to try?

Me: Let's talk about similarities for this lesson.

Student: Similarities?

Me: Yeah, you know, things that Japanese people have in common with other people of the world.

Things that are the same in Yokohama as they are in New York. Stuff like that.

Student: I don't understand.

Me: Ummmm.for example, the McDonald's menu is basically the same here in Yokohama as it is in NY.

Student: American hamburger is bigger than Japanese hamburger.

Me: —

Student: Deshou?

Me: Ok. How about rice? Back in the U.S. my family ate rice all the time. And Japanese people eat a lot of rice too, right? That is one clear cut—

Student: American rice is dry, and a little hard, I remember. Japanese rice is moist and delicious—

Me: Ok, Starbucks! Starbucks is essentially the same in both cities; I think we can agree on that. Coffee is coffee. So that would be an example—

Student: The cup size is different. Japanese large size is a small size in America, I think.

Me: I don't think so.

Student: I could not drink the whole cup of coffee. It was too big!

Me: —

Student: Americans like everything too big deshou?

Me: I think you're missing the…ok, ok, I have a nose and you have a nose, right? Both our noses serve the same purpose, right? This would be an example of a similarity.

Student: (Studying my nose) —

Me: Since I've been living here, most Japanese people I know will make a point of noting the differences between things here and things in America, but no one ever mentions the similarities.

Student: I see.

Me: When people constantly point out the differences, it feels almost like you're isolated, like you're being pushed away. You know? I mean, imagine two countries negotiating peace when they can't find any common ground.

Student: Hmm…I think I understand.

Me: Great. So, can you think of a similarity?

Student: — (silence for 20 seconds)

Me: Just one thing…anything'll do.

Student: — (another 30 seconds)

Me: Anything!

I I

THE ENVY OF WE

It's totally my fault. I unlocked the cell and turned my back, and my racism strolled right out of the penitentiary where I kept it; and it wasn't the least bit penitent, either.

I know the human tendency is to seek externally for problems caused by internal issues, to blame others and ignore one's own culpability. But I take full responsibility for my carelessness and what's more, I should have known better! From the moment that first negative feeling I had for Japanese people and culture revealed itself for what it was, I should've been, at least, on Yellow alert (no pun intended).

The feeling was envy.

Encountering envy in your heart is like coming across a dandelion in your garden. If you're wise and if you want to have flowers in your bed and not a bunch of flower devouring weeds, then you had better get to work on eliminating all traces of infestation immediately, or its pretty much guaranteed your garden will become a resort for botanical nuisances before you know it.

Needless to say, I didn't pull the weed.

Sure, there are certainly darker facets of the human psyche, but not many pollute and pervert the thinking process, strangle goodwill and obfuscate the intentions of others as effectively as envy.

Even when I felt this envy for Japanese starting to tamper with the feelings I thought I had resolved about white people, I *still* didn't assemble a search party and release the hounds to find that fugitive and shove him back in his cage where he belongs. Maybe I figured because I was dealing with an entirely different race that everything would be different. Maybe I didn't realize I was looking at warning signs of troubled times to come.

Or, maybe I didn't think at all. That seems more likely. Like I said, definitely my fault.

It's not like I hadn't had experience with this kind of thing. Envy had revealed itself to me as a trigger of racist feelings several times over the course of my life- not only within myself but within friends and family, as well.

*****

Something extraordinary happened in New York during my last year at LIU, something so surreal that, at least politically, I wouldn't feel anything even approaching it again until Obama's campaign for President nearly 20 years later. There had already been black local politicians at most levels of city government in New York. But, the political face of New York, Hizzoner, the Mayor, had always been Caucasian until David Dinkins came along.

I was just getting politically active around this time, and Dinkins was actually the first politician to shine through my blinders of apathy and really open my eyes to the political landscape in NY. And though I'd been able to vote for several years before the 1990 mayoral election, this was the first time I'd actually exercised the right my parents, grandparents and ancestors had been deprived of until 1965.

The previous Mayor, Koch, was very charismatic and in-your-face with everyone, a prototypical New Yorker, and thus was pretty popular. He'd been mayor since I was a kid. But, Dinkins came along, with his laid back style, and had a calming effect on people at a time when racial tensions in New York were intensifying. I think that was an important factor in his miraculous victory. That, and he had "juice" (meaning power in NY politics, meaning he knew where the bodies were buried and he knew how to get the money, having been a player for many years).

His aura of tranquility wouldn't last long, though. It was barely a year after his victory when the melting pot boiled over, practically right outside my window.

I was living on Eastern Parkway at the time, in Crown Heights. Crown Heights was not so much a melting pot community as a gumbo. Immigrants from many countries brought their cultural distinctiveness to this Brooklyn hamlet. Aside from African-Americans, it was made up mostly of ingredients imported from the developing nations of the West: Jamaicans, Panamanians, Puerto Ricans, Dominicans Trinidadians, Haitians and many more, predominantly Black and Latino.

However, there was one untraditional ingredient in this ghetto gumbo: a little colony of Chabad Lubavitch Jews. Within this Jewish enclave, many of the homes, businesses and services were owned and operated by the Lubavitch. It had its own private security patrols and even an ambulance service. It was basically a self-sufficient community, a micro-nation. While most of the white people that lived and owned businesses in Crown Heights had long since headed not so much *to* greener pastures in the suburbs as *away* from a darkening and increasingly neglected inner city (in a mass exodus known as *White Flight* — which is, ironically, very similar to the migration away from the hate crimes and deteriorating economies that brought blacks north to the inner cities in the first place) the Lubavitch were only just arriving and had no intentions of going anywhere. They were in the hood for good.

While some of my friends, and family, held the most

preposterous notions about this anomaly and about Jewish people, in general (most people have had their minds tainted by a centuries-long widespread promulgation of anti-Semitism) I viewed this community for what it really was: The fruition of what my elementary school had attempted and failed to do (in many respects) when I was child.

My elementary school was founded by prominent Pan-Africanists of the time — educators mostly — who wanted to decolonize the minds of young African-Americans by systematically dismantling and removing all the oppressive ideas planted there by their former enslavers (whites) in order to, among other things, heighten self-esteem, inspire spirituality, diversify cultural references, mold social values, and increase political awareness. In this, they were very successful. I benefited a great deal from their efforts.

However, the organization that formed my school had another goal. And, in this undertaking they were considerably less successful. This other aim was to build a self-sufficient black community, able to sustain itself economically by keeping the substantial buying power of black people *within* the black community, where it could do the most good *for* the community. To this end, the organization opened a number of shops and businesses including: a book store, a food co-op, a restaurant, and even started an African cultural festival (which continues until this day and draws thousands of visitors every year). We wanted to show the greater community, by example, what could be accomplished if black people would just follow the guiding principles set down by great Pan-Africanist minds like Maulana Ron Karenga, the founder of Kwanzaa and author of the Nguzo Saba, or the Seven Principles of Blackness.

If it had been successful, it would have been, essentially, a black version of exactly what the Lubavitch Jews have done in Crown Heights and in other communities in the U.S. and around the world.

When I walked through this Jewish community, seeing what my community had tried and failed to do (for a number of reasons) oh man, was I envious! I just knew that if we hadn't been brainwashed as a people to distrust one another and self-hate, by whites, that we too could be enjoying the same success as the Lubavitch. And, resentment for *them* grew out of this envy. It fitted in nicely with the overall resentment that had accumulated among blacks in Crown Heights. It made it easier for me to view the positive achievements of Lubavitch collective work and cooperative economics as the result of preferential treatment and racism.

All of that negativity came to a head in August of '91, the ugliest August of my life until that point. And, our first black mayor, already warding off the racial backlash of breaking a color barrier, was caught in the crossfire: Jews and cops on one side, angry blacks on the other, two dead bodies at his feet (one black, a child, accidentally killed in a traffic accident by a Jewish driver, and one Jewish, lynched by an angry mob of blacks) and a race riot on his watch.

What a damn shame!

*****

You're probably wondering what it was exactly about the Japanese I was so envious of.

Envy, simply put, is when one resents that another person has something they perceive themselves as lacking, and wish the other person to be deprived of it. So envy, though I hear it tossed around rather lightly sometimes, is potentially a deadly emotion. Thus it is known throughout the Christian world (as well as other religious worlds) as a Deadly Sin.

I didn't wish to see Japanese deprived of this enviable attribute...at least not at first. I simply acknowledged and admired it for what it was: something I had come to believe had been the missing ingredient in the world I'd grown up in. A very complex thing but, like most complex things, it can be reduced to a very simple concept.

Sometimes even to a single word.

In this case the word is, an all-caps, WE.

As a NEON instructor back in my early days in Japan, I'd find myself on a daily basis seated before a quartet of Japanese English students. Sometimes there'd be a housewife, bored out of her wits but with money to burn, there to be entertained more than anything else. Maybe a manga artist and writer studying me (and the other teachers) as much as he was English, so that he could give the gaijin characters in his comics more depth. There might be a salaryman, breath spiked with the compulsory alcohol he'd consumed after work, studying English in preparation for his pending transfer to one of his company's overseas offices. Sometimes there'd be a lovely young lady who worked at a hostess club in the red-light district of Shinjuku, trying to brush up on her English in order to serve her growing clientele of well-to-do foreigners better. NEON drew people from all walks of Japanese life.

Four people as different as different can be — as far as appearances, lifestyles and priorities were concerned. But there was always one thing they could all agree on: This WE business.

"WE are shy." "WE are humble." "WE are polite." "WE eat healthy food." "WE are not like foreigners. Why? Because WE are Japanese!" "WE don't do it that way. Foreigners do it that way. WE do it *this* way!"

A constant barrage of WE this and WE that, accompanied by nods of agreement...no coercion required, no opposition, no dissension. They seemed to proclaim, as a unit, WE hold our truths to be self-evident that WE, Japanese, are created equal! United WE stand, for better or for worse.

I'd never seen a WE up-close and personal before I came to Japan. At least not a whole nation of WE.

Sure, the American Constitution waxes poetically about a "*we* the people" but, until Obama came along, I'd never felt myself to be an acknowledged and integral part of the formation of that *we*. To me, that *we* always meant a bunch of rich, white, slave-holding hypocrites who decided tax evasion and revolution were preferable to taxation without representation. Oh, and of course their progeny, the beneficiaries of this treasure trove of blood money, plunder and deceit, as well.

You might say that America had become a *we* of sorts after September 11, 2001. But I also took issue with that kind of *we*. The "*we will rid the world of Islamic terrorists (and anybody that even vaguely resembles them), and you're either with us or against us*" kind of *we*, to me, is clearly an example of a very dark *we* forged by some shit kickers exploiting a nation's fear and grief under the guise of patriotism.

I'd personally used *we* before but usually as a way of establishing the exclusivity of my club, crew, clique or cult. Rarely did I use it to mean black culture, and rarer still for the black race.

My elementary school, though successful in edifying me with a heightened sense of cultural awareness had, unintentionally, made me a bit of an elitist. While a good number of my friends were products of the public school system and emerged from it with minds poisoned by Eurocentric indoctrination, me and my fellow alumni had been the beneficiaries of a *superior* Afrocentric education. So, I had difficulty including *average* brainwashed black folks in any *we* scenarios, and would find myself silently condescending to them way too often; sometimes even noticeably. I was all fucked up, too.

Moreover, I knew that even among white people there were a great many opposing viewpoints based on whatever precepts they'd been exposed to. As a child, most of my white friends were Jewish, but as I grew up and my circle of white friends expanded to include WASPs and Catholics, I learned that there were more points of contention among whites than I thought, and some were pretty deep and ugly.

Some melting pot America was. Melting pot, my ass.

So, I always felt strange including people I didn't know *personally* in a declaration of *we*. In fact, if I even heard anyone speaking of a race, referring to it as a *we or they*, at the very least I'd be on alert. I'd instinctively think that person was either an idiot, ignorant, joking, race-baiting, or trying to sell a product or idea. If I was asked a question, to which my answer was expected to represent the views of a race, culture or nation, I'd look at the questioner as if they'd just arrived from Planet *What The Fuck*?!

I realize now that these initial encounters with the Japanese WE constituted my first case of not so much culture shock as being struck by a bolt of cultural lightning.

My restless mind, though, was fascinated! I tried to imagine what a black WE would be like, and all the things it could accomplish. I thought about all the leaders throughout African, and her Diaspora's, history who had dedicated their lives to this idea of a black WE. Some were more successful than others, but all were motivated by a vision revealed to me in those glass cage-like classrooms at NEON. They'd envisioned a people who drew pride and strength from their commonality, bound by single-mindedness yet diversified by ability and aspiration. Like a bee hive, only each comb distinguishable from the next, each bee tasked according to its capabilities.

It was an awesome sight, this WE.

I imagined I could see the beneficial impact this Japanese WE had on Japan. For example, WE, (I told myself) was responsible for the low crime rate in Japan. Why would WE rob WE? Or intentionally hurt WE? Or, god forbid, kill WE? It's like robbing Peter to pay Peter, like killing your own flesh and blood. Why would WE break the rules WE live by?

And, I wondered (more like fantasized) if I studied this Japanese WE could I learn something useful. Perhaps go back to my home world with renewed optimism, and even figure out a way to institute this idea of WE in America. (Obama would eventually use a similar *we*, as in "Yes *We* Can," and that slogan would carry him to the pinnacle of Western power).

But, this admiration didn't last long.

CONVERSATION #4

Are You A Pure Blooded Japanese

A conversation with my student over coffee at a Starbucks in Yokohama:

Me: So what did you do yesterday?
Student: I went shopping at Jiyugaoka.
Me: ...*in* Jiyugaoka...
Student: Sou sou sou sou...in, da ne.
Me: That's good. So, what did you buy?
Student: I bought nothing, but I meet...met a very nice woman.
Me: Really? In the store?
Student: Yes, she was shop staff...she want to meet you!
Me: She wants to meet me? Why me?
Student: Before, she live at...*in* Brooklyn.
Me: Really? But how does she know about me?
Student: I talk about you, of course.
Me: You told a stranger working in a shop in Jiyugaoka about me?
Student: Yes! She is very exciting. Me too!
Me: She was very *excited*, you mean.
Student: Yes yes yes yes yes.
Me: I'm sorry, but you told me to correct you every time. I can stop if you like...

Student: Yes, please, today. No fix my terrible English. I want to be like natural. Just today.

Me: Good idea.

Student: So, at the shop, ne. She see me in the shop and she say 'am I Hawaiian?'

Me: Why?

Student: Because my hair…it's not usual hair for Japanese, very long, and my, how you say, sun tan?

Me: Oh, I see…go ahead.

Student: So she asked me am I…junsuina…pure… bleed, pure brood…how you say?

Me: Huh? How do you say what?

Student: For example…if your mother is Japanese and your father is gaijin…like so…

Me: You mean Pure*breed*? Pure *blooded*?

Student: Sou sou sou sou sou. I tell her of course I'm junsuina nihonjin, I 100% Japanese…And she…

Me: I'm sorry to interrupt you, but…maybe I don't understand correctly…a staff person in a shop asked you about your blood status?

Student: Huh?

Me: She asked if you are 100% Japanese?

Student: Yes…all the time, you know. Because of my hair and….

Me: ….and your suntan. Yeah I got that.

Student: And she want to meet with you…what's wrong?

Me: I was just thinking about Muggles. And the axis of evil…

Student: The…nani?

Me: No, the *Nazis*.

Student: Wakannai!

Me: It's not important...and I'd be happy to meet her...why not?

Student: That's wonderful! I will tell her...

Me: Can I ask you a question?

Student: Of course.

Me: Don't you think that is a personal question?

Student: What question?

Me: About junsui...about your blood status, your pedigree.

Student: Ee! Personal?

Me: Yeah, VERY personal, I think. And very irrelevant, too. I mean, to a salesperson anyway.

Student: Irrelevant?

Me: Kankei nai.

Student: Sou deshou...demo, to Japanese not irrelevant. Not personal.

Me: Why?

Student: Wakannai

Me: Okay...well, anyway, let's start the lesson, shall we?

12

THE DARK SIDE OF WE

The admiration began to fade around the same time envy came a-knocking, as a matter of fact. Envy showed up wanting to know just who the fuck did these little bastards think they were, jabbing me with their WE at every goddamn opportunity. Envy understood me like Crack understands a Crackhead cause I too felt the effrontery of it all.

"Yeah," I said to Envy."They need to cut that shit out! Can't they see I'm just trying to get along and learn something?"

But, apparently they couldn't, cause whenever the opportunity presented itself they didn't hesitate to insinuate (politely, but in no uncertain terms) that I could never be a part of WE because I lacked what WE Japanese have in abundance: A shared history and shared cultural values, like a love of good health, good food, a safe environment, the family unit, peace, and, of course, a profound fondness for all things cute and small (of which you are not).

And, it seemed, the more I tried to fit in, the more relationships I eked out, the more immersed I became in the culture, the more intense the WE became. It's so persistent, so matter-of-fact and pervasive, yet done with such purity and innocence. Like being struck with a wiffle bat upside the head over and over by a mentally-challenged child, smiling and giggling all the while. Living amid such guileless and unwitting hostility was emotionally confusing. I didn't know how to feel about it.

Deep down, you know they're ultra-good people. Would sooner catch a mosquito and set it free outside the window than kill it. But, it becomes increasingly difficult to see Japanese as anything but some bizarre cult of personality, like North Korea. Only there's no Kim Jong-Il. No charismatic leader. The nearest I've seen to a personality everyone here can get behind is the charismatic *leader of the club that's made for you and me: M-i-c-k-e-y M-o-u-s-e.*

Sometimes the ignorance rises to a level where it gets difficult to believe its source is naiveté, and you say (to yourself), *oh, they've* got *to be shitting me! They know what they're doing! They know this WE business is aggressive, a big glob of phlegm in the face. I can see through that WE smile and WE bow of theirs. It's all a façade!*

And, what happens? Your smile becomes as plastic and disingenuous as you perceive theirs to be. Your thoughts become as devoid of inclusion as you perceive theirs to be. You begin to surrender to the WE and forge your animosity into an US!

US initially took on the meaning: *people who are not included in this WE business.* And the longer you stay amid this obsequious hostility the more likely your definition of US evolves into: *people who realize that this WE business is some insipid shit and wouldn't want to be a part of it if you paid them!*

And, if you're like me, you start to instinctively self-preserve and protect yourself from WE. You might even develop an odd compulsion to find holes in it. Get to thinking of how this WE thing they swear by could be weakening them somehow. You even think of ways to ridicule it. I armed myself to the teeth with enough refutation ammo to launch a one-man blitzkrieg on WE.

`When a student would thrust at me with a WE blade, I would parry with an US sword, and try to decapitate his ass if he didn't back down, by blaming Japan's Bubble Burst and economic decline on their lack of individuality and this obsessive need to group-think every goddamn thing (politely as possible, of course). Or, when some half-drunk salaryman at a bar would fire a few WE rounds at me I'd retaliate with a little overkill, twist-pull pin and lob an incendiary grenade in his lap, spitting something like how this WE bullshit you guys got going over here is the same nonsense that got your asses nuked in World War II (again, in slightly nicer words, of course).

Though statistically most of the crime in Japan is Japanese on Japanese crime, the crimes sensationalized the most are those committed by foreigners, especially the Chinese and Koreans, (because WE are too civilized to commit crime, the insinuation seems). So on the rare occasion I'd see a story on the news about a homicide, rape, or robbery, I'd secretly hope it was a Japanese suspect; more ammo!

When the train lines launched the *Women-Only* cars as an, albeit, impotent response to the groping problem here in Yokohama, I smiled as I thought, *Next time one of them tosses a "WE the inhabitants of the safety planet are not safe in your criminal-infested home world of New York" dynamite stick at me, I'm gonna piss some "I'm afraid to bring my teenage niece here cause she might get molested on the train by some perverted salaryman," right on the fuse!*

This was envy talking, though. And, as you can see, my envy of WE and my detest of having WE unleashed at me at every conceivable juncture, even when it was apropos of nothing, had made me quite irrational, and diminished my respect for my hosts…as a group!

In fact, envy had begun a chain reaction that opened up a whole can of intolerance.

*****

Since I wasn't one of those people who are just dying to be

Japanese (and there are a bunch of them here), or so enamored with the culture, language, women and oddities here that I've been able to mindfuck myself into utter blindness or selective vision, envy, like admiration, didn't have much a shelf life, either.

The environment I worked in at the time certainly wasn't very conducive to envy. While NEON was a kind of incubator for the US versus WE mentality, it didn't nurture envy much. At times it seemed to even be structured in such a way as to kill envy.

I mean, there we were, a bunch of Australians, British, Americans, and some Canadians, fresh off the space shuttle from the outside world, eager to try out the rides in this cultural theme park we'd heard such amazing things about.

Some of us had read or seen "Shogun" and had visions of becoming latter-day Anjin-Sans. (I know I did). Some of us had even been big fans of martial arts films and anime, or read manga extensively, or had grandiose ideas about immersing ourselves in Zen Buddhism, Judo, Kendo, sake... anything Japanese. Some of us were just aching to prove our mettle by mastering this purportedly difficult language and navigating through this infamously close-knit culture.

And, yes, some of us had heard, read, or watched videos about how supposedly easy and eager Japanese girls are — and how much fun a foreigner can have with them — and couldn't wait to get our paws on some perpetually prepubescent poontang.

Optimism, enthusiasm and libido run amok. That was NEON to the New Jack.

To be fair, the opportunities to do much of the above were there. When there's a will there most certainly is always a way.

And, some did, by God.

But, most? Meh, not so much.

You see, when you start working for a company like NEON, where the company policy prohibits fraternization with essentially the only Japanese people you're going to get to know for a while, you start out with a couple of strikes against success. I mean, naturally you're going to covet first what you see every day, and NEON knew this. But, the risk to the company was too great, I figured. Teachers knocking up students, for example, just didn't look good on an annual report. So, yes it was a silly rule, thus broken quite a bit, but quite necessary for the company to at least reduce the number of incidents.

On top of that, the cross-section of the Japanese populace that an English conversation school like NEON attracted often offered a warped view of what was really going on out there. A good number of the students were what my girlfriend at the time referred to as Gaijin Freaks, the type of Japanese person who is infatuated with foreigners and foreign stuff. Especially when said of the girls who chase foreign guys around.

Some of these students were just dying to know all about you, questioning you incessantly about topics unrelated to English; questions, asked with syrupy sweetness that would be very non-specific to the point where you wanted to reach across the table and ring their necks. "Do black guys like Japanese women?" "Why do black women have such big behinds?" "Why do Americans like war so much?" "Do black people..." "Do American women..." "Do black men..."

At first, these types of questions were tolerable. When you first arrive, you're feeling kind of like an ambassador anyway and, admittedly, sometimes I'd take off my *thinking cap* and

311

take a perverse pleasure in speaking on behalf of my race and nation. After all, the Japanese had handed me the influence of an opinion maker like it was my due, so I ran with it, thinking this was an excellent chance to do some PR on behalf of black people everywhere. And, with all the damage Bush had done to the image of Americans with his warmongering, it was an opportunity to show that Americans were not a bunch of war happy Bush disciples, as well.

Only, by the time the number of "Do black people..." and "Do Americans..." questions reached into the triple digits, I felt cold and naked without my cap. Once my thinking cap was firmly back on my head, I realized that the vast majority of the questions were directed at the various groups I presumably belonged to, but there was a distressing lack of "do *you*..." in their questioning. It stood to Japanese reason that I could speak for everyone. After all, that's exactly what they do with the WE thing. Answering their questions, I found myself repeatedly saying, "I can't speak for all black people, but I..." to the point where I didn't even want to, and began to refuse to accept their questions anymore if they weren't addressed to me personally. My pat answer became, "how (*the hell*) should I know? If you really want answers you can trust, you should conduct a survey!"

Some of these NEON students just wanted to touch your skin or your hair and remark on its differences from their own, or observe your daily rituals, taking careful notes on the differences (always the differences), or simply see how it felt to be in a room alone with you.

All in all, it made me feel like those glass-walled rooms were cages and my students were patrons of PETA.

Or, vice-versa.

Some of them would take it too far, and their need to see how you lived drove them beyond the acceptable. Some would stalk you after work, following you home and whatnot. You'd look up on the train to see your student standing there staring at you. Sometimes they'd pretend that it was a coincidence. Sometimes they didn't even bother. Some were actual mental patients whose therapist had recommended that they study English in order to relieve stress (they'd confess to me on occasion). It was rumored that NEON had a special business relationship with the mental health community, but that's not confirmed. It wouldn't have surprised me though because there were always quite a few students that I felt to be certifiably bonkers. I mean, really creepy shit.

You might consider this an upside (and many teachers did) but some students simply wanted to take you to bed. They'd play coy for a while, but their intentions would surface sooner than later. Some of the younger girls (HS and College) wanted to be the first on their block to cherry pick a gaijin from the tree, so to speak (I mean, there was always new blood coming in), and make a boyfriend out of him. Or just experiment with you. Some women (usually Office Ladies, mid-thirties to early forties, and thus ignored by a society that worships youth) came there with the expressed purpose (and weren't so shy about it either) of finding a gaijin who couldn't see them for the Japanese societal road kill they were, bedding and wedding him.

Some of my students were pretty cool, though, and wanted to make foreign friends, but unfortunately it was difficult to tell the difference between those who genuinely sought friendship, and those that just wanted a pet gaijin — someone to show off to their friends, living proof that they were internationally-minded, or something. There'd always be offers. "Let's go drinking. Let's go clubbing. Let's play pool." To which you were strongly encouraged by NEON to refuse...but sometimes you didn't, only to find out two or three months into the "friendship" that the student was using you as a social accessory.

And, yes, some came there with the sole purpose of learning English. Maybe the ratio was 50 / 50, at best.

But, all of them came equipped with the WE.

So there you are, a NEON Instructor (which, despite your college education, carries its own stigma – with Japanese and Foreigners alike – branding you at worst, a total loser and at best, a teacher whose only qualification is being raised in an English speaking country), spending nine hours a day with people who had been reportedly coerced into paying exorbitant fees to be in your company; studying them as they're studying you, learning about this fabled culture from the gaijin freaks of the WE world. And, little by little, it takes its toll on you.

It starts with off-color mockery and illicit jokes – mostly condoned, followed by culturally-based complaints. And, soon it builds to a crescendo where all semblance of respect for the people you're there to service is lost.

Even management could barely contain their contempt for the WE nation. They were just going through the motions and regurgitating the party line: "These are our clients, they pay the bills, and here in WE land, the rule is okyakusama Kamisama (The customer is God). So kneel and suck on it, change your line of work, or go home!"

And most did just that; after their one-year contract was up (if they could even take it that long...most of the women couldn't) they got themselves tickets on the first thing smoking out of Asia.

But those that found love, or paradise (when compared to their hometowns), or were in possession of profound patience, or had alternative missions (like belt notching, ghost-town photographing, anime character stalking, and so on) or had just managed to find a relatively comfortable niche, they stayed. (I stayed for Aiko, and have no regrets).

So, as you might imagine, the envy I harbored for Japanese didn't last long. All the above mentioned bizarre behaviors – the dark side of WE – dashed my silly visions of assimilating on the rocks off the coast of Yokohama.

So, what began as admiration for Japanese people, culture and customs devolved into envy. Then, slowly, envy – no longer able to feed on WE – began to metastasize. Tumors popped up randomly all over my mental well-being, no longer relegated to areas associated with Japanese.

One tumor predictably attached itself to the place in my psyche where I kept all those ugly thoughts and feelings about white folks sealed away, the ones I thought were well under control. The envy I'd held for Japanese made me susceptible.

You see, while the Japanese had this WE thing they loved to bombard foreigners with, they also had their own brand of admiration and envy, and this too they loved to heave. Sure, a small segment of Japanese admired not so much *me* as their *image* of me (an image cooler than I'll ever be), but the vast majority worshiped white people, or rather, the ideas they associated with white people.

I mean, ridiculously, eerily so.

CONVERSATION #5

Everybody knows White People Are More Beautiful Than Japanese People

Conversation with a Japanese friend at a café in Yokohama

Me: Can I ask you a question?

Friend: Sure. Go ahead...

Me: Well, last week my student told me that a staff person had asked her if she were 100 percent Japanese...

Friend: Really? A staff person? Why? Does she look like a foreigner?

Me: She has long dark hair and a suntan and sometimes she wears Hawaiian accessories. Jewelry and whatnot...

Friend: Sou desu ka. Ja, the staff maybe think she wants to be like Hawaii's people.

Me: Yeah...And??

Friend: Well, the staff was probably...oseiji...do you know oseiji?

Me: Yeah, you mean like flattering or ass-kissing...

Friend: Sou sou sou sou! Staffs do it all the time!

Me: But, how is asking someone if they are purebred or pure blood considered ass kissing? I don't get it.

Friend: Well, we are Japanese. Almost Japanese want to be like another people.

317

Me: What? Japanese don't like being Japanese?

Friend: No, we like our culture...but we like another cultures too.

Me: Huh?

Friend: Your student...when she tell you that, her face was happy deshou?

Me: Kinda...I mean it was more like indifferent...not happy, not disappointed.

Friend: If she tell you the story that means she is happy. If she didn't like it she don't tell you about that, I think.

Me: That makes sense...but why does she like it?

Friend: She wants to look like Hawaiian, so the staff oseiji to make her happy.

Me: I guess I understand. I had the wrong idea...

Friend: Japanese is very difficult culture.

Me: Sou da ne. So if I say to a Japanese person that they look like they are mixed blood, it's *ok*?

Friend: Yes.

Me: It's confusing. One time I told my girlfriend she looks kind of Chinese and she almost started crying...

Friend: Eeeeee! Never Chinese! Japanese people do not think Chinese are attractive.

Me: What? So if the staff person had said my student looked a little Chinese then...

Friend: Ohhhhh No! They never say that! *Everybody* knows it's rude to say Chinese!

Me: *Everybody*?

Friend: All Japanese know!

Me: Why?

Friend: Muzukashii kore (this is difficult)

Me: Do Japanese people hate Chinese people?

Friend: No, we hate no people. But, eeto ne, we think Chinese people hate Japanese people so...

Me: So, what?

Friend: So...that's what we feel.

Me: Paranoia's not a feeling.

Friend: Nani sore? (What's that?)

Me: Betsu ni nani mo nai (It's nothing, forget about it) What if the staff said she looks mixed with white?

Friend: Oseiji! White people are very attractive to Japanese people. Japanese people like blond hair and blue eyes...

Me: Most white people don't have blond hair and blue eyes, though...

Friend: Don't care. White people are kawaii... Japanese people think white people are more beautiful than Japanese people.

Me: What about black people? If the sales staff says you look mixed with black...

Friend: Eetoooo ne...If customer is B-boy or B-girl, it's ok.

Me: If not?

Friend: Not oseiji...normal Japanese people don't like to compare to black people.

Me: *Normal?* Nevermind...Why?

Friend: We are so different...

Me: I see.

13

IN A WORLD OF SHIT

I t seemed to me that, through Japanese eyes, white was the ideal. I can hardly fault them for this affliction, though. There's a global perennial PR campaign that supports this thinking, and no country, no culture, no*body* (except maybe some areas in China, North Korea and other MTV-free zones) is completely immune.

I'd seen this soul-snatching malady afflict many black people back home, as well. Michael Jackson is often held up as the epitome of the damage it can do for his disfiguring attempts at physical metamorphosis, but with the majority of the sufferers it's their minds and souls that are disfigured more so than their bodies.

For centuries many black people have associated all the good things in life with white people and white culture. Whites are held up as the ultimate social achievement; the consummate aspiration. And why shouldn't they be? White people seem to hold all the power, money and influence. Beauty, business, technology, entertainment, the Arts...almost all positive facets of life somehow get attributed to whiteness. It almost seems rational, even natural, to covet what *they* possess, to envy them.

The PR machine informs us that the American dream is to live the dream white people were already living, to have access to the things white people already have.

My elementary school had immunized me as best they could against this, and I'd gotten booster shots with the Five Percenters. But, these inoculations were poisonous as well; like treating cancer with chemotherapy. Sure, you'll kill the cancer, but you'll kill a lot of healthy cells, too, in the process.

Nevertheless, it's a condition, I've learned, you must be constantly vigilant against. Like colds or weight gain. Otherwise, it'll sneak up on you and gag you when you least expect it. It's an insidious assailant, a social Ninja, this envy of whiteness.

I still remember well my first bitter taste of Japanese-style white preference.

I was still working for NEON at the time. I came into work that afternoon and, as was the practice, I checked the schedule on the wall to see what classes and at which level I would be teaching that evening, made a note of them and prepared my lessons.

One of the Japanese staff people came into the office a little before classes were to begin to change the schedule. This happened occasionally and was always accompanied by apologies. I saw that one of my classes had been switched from a high level class which I liked to a low-level class which I could live without. I asked why the change was made. It seemed arbitrary. The staff person blushed and confessed- via a troubled look- that it was for a reason that she didn't exactly feel comfortable explaining to me. Not much of a poker face. But, in words she told me only that it was the student's request. Her blush had raised a red flag though, and I smelled a rat so I didn't let it drop.

She informed a head teacher of my concerns, a white guy. I watched them discussing it in Japanese which I could not comprehend at all at the time. Occasionally he would glance at me and also looked uncomfortable.

Finally, he came over to me and said, "The student wanted a different teacher…it's not a reflection on you, Loco. She wants to go to England someday so she would like to study with a teacher from England."

There were several British teachers, all white and all preoccupied that period. The teacher that was to replace me was Australian, also white (with decidedly a different accent from the British). I pointed this out.

The head teacher had screwed up; otherwise I'm sure he would have said the student wanted to go to Australia and not England. He just stood there beneath my scorn looking like he wanted to take his own life for being so stupid. I wasn't sore at him, though. He was just trying to make the best of a really crappy situation. I wasn't sore at the Japanese staff person, either. She too was just doing her job which is primarily to keep the client happy. I wasn't even especially pissed at the student. She was just expressing a preference based on whatever criteria she had in her head.

It would take several more of these type incidents, and stories from other non-white coworkers of similar occurrences, before it got through my benefit-of-the-doubt giving heart that something was amiss; something that was not aimed scattershot at "foreigners" but sniper deadly at *non-white* foreigners.

And, these incidents informed me in no uncertain terms that I wasn't in Kansas, or anywhere near America, anymore, and that I was now dealing with a people whose ignorance and racism would be tolerated as a matter of de facto company policy. Initially, I pushed back against the company, with notes in the suggestion boxes, tersely worded letters and such. The policy didn't budge, though. In fact, my complaints, aside from speculative stares and ominous smiles whenever upper management would pass through my branch, went unacknowledged; forever floating in a bottomless box.

*****

This actually surprised me, though. Why? Because, I half-expected Japanese people to feel they had something in common with people of African descent when I first came to Japan.

Seriously, I did.

I mean, here was a country that was actually nuked by white people (Roosevelt approved them, Truman ordered them dropped), the only country to hold that distinction. So, naturally, I thought that there might be a certain kinship with other people who have seen the dark side of so-called Western civilization up-close and personal.

After all, modern African-Americans are the survivors of a holocaust that has lasted over 400 years, and most modern day African countries have suffered even longer due to European imperialism, exploitation and genocide. A couple of nukes and a few years of occupation are nothing in comparison to that, I know, but I thought Japanese might draw some commonalities.

I was wrong.

It's a virtually inescapable phenomenon, the power this PR machine wields. Even here in Asia.

For three years on a daily basis, I sat and listened to Japanese students *share* their ideas about the world. It would be almost impossible to overstate how much they wished to be associated with white, though they often seemed to be unaware of this. It took on the appearance of a natural aspiration, as if the thinking was: *The Western World is white, so if one wants to be like Westerners then one ought to want to be like those that reside at the pinnacle of Western civilization* (by all appearances. Mind you, this was pre-Obama).

Before coming to Japan, most foreigners are made aware of the stigma Japan rightfully retains of being a xenophobic country. NEON even gave us all the *brace yourself* orientation twice, once stateside and once again in-country. "Please be tolerant of the Japanese," they told us as we sat there enthused, en masse. "They are a homogeneous people and thus have certain xenophobic tendencies..." Keep it simple for us new jack instructors seemed to be the order of the day. But it *wasn't* as simple as that. Soon enough you realize, especially if you're not white, that that xenophobia label has degrees. Some foreign people and foreign things are feared more than others. And at the top of that xenophobic food chain (so to speak) resides this image of white people and white culture.

Doesn't it matter that members of the race you idolize were the ones that unleashed hell on your country and got medieval on innocent Japanese women and children not so long ago? This too could be rationalized, believe it or not, and I've sat and listened to dozens do it. They'd tell me that the blame for this tragedy was the Japanese imperialist, the unyielding emperor and the blind obedience of his legions going about Asia (and Hawaii) committing all sorts of atrocities. That Japan *deserved* to be nuked is the implication. That suffering the wrath of the West was their comeuppance, and in a way a blessing because White people, through nuking, had helped transform Japanese into the gentle, cuddly peaceniks they are today; the way a microwave oven turns hardened kernels of maize into fluffy tasty popcorn.

I would have to hold my head to keep from shaking it while I listened to such tripe, very reminiscent of the rationalization many whites (and some very brainwashed blacks) used to argue the merits of slavery back in the *good old days*. That being, European invaders actually saved my heathen African ancestors from a savage way of life, running butt naked in the jungles, fornicating with animals, eating one another, with nothing to look forward to but eternal damnation. But, the slave trade saved them from all of that.

The Global Perennial PR campaign for white superiority is an ancient awesome machine.

I never suspected how overwhelming a force it really was until I came here. I was simply too close to it in the U.S. to truly see it objectively. Now I can see clearly that it's like the Jedi mind trick only broadcast via satellite. It's in every movie theater, on every computer screen and even on your iPod. Don't have access to the net? No problem. It'll find you, unless you make a concerted effort to avoid it, which would be difficult because it's so ubiquitous as to be virtually invisible. It's a relentless campaign, sponsored by the companies that sell everything you want and have a monopoly on everything you need, financed by an endless revenue stream that has, over the centuries, worn, paved and tunneled a path of least resistance to hearts and minds worldwide, powered by a renewable energy source: us.

I'd never come across a people with so much white envy in my life. It was like encountering an arrant strain of the virus I was inoculated against. And with my defenses down, the infection quickly took hold and spread.

Luckily for me, though, I went home to my roommates, the Aussie and the Kiwi, Joe and Greg, and often I'd find them hammered, sprawled out on the sofa or floor, the living room littered with beer and liquor bottle, or they'd be preparing to tie one on and just waiting for me to come home and join in. They were just what a therapist would have prescribed for any racist notions I might have been afflicted with…at least against white folks.

My roommates and I had worked through a number of issues, race among them, as I discussed earlier. The minor racial wrinkles had gotten ironed out pretty quickly…nipped in the bud in the first couple of months, in fact. Before long I hardly saw them as white boys. They were just two really cool guys.

But, envy was another story. And when I turned green, they turned white!

Like when Joe and Greg would have their posse of Aussies and Kiwis (all white of course…I've never seen an Aborigine or Maori) over to the apartment drinking, laughing, and fucking off til dawn; just having the time of their lives. You wouldn't even have known they weren't Down Under if it weren't for the complaining Japanese neighbors and the threatening phone calls from NEON.

Though I was always invited to join in, I'd often pass. I wasn't much of a drinker back home and didn't long to do it here in Japan, either. They'd be disappointed, of course. Couldn't figure me out, those two, nor could their friends. Whenever I did hang out with them we'd all have a great time, so they couldn't make heads or tails out of why I passed on it so often. And, I couldn't rightly explain either, at the time. I'd just make up some excuse they never bought, and they'd just shake their heads and go, "uh huh…"

Maybe they even thought it was racial, that I had some reservations about being the only black guy in a posse of whites, carousing in the streets of Saitama to the wee hours of the night, getting into all kinds of misadventures. I sincerely hope not, though, because it was nothing like that. Over the course of my lifetime I've been the solitary or one of a couple of chocolate chips on a vanilla ice cream cone a number of times, and had developed a measure of comfort with that scenario.

What was really fucking with me was the camaraderie among them. I'd observe their fellowship of the Spirits, or listen to them through the thin walls of my bedroom, all together, a circle of friendship, kinship, and support through the tough patches here in WE land. And I'd be green as a bell pepper with envy. I mean, to them, it made perfect sense to find a group of like-minded, similarly oriented individuals and make the best of the challenges they faced here. But, for me, and for the other African Americans here...yeah, not so much. I simply didn't feel that way about Americans...*particularly* African-Americans. And, I got the distinct impression that the feeling was mutual.

The African cats were the complete opposite. They were more like the Down Under posse and the Japanese. They have their own version of WE. They congregate all the time. And when they see me, it's nothing but love. They'd holler "my brother!" across a Boulevard, blow their horns when they pass by me in cars, or even walk through a crowded train from the opposite end just to shake my hand and make my acquaintance. I mean, they'd totally go out of their way to show some love.

However, if I ran into an African-American guy (and I could usually tell at a glance) fuhgeddaboudit. We'd nod at each other and maybe mutter a few words if we found ourselves in a situation where the weirdness would be too blatant if we didn't engage in some kind of conversation. But, for the most part, it never went beyond that. If emails or phone numbers were somehow exchanged, there'd be no follow-up. Sometimes, I'd get a vibe from the person...a feeling like maybe they were on the run from the American authorities, hiding out here in Japan, and afraid I might ID them and text John Walsh at *America's Most Wanted*. Or, that they'd felt I was a saboteur looking to fuck up whatever scheme they had going over here, something fragile and lucrative, and the last thing they needed was Homie the Clown (me) fucking up the works. Either that or they were so clueless or geeky I'd see no common ground aside from race and nationality.

As for the handful of African-American women I'd run into here…well, I'd wager cockroaches get a warmer reception at the dinner table. The hostility is so potent, so open, you feel like the reason for it is obvious and personal. Their eyes would say, "you can front all you want! You might have all these Japanese bozos fooled but I *know* you and I *know* why you're here, so don't even *think* about getting in my face!"

There was, often, absolutely no love in the air. And I couldn't understand why. All I knew is I wasn't sending any and I wasn't receiving any. And, actually, to be honest, in the early years, I didn't feel bad about it. I felt like I was on my own private adventure…not to be shared, *particularly* not with other black folks. I rationalized it to myself this way: *I didn't come to a foreign country to hang out with cats from around the way.*

So there I was, an angry, pitiful and lonely black man abroad, with a burgeoning hate for Japanese, a contempt for whites threatening to resurface, and, to top it off, a disdain for blacks I wasn't even aware I retained rearing its ugly head at this most inopportune and vulnerable time.

All thanks to envy.

Envy had lived up to its reputation. It had undone the fly on my soul, leaving me exposed to the elements.

I was in a world of shit!

And, I missed Aiko so much…

14

A DECENT HUMAN BEING

I thought about Aiko a lot. How would things be different now if she were still around? Would I still be wrestling with these same demons? To her, life was much simpler. She didn't dwell too long in the grey areas like I tend to do. Not to say she wasn't complex. But she saw the complexities as hindrances and distractions while I tended to think of this proclivity of mine to consider the grey as an annoying advantage.

As a product of a city like NY I imagined I had advantages over people from less diverse areas, but in reality I had to work as hard or even harder to ward off racist thoughts, feelings and behavior. The upside of diversity is you actually get to encounter and interact with people from various races, cultures and backgrounds. The downside is if you or anyone around you should develop into a racist in such an environment, the resulting resentment is much more intense, the anger so much more violent because, goddammit, you should know better! With so many contradicting individuals at your disposal, so much information within your grasp, so many arguments against any racially divisive stance you might take, to allow yourself to become a racist becomes virtually a willful act, beyond ignorant, beyond offensive. It becomes contemptible.

Plus, there's this whole history thing.

American history, as it pertains to race- which it inevitably does- is filled with events that many (I want to say most) Americans wish had not occurred. It's a dark painful saga of dehumanization for all involved. The whites (and the government) who perpetrated these crimes and the blacks (and others) who were victimized. I've come to believe that every American was significantly damaged by this. And, as much as I would like the slate to be wiped clean, and all parties to start from scratch, that just ain't the way human beings do things.

We depend on history. History is the foundation of everything we stand for and upon. Everything we do, everything we are, is measured by and against what has happened previously. Records are kept, memories are cherished, and history is taught, fraught with distortions, willful misrepresentations and sometimes indelible truths about who we are as a people and from whence we've come. We define success and failure based on what has occurred previously. Experience is learning from the past, using this knowledge to enable ourselves in the present, and to plan for the future. Even originality is based on comparison with what has been accomplished already. That's just the way we are. That's just the way it is. That's a huge part of what makes us human.

There's not a moment of my past I regret or wish I hadn't gone through. Not that I think it has made me a better person, or even a wiser person. I couldn't make that claim with a straight face. But it has made me who I am today. With all my virtues and faults, my strengths and weaknesses, I am alive, in every sense of the word, because of what I've experienced.

This life and this history I brought with me to Japan.

And, almost immediately, almost collectively, Japan said, "Fuck You!" (Politely, of course).

It was a humbling experience, and not altogether awful... at first. I mean, I admit, I needed to be taken down a peg or two. I came here replete with these ideas of how things are and how they ought to be, and although I was wary of broadcasting them, they were always teeming just behind my guile-less eyes. I came here harboring a superficially high but arduously tempered opinion of myself and of the culture (meaning African-American, not just American) from which I sprang.

But, I realized early on that if I was going to learn anything from my time in Japan then I had better do more listening and observing, and less proselytizing and judging.

And, yes, this was as difficult as it sounds. Maybe more so because of my character.

My sensitivity, in every respect, has always been rather high. I can intuit a slight, even an unintentional one, rather quickly, and respond to it appropriately, even if the most appropriate response is ignoring it. And, I was well-equipped to defend what I hold dear, be that cultural, racial, personal, or what have you. I could hold my own against most comers, be they Asian, Caucasian, or even my fiercest opposition: people who share my racial designation.

I was a one-man Anti-Defamation League.

Only problem was, for the first time in my life, I found myself living in a country amongst a people who would delineate my doctrines of defamation as common sense. Here was a people, I ascertained rather quickly, to whom the sum total of my life and history was reduced to something to be feared and evaded if at all possible, as a matter of course, with no more consideration nor ill will than a driver might have for a pothole in the road. Here was a nation no more worthy of my contempt for full-blown ignorance than children or mentally challenged people are.

At least I came to believe so in my early days here.

So, when and why did that change?

The answer to when is in 2006.

The answer to why is still elusive. At least the complete answer is. But, I'm sure a big part of it was losing Aiko.

She was more than this country's saving grace. She'd *become* Japan to me. But, after I lost her, I got lost, too.

She came along at a time when I was still assembling my ideas about life in Japan and Japanese people, particularly women. She managed to simultaneously reinforce and undermine the stereotype I was constructing at the time. In other words, in many ways, she was just like me: Just another human being, a random and not-so random mosaic of life experiences.

I love basketball, and fried chicken, and watermelon, and hip-hop (mostly old-school, though), and any number of other stereotypes that might come to mind. But at the same time I've never been to jail, never harmed anyone (not mortally, anyway), never owned a gun, I graduated University, I'm still alive post-30, I love Bette Midler, Pre-Disney Elton John, The Beatles, Nirvana, Mozart, etc.

Aiko wasn't dainty, but she could wear a Yukata and Kimono like nobody's business, and look as fragile as a porcelain geisha in it. She was passive occasionally, but you'd soon forget that once she got a full head of steam. She loved cherry blossoms, fireworks and cute little cell phone doodads, like any stereotypical description of a Japanese person would contain, but she'd be the first to say "fuck Mickey Mouse," "Temples and Shrines are boring as fuck," and "I'd rather fuck than go slave away in an office!" (And, she loved to say, "fuck" too, if you haven't guessed). Certainly far from a stereotypical Japanese girl.

She was *my* kind of girl, regardless of race.

I know I shouldn't have placed such a heavy burden on her but she was strong. Stronger than me. She redeemed Japanese and, in the process, redeemed me. She set me free from the thoughts that were conspiring to corrupt my soul. Her very existence spoke so highly of Japan and its capacity for greatness. Her essence was an irrefutable argument against pigeonholing her people.

She made life here beautiful. She'd make life *anywhere* beautiful. She was the light.

But, once she was taken from me – and the way she was taken from me – life got darker, and Japan got darker.

And, eventually, I got darker.

"You're a writer," Aiko had said on one of my final hospital visits when she still had enough strength to get around. I just knew she'd beat whatever it was that was ailing her. A belief that held out even up until her last couple of days. If someone had told me that day that I'd be writing about her *in memoriam* someday soon I would have smiled and told them that they just didn't know her the way I did. But, I would find out this day that she'd held no such illusions. "So, you had better write!"

"I will, don't worry," I told her.

I didn't know that it would be a couple of years from that day before I'd actually get to it.

We were seated on a lounge in the Visiting Area, surrounded by dozens of other people visiting friends and family suffering from various maladies. Every time I looked away from her there would be Japanese people peering at us- the incongruous couple that we were- their invasive eyes seemingly recording everything, irritating the shit out of me. Once they'd notice me looking back at them (and sometimes this would take several moments, they'd be so entranced) they'd look away, or whisper to one another, glancing over their shoulders, rubbernecking around people or obstacles, checking to see if I'd turned away yet so that they could resume their ritualistic gaping. Staring at us out of the sides of their heads, like human fish, or any number of other all too obvious surveillance quirks people here use to satisfy their need to espy.

They simply couldn't help themselves. Not even for a man visiting his seriously ill woman, they can't.

These motherfuckers!

When I turned back to Aiko she had an expression of complete comprehension.

"It's gonna be alright," she soothed. "You'll see."

"I'm sorry, baby," I said. "I'm supposed to be cheering you up, and here I am letting these motherfu — these *people* upset me."

"When I get outta here, we're gonna go to New York, right?" she asked, changing the subject in that way of hers, speaking with the Brooklyn accent she'd acquired from me.

"Yes!" I said, cheered by thoughts of a future with her, visions of us walking hand in hand, enjoying the wondrous sights (at least for her) of my hometown. She always knew just what to say to bring me back. "You're gonna love Brooklyn!"

"I know!" she said with a smile. The medication had been doing a job on her teeth, corroding them, so she was not keen on smiling. And, she wore a headscarf, most of hair having fallen out. "You think you're mother will like me?"

"I don't care if she likes you or not!" I snapped. "You're mine, not hers."

"What about your friends?" she asked. She was always worried that my friends wouldn't accept her because she was Japanese, for some strange reason.

"I don't give a fuck what they think, either," I cried, righteously. "But, I think they'll love you, and so will my mother. How could they not?"

I looked around again, and a dozen sets of eyes darted away, again, moments late as usual.

"My people aren't like your people," I said, a little vexed.

"Nobody cares about your race back home."

"Really?" she asked, sensing my exaggeration.

"Well, mostly nobody, anyway," I said, and winked. "But, they definitely won't be mistreating you or staring at you like you got three necks."

She laughed, and all was right in the world.

Thinking back, I probably should have gone home right after her funeral, cause the world ain't been right since. But, if I had, I tell myself, I would have missed out on all the things living in Japan still had to teach me about who I really am and who I am not. I would have remained oblivious of certain strengths I possessed and certain weaknesses that were flying below the radar, eluding my detection.

"I want to go to New York," she proclaimed. "...with you. I want to meet your friends and family, and see everything!"

The way she'd said it scared me. It was like she wasn't speaking to me at all, but to God. Aiko was a Jehovah's Witness, but obviously not a full-fledged one. What, with all the smoking, drinking, and fornicating we did. But, I'd never heard her pray or speak to God before. I pulled her to me.

"We're going, baby, this summer," I said, kissing her. "But first you gotta get well."

She held on to me with a desperate embrace.

"What's wrong?"

"I'm scared," she said, tears flowing. "And I hate this fucking place!"

That was the first time I'd heard anything from her to suggest that she didn't have every confidence that she was on the mend. In fact, it was the first time I'd really ever heard fear in her voice. On some unconscious level I realized that she was sharing something with me. Something she'd withheld out of pride, or out of her concern for how I'd handle it, or maybe she'd just refused to accept it before. But, the time for denial had passed.

She was bracing herself, and me, for what may come to pass.

She rested her head on my chest and I stroked her silk scarf and the warm scalp beneath. I looked up and more eyes were trained on us…un-caring, curious, judgmental, cold little black…fucking…eyes. Little children, adults, old folks and nurses.

"FUCK ARE YOU LOOKING AT!!??" I screamed at the room, almost hysterically, and the room collectively looked away. "FUCK *ALL* YOU MOTHERFUCKERS!"

Aiko didn't even start, just nestled closer.

"It's gonna be alright, you know," she'd said. I could feel her skull moving against my chest, the sharp edge of her jaw bone through my sweater. "Can we go to where the Towers used to be?"

"Huh? Wha.?" I couldn't understand her through my fury.

"You know, what do you call it? Ground Zero?"

"You want to go to *Ground Zero*???" I asked, bewildered.

"Yeah…is that ok?"

"Darling," I said, holding her even tighter. "We can go anywhere you wanna go!"

"Really?" She pulled away, sat up and looked at me. Her face taut against her skull, her skin luster-less, her lips dry and cracked, her eye brows thinning and eye lashes almost non-existent. She hadn't made-up her face for this visit. She'd saved her energy for me. Or, maybe she'd wanted me to *really* see her. "Thank you."

The way she'd said "thank you" nearly broke my heart.

"Anata," she whispered, and smiled. That was what her

mother called her father. It means "you" but it's a term of endearment for a beloved one in this context. "I'm tired. I think I need to get some rest."

I wanted to protest, but I glanced at the nearly empty IV bag next to her on the rolling IV carrier and I swallowed my desire, along with a lump of anguish that could choke a child.

She eased herself up off of the lounge we were seated on, allowing me to help her...another first. Then, she looked around the room, at all the eyes watching us.

"When are you gonna finish your book?" she asked, turning back to me, like the atrocious behavior of our audience had reminded her. She'd been asking me that question for almost two years, though. She knew I hadn't really been writing at all. "I want to read it."

I took her hand and we walked towards the elevators.

"Don't worry about that," I said, evasively. "You just get well."

"You're a writer, right?" she said, kissing me on the cheek. Then whispered in my ear, "So, write!"

"Ok, ok," I said, like she was nagging me. Like all systems were normal. Like this was just another visit.

I hugged her gingerly. Her body ached everywhere. I tried to kiss her on the lips but she turned her head.

"People are watching," she said, with a slow-motion wink.

I laughed. She was as bashful as a stripper doing a pole dance. And, I kissed her on the cheek.

"I'll see you soon," I said as she stepped into the elevator. I didn't know that was the last time I'd see her walking, or even standing.

"I'll try to text you later, but with the medication..." she frowned.

"I'll text you. Don't worry about responding."

Her frown blossomed into a smile. She blew me a kiss and waved slowly as the doors slid closed.

I turned around to the room, and dozens of heads turned away *almost* simultaneously, like they'd wanted to drink in every last second of my interaction with Aiko, with one they would claim as their own. And those eyes, those *fucking* eyes, scurried every other direction but mine, like rats on the run.

As I walked through the visiting area to the exit, I watched all of them, a tableau of alienation. No one dared to look at me. No one cared. I was the Invisible Man (not Wells', but Ellison's), a black hole moving through the hall.

One little boy broke rank and turned as I passed. He looked at me and, for a moment, I felt real. He didn't have rodent eyes. There was warmth in them, sympathy, like he was in possession of a presence of mind way beyond his years…and I was moved, deeply; a human among them, decency amid the stolidly oblivious and the psychotically indecent. I nodded my head; just a tiny bow to show my gratitude…But, in a blink, his mother handily turned the child's head away, and said to him, scornfully and pointedly, "da-me" (that's a no-go).

Another recruit to the cult; a future rodent.

Once outside the hospital, I stopped and, trembling, heaving, I struggled to breathe.

I didn't realize that I had been crying until then.

15

OUR EYES WERE WATCHING GOD

"I know you're supposed to be
My steering wheel
Not just my spare tire
So Lord, I ask you
To be my guide toward the truth…"
　　　Speech (from "Tennessee")

I was about to leave home for work. My office was a mere five-block walk from my apartment in Bed-Stuy, Brooklyn. I had been living on the top floor of a four-story Brownstone for about seven years. The woman I rented from was the mother of my best friend and I had known her since I was a child. My best friend also lived there, on the ground floor. I had a great relationship with both of them, and they were both very supportive of the changes I had set in motion in my life.

I had quit my secure and fairly well-paying job of six years a few months earlier in order to have more time to do revisions on the book I'd written. I had secured one of the most prominent black literary agents in the country on the strength of that manuscript. And it had been one hell of an undertaking. For example, I had changed the entire 340-page manuscript written in third person to a 275 or so page first person narrative, so you can imagine all the work involved. But, this was soul work, the kind of work you wake up in the morning to with the eagerness you might wake up with on the morning of your big vacation to some Caribbean island off the grid.

I'd also secured a consulting job where my main responsibility was to raise awareness in Bed-Stuy of funding that was available for corporate sponsored beautification measures. I was responsible for scouting locations and securing the contractors necessary to convert empty lots into awesome gardens. I was volunteering (again in my community) with a neighborhood home owners association, going door to door or giving presentations at Block Association meetings to residents, bringing to their attention the efforts of predatory lenders to separate them from their property through shady re-financing products, and the complicity of certain government agencies in this. On top of that, I was working freelance for a local newspaper raising awareness of the above issues, writing articles and editorials on the players involved, for which I had gained a certain amount of notoriety and respect in the community, viewed as a "comer" or a person to be reckoned with.

I was high on life. It was an awesome time to be Loco.

It was a beautiful day; blue skies, warm breeze and sunshiny. I was dressed in jeans and a T-shirt with a light Polo jacket. I had an Afro then and it was freshly braided tight to my scalp in cornrows ornately and uniquely designed by a woman I paid 20 dollars plus tip to do every other week. I had a little money in my pocket and a lot of joie de vivre in my heart as I descended the stairs from my apartment.

As I was opening the door to walk out into the glory of another day being me, I heard my best friend call my name.

"You seen the news?"

"Nah, what's up?"

"A plane crashed into one of the Twin Towers!"

"Say word!" and I came back in and joined him in front of the TV set. And, sho nuff, one of the buildings had a cavernous hole in it, coughing flames and smoke. "Shit!"

While it was most certainly news, it was merely the kind of news that would make for semi-interesting conversation for the next week or so, by NY standards. Just another saga in the ongoing saga of life in the most major of major metropolises. Seasoned New Yorkers can roll with just about anything.

I basically made my own schedule as a consultant so I wasn't stressing over being late to the office or anything. So, my best buddy and I were sitting there watching this scene play out, listening to the reporters' speculations while speculating ourselves about the size of the plane and the chances of survival of the people above the floors now aflame, when the next plane hit right before our eyes.

"What the fuck was that?"

We found out a few moments later...along with the rest of the world.

While the CNN guys were talking about more planes being expected I remember grabbing and holding myself, like a mother might hold her child...kind of protectively, and thinking aloud, "my God, we're at war!"

And not that *Smart-bomb-down-a-chimney* in some Muslim country *Wag The Dog* kind of war, but the kind of war *other* countries have all the time. The kind of war the U.S. always wages on others had, after a 60 year lapse since the Japanese pimp slapped Pearl Harbor, finally come home. The kind where the enemy is dropping bombs (and planes) on U.S. cities!

The kind of shit you never imagined happening.

And, I was living in ground zero, apparently.

My friend and I looked at one another and a new fear, like a fear of God, was in both of our eyes. More so in mine than his, though, I think. He was always better able to compartmentalize and rationalize than me, something I've always admired about him. He was also more cynical than me, I think.

Or, rather, I felt.

Thinking had been put on hold for longer than I like to remember. All I could do at that moment was feel. Feel my own mortal vulnerability, and that of my family.

I feared for the safety of my sister who took the subway to work, her train passing just beneath the towers. I snatched my cell phone from its holster at my waist. No service. The Land lines were out, too.

No communication only exacerbated the rising panic I felt.

Back to the TV. Back to the talking heads talking Doomsday scenarios, end of the world as we know it shit while in the backdrop of their prognostications the symbols not only of American financial might, but of pride for us New Yorkers, burned, and people leaped to their deaths live on TV.

This can't be real...

I felt myself shaking, trying to process my place in this new paradigm, if I should survive!

"Let's go up on the roof!" I shouted and was headed that way even before I finished the sentence.

From the rooftop, the two towers were clearly visible, the smoke from the fire was drifting over our heads (and would be in the air for days), a metallic chemical taste to it. I was breathing in the incinerated lives of hundreds, and God knows what kind of chemicals. Then, we heard a rumble and looked around as what looked like fighter jets shot by overhead. But the rumble continued even after they'd passed. I looked back to the two towers, and realized there was only one. The other was falling from view like some kind of house of dusty cards.

"Ohhhhhh Fuck!!!"

My heart was jumping all over the fucking place...there were screams from other rooftops.

I remember thinking I might as well jump off this fucking roof. Change doesn't happen this fast...something is wrong with the world, with life. Everything I believe is wrong. Everything is wrong.

Everything.

I was pacing around the roof, looking for something to hold on to. It felt like the house was shaking, like the ground was going to open up and swallow us at any moment, the same way it had just taken one of the world trade buildings.

The roof was the worst place to be.

I climbed back down the ladder into my home. It took much longer than the climb up to the roof had taken. My legs weren't sturdy. The ladder felt rickety. I didn't feel safe. I felt helpless as a baby minus that carefree-ness of not knowing that danger lurked everywhere, that fire burns and water drowns and plastic suffocates. There was no mommy and daddy to protect me. There were people dying, jumping from a burning building into the debris of a tower that didn't exist anymore.

I couldn't walk or talk...I just had to get back to the TV. I don't remember how I got back to it. Did I crawl? I got back though, and I just stood there watching that building crumble to the ground in a sandstorm of dust and debris that swarmed through the air like it was in possession of intelligence of a limited variety, like a plague of locusts swarming down streets I've walked thousands of times. I covered my mouth watching on the news terror-confused people running hither and thither through roads I rode upon often on my mountain bike, shocked people standing on corners I've frequented, holding their mouths same as I was.

I don't know how long I stayed that way. Maybe until the second one dropped.

Somehow, though, the collapse of the second of the twins snapped me out of it. It had a certain finality to it, like a crescendo had been leading up to that moment. I was almost relieved to see it go. Like maybe this had been the goal all along by these forces that sought to change the world as I and everyone I knew saw it, and now that they'd accomplished that, they would cease and desist, show mercy, pull back and let us collect our wounded and fallen, pick up the pieces of our shattered images of safety and delusions of superiority and invulnerability and, at some point, God willing, use our brains to think again.

It would be a few hours before I could think clearly, though. Before I realized that the fear I had experienced, and the shock, had traumatized and paralyzed me. A paralysis during which I'd felt a strong and poignant, almost desperate need to move. And not just to move from the spot where I stood but from the life I'd built. That life was over...I had gotten as much from it as I was likely to get.

It would be another two years before I got sick — sick to death — of living in a city and a country still traumatized so much that it actually supported a man who instructed them (among many ill notions, including, the detention camp in Guantanamo Bay, the Bush Doctrine, USA Patriot Act, etc,...) to go *shopping* and show these terrorists that they haven't destroyed our way of life.

Such flagrant earth-scorching atrocities from our supposed leadership made it easier to cast my shattered life aside, turn my back on that Loco, put my soul work on hold, pack up my shit and move abroad.

I felt at the time that this was what The Creator intended. After a few years in Japan, though, I wasn't sure anymore.

But, exactly nine and a half years later, on 3/11/11, The Creator was back.

*****

Eight years living on this island, among these people, had already rocked my world, in a slow incremental way. So much so that I took on a new moniker, Loco. So much so that I didn't think it could be rocked much more.

I've confronted, endured and in some cases overcome all manner of provocation. In some cases, doing so has changed me for the better, and in others, well, not so much.

For example, one change I'm particularly pleased with is that I've learned how to channel much of my frustration, resentment and anger into my writing, transforming those often overwhelming emotions into creativity, like converting a hot serving of maggots into a five-course dinner at a four-star hotel.

An example of a change I'm not so proud of is the habit I've embraced of not looking at Japanese people when I'm out and about. I've found that the less I see of them and their sickening behavior (not all but more than enough of them) the less I have to restrain myself from acting on the thoughts (some violent) triggered by their actions, which would likely result in my doing something regrettable. Not looking helps me achieve my version of patience and tolerance, of keeping my temper in check and reducing stress.

Definitely nothing to be proud of.

Which is what I just happened to be doing at the time the Earth decided to make a few ultimately minor alterations somewhere in the Pacific ocean off the coast of Japan.

I was walking toward Kikuna station in Yokohama. The closer I got to the station the more populated the streets became. As soon as I entered the area in front of the station the Japanese shifted into *Antoine Dodson* mode ("Hide your kids, hide your wife, and hide your husband, too!") giving me the perimeter or making unnecessary detours, leaping from the sidewalk into the street to make way for me; the usual Japanese foolishness. I shifted into "See No Evil" mode, turned up the volume on my tolerance, put my head down, gritted my teeth and carried on...trying (and failing) not to think hateful shit.

It was about at that moment that the Earth, as if reflecting the rumbling vexation within me, started doing likewise. I didn't notice, though. I was so busy doing battle with my lesser angels.

Until I saw two cops running towards me.

Great!

The Thought Police. They'd be justified burying me under the prison for all the homicidal scenarios that go through my mind!

But, they weren't looking at me, they were looking up! I followed their line of sight and saw that the power lines were swinging, and so were the poles they were connected to. Wait! Everything was swinging and shaking!

That's when my legs got wobbly, like someone had given me a charlie horse. But I was cool. Eight years in Japan and you get used to the terrestrial hiccups that occur here on a regular basis. The tremors have their NY equivalents in my mind so I've gotten pretty comfortable with them.Like an underground subway train rumbling beneath your feet, or the vacuum caused by an 18-wheeled tractor trailer whizzing by your windows, rattling them. And these tremors are usually pretty short. You can forget they even happened in a matter of moments.

But, as I looked around, my hands stretched out before me like a blind man, trying to keep my balance, I realized this was not the usual tremor! Watching power lines and even light poles sway and swing is one thing, but watching train stations and buildings do so is another. Loud rattling, clinging, banging metal and rattling glass rang out from all directions, like a thousand chandeliers shattering; like the street was screaming.

And the people all around me who were, just moments ago, acting the fool, were now at a loss for how to act; just looking around at one another, waiting for the end, whether it be in death, injury or other.

I was, too. If the tachycardia in my chest had it right, I might be looking at the last people I'd ever see!

I staggered out of the street onto the sidewalk because traffic was still moving — some motorists were perhaps unaware of what was happening — and I groped for a building. I looked above my head. A sign was swinging on flimsy hinges. I moved away into the path of a building what looked like a lean-to, made of wood. Surely it would collapse any moment. To my left and right were things that could kill me. Structures had become lethal. The dry cleaner was a two-story tall brick executioner on the Creator's payroll. Sukiya (the fast food joint) was a ninja, armed with hidden secret weapons, ready to kill anyone who came near.

So, I stopped trying to outthink God. And God acknowledged my acquiescence by exploding a window near the area I had thought about running to for safety!

No screams. There would be screaming in NY. There was none in Yokohama.

In surrender, I looked around into the faces of these people, these strangers I usually hold in such contempt, and felt no spite, no disgust, and no contempt whatsoever for them. The slate had been wiped clean. All I saw were people scared shitless. They looked at me and saw no threat, no fearsome foreigner. I had been promoted to the office of just another scared shitless human being. We were one and the same! We were all in this together.

In actuality, we were looking at each other but, to borrow

the words of the late, great Zora Neale Hurston, our "eyes were watching God!"

It was a moment. One I'm not likely to forget.

Then, like an old car engine, with jolting fits, the quake subsided. Nobody moved for a solid 15 seconds. If they were like me they were trying to hold on to that lovely and rare view of eternity we'd all been given, that ethereal glimpse of the inner workings of the Universe, and our place in it. Just for a moment longer; savoring our smallness, our triviality, while at the same time silently extolling the bonanza life is.

My first step was Armstrong's first step on the moon.

I followed it with another and another and before I knew it I was walking among the stunned masses without being noticed, feeling our equality. Everyone was my kin. We'd shared something that no one — at least not immediately — wanted to discard.

Trains were shut down, naturally, so I went to a cafe next to the station, and took a table, amazed at how the staff was hardly behaving like they'd just experienced the worst earthquake in their lifetimes. I took a seat and ordered coffee. Others, realizing the cafe was open for business, followed suit and before long the cafe was full. The table nearest mine was not the last to be taken I noticed because it was so jarring an aberration from the norm.

Some of the older patrons were reading newspapers or chatting with friends. When the first aftershock hit, a pretty big one, the light fixtures started swinging like pendulums and from my window I could see flimsy wooden buildings waving like metronomes. Some dishes fell behind the counter, crashing to the floor. The staff apologized for the disturbance like there wasn't a clear excuse for it, like death wasn't in the air. And everyone else also had a prayerful nonchalance; still reading, still chatting, stealing glances at the swaying room between breaths. There was beauty in their defiance.

I loved them all!

It was about then that I thought about 9/11.

How at that time I had been so focused on my fear, so young, that I didn't take a moment to see the beauty of fear...I was so afraid that I'd gone blind.

I've changed in the nine and a half years since 9/11, most of which were spent here in Asia. Being the object of fear for so many years has slightly altered my relationship with fear, the same way the Earth had slightly altered its position a few minutes earlier. Changing that relationship in ways I had been too busy writing about to fully appreciate.

I remember thinking (an epiphany, really) that my writing is the earthquake resulting from this alteration; every story a tremor.

It was the most profound and inspiring thought I'd had since 9/11.

It took me back to the time in the days before 9/11, when I was so beautiful, so unstoppable, and so unflappable. I could do ANYTHING!

And it informed me, in no uncertain terms, that that beauty was still there, in me, and in everyone around me.

It took an earthquake to awaken the sleeper in me! Talk about *mysterious ways...*

On September 11, 2001, I closed my eyes.

On March 11, 2011, I opened them

****

A couple of days later I was to return to work. It was to be my last day for the school year. Until April, I would be on Spring Break. And it couldn't have come at a better time!

Before 3/11, I had planned to spend this 2-week vacation putting the finishing touches on the book you're reading now.

I had it all mapped out.

Then, this bit of ongoing unpleasantness began. Earthquake (upon earthquake, upon tremor, upon aftershock), tsunami and the most dreadful for me: a nuclear meltdown somewhere over the rainbow. So, now, instead of preparing to embark on a literary adventure, I was faced with making crucial decisions, quite possibly (though I loathed to think of them as such) life or death decisions.

I woke up that morning 6am-ish to a phone call from my Boy, Dee, informing me that it was time for the exodus.

We'd talked about this eventuality the night before for several hours amid persistent aftershocks giving an ominous severity to our already dark conversation, dissipating our wistful, hopeful thoughts of this crisis coming to a miraculous conclusion; of experts and professionals who live for this and drill for these moments, performing their perfunctory tasks in heroic fashion and bringing under control what the world media proclaimed out of control at every opportunity, 24 hours a day.

I'd left his apartment feeling none too cheery only to find a 24-hr McDonald's closed. A harrowing sight, I gotta tell you.

On the way home, my heart had begun racing. I took deep breaths and sighs and kept it moving. I had to get home. The Yokosuka line came, a notoriously crowded train this time of evening. It was virtually empty. I sat down and looked around at the faces of my fellow commuters, all in varying stages of over-nonchalance. So much so that I knew it had to be a facade. Kind of. You never can tell sometimes.

From the station I had set out on the 15-minute walk to my home. Midway, my mind filled with thoughts of widespread panic engulfing me, thwarting my desperate attempts to reach safety, my heart skipped a beat. A couple of beats, actually. And I almost blacked out on the street. If I hadn't stopped and sat down I most certainly would have.

I stopped in front of the 7/11, empty shelves glaringly visible through the windows, people rummaging through what was left like shoppers doing their Christmas shopping on Christmas Eve at 11pm. I turned away, sat on the ground, leaned my back against the store's wall — like I'd seen the young guys do on warm summer nights — and looked to the heavens. It was nippy out, cold even, but the sky was clear, a crescent moon and a handful of stars were visible. It was the kind of night that would find me cruising around Yokohama on my bicycle, taking a ride for the pure pleasure of it.

The sky was really beautiful until I imagined a radioactive plume gliding in upon that deceptively refreshing breeze. My right hand was massaging my chest, caressing my heart, feeling it race at breakneck speed; the kind of speed that usually accompanies an exertion of some sort — running for a train, playing with my kids, making love to my girl. Not just thinking.

Panic attack? *Heart* attack? I'm around that age range where shit happens!

I forced myself to think of good things. A Japanese couple came out of the store. Their hands intertwined, smiling. She actually giggled. I felt happy for them. I didn't care whether they were oblivious to the approaching plume or not. They were alive and in love. I smiled at them. I told myself that radiation wouldn't kill them; that, perhaps, love was stronger than manmade poisonous particles. Sure, I was lying to myself, but in a good way for a change. They noticed me sitting there — a black guy, his hand inauspiciously inside his jacket, with a look of desperation, groping for something hopeful on his face — as they passed, and their joy vanished as they sped to their waiting car. I wasn't surprised. I laughed at the irony.

Once my heart slowed to a fairly normal speed I resumed my walk home. The gaijin house where I live has five rooms. Three occupied by German guys, one Thai girl and me. The German guys had abandoned ship two days earlier leaving in their wake everything they couldn't carry on the fly. I heard they were still in Japan somewhere in the safer southern prefectures but they'd left me no forwarding address so I couldn't say for sure. The Thai girl heard me come up the stairs and popped her head out of her room to tell me she was about to go, too.

"Where you headed?"

"I have a friend in Osaka. She says I can stay with her."

"That was nice of her..." I said, fumbling with my keys.

"You're not gonna stay here?" She asked with almost frantic concern in her voice." *Are* you?"

"Nah, I think I'm gonna be right behind you...tomorrow's my last day at work. I'm gonna go to my job, get my stuff and then I'll decide where."

"Oh, ok..." she said, almost teary eyed now with the shocking and upsetting developments that have altered all of our plans of late. "If you don't see me, that's where I'll be. My family says come home now but..."

Then, she hid her face. I gave her a hug around the shoulders. "It's gonna be alright."

We said our farewells and I went into my room, turned on my computer and absorbed as much bad news as I could, trying to weed through it for some sprouts of optimism. Finding none, I drank heavily and crashed.

Then the next morning I awoke to my cell phone's ringtone Yo, negro, it's time to go!"

"What…what…who?" I was still in a whirlpool surrounded by toy cars and boats and swirling corpses, a dark cloud raining black raindrops hovered overhead. I shook my head loose of the grip the dream retained.

"Yo, I'm outta here…this shit is crazy. The U.S. Embassy extended that shit to 50 miles. 50 MILES! So you know if they say 50 it's probably double that. That's puts it in Chiba or Ibaraki."

It.

I knew what it was. I pictured it like that smoke that went from door to door, slipping under the cracks and through the windows of the homes of Egypt's first born sons, killing them, at Moses' behest. It was that cloud of poisonous debris that swept across lower Manhattan chasing away, or consuming in raging billows, rescue workers, firefighters, police and citizens alike, when the twin towers collapsed.

"Time to go, Bro!" he said, like that bit of news from the Embassy was all the foot in the ass he needed to alleviate his procrastination and accept the reality of what was happening. Things had indeed changed, for the worse, and he'd be damned if he was going to sit by idly while *it* coursed over mountains and through valleys and ultimately through the walls of his cell membranes. "You packed, right?"

"Yeah, but, I don't know…" I said, wiping the sleep out of my eyes and lifting the lid on my laptop.

"You're not gonna stay here?!"

"Hell nah..." I said with twice the conviction I felt. "Fuck I look? Suicidal?"

"Where you headed today?"

"I don't know, yet," I said. Then I remembered the rolling blackout schedule was either for that morning or in the evening. It had been erratic. "Shit, let me take a shower while I still got lights. I'll holler at you in a bit!"

In the shower I thought about what that increase from 30 miles to 50 miles meant. Over the past couple of days I'd learned more about nuclear power plants and how they work than any C-minus science student would ever believe possible.

50 miles...almost half the distance to where I was standing at that very moment! My heart started racing again, same speed as it had the previous night. I stood in the shower room feeling more naked and exposed than I was.

I gotta get the fuck outta here!

I jumped out of the shower, frantically drying myself, my body still soapy. I ran back into my room and turned on the computer, expecting tweeted announcements of a mass exodus of all those foreigners who had previously declared their intentions not to overreact to the news stemming from the West (or the lack thereof coming from the local news agencies).

No tweets jumped out at me. Facebook, however, was crammed with "Run for your life!" type messages. But, none of these folk were on the ground here. The message light was blinking on my cell phone. My friend had sent me a link to the source of the alarming 50 mile verdict. I went to that site, my stomach churning and my hands shaking as I read the wording my government used. Then I read it again.

My eyes kept returning to 50 miles! A 30 mile extension in

one day!

I am sooooo outta here!

But, not like my hair's on fire!

Breathe, relax, I reminded myself.

Fukushima wasn't exactly my backyard. I was no closer to it than I was to *Three-Mile Island* back in NY, in 1979 (and I couldn't remember if NY had planned any evacuations back then, but I doubt it). I decided I would go to work for my last day, say goodbye to the kids and co-workers, and hope for some good news in the mean time.

The bus was late and packed to the door but the train was much emptier than usual. It was cold, but the sun was shining and the skies were clear I could see from the window I stood next to on the train. Other than the welcomed reduction in the number of people commuting, there was nothing different. No hysteria. No panic. No conversations about the encroaching disaster. No worried faces, no desperate eyes. No Smoke Monster like the one Mr. Eko faced down on "Lost".

What's wrong with these people? Don't they know it's the end of the world as we know it?

When I arrived at the school, Takahashi-sensei, my fellow English teacher, met me at the door.

"Loco sensei, are you ok?" She was grinning nervously.

"I'm keeping it together," I said, feeling like I was lying. "How you holding up?"

"Eeeee??"

I'd spoken naturally to her, responding to her sincere concern, and used expressions I'd never used before with her and apparently she'd never heard before.

"I'm sorry. I'm OK. How are you doing?"

"I'm OK, but the principal wants to speak with you."

We walked together into the principal's office where we were met by both he and the vice-principal and some pretty formal welcomes and bows.

"Loco-sensei, how are you?" the vice-principal asked, in English, the extent of it from my assessment of his ability, offering me a seat.

"I'm OK, I guess. A little upset by everything going on," I said in Japanese knowing he would look to Takahashi to be our intermediary if I'd replied in English.

After some brief discussion about the state of things, he asked me was I going back to New York.

"I'm not sure. But the U.S. State department…" I turned to Takahashi-sensei to make sure I'd gotten the words right. She nodded. "My State department has suggested Americans leave Japan. Some of my friends here have already left and my family and friends back home are very worried."

"As they should be. It is a very troubling situation," the principal said to nods around the table.

"That it is," I said.

"Do you know if you will be back in April for the new school year?"

"At this point, no, I don't know, but I certainly hope to be," I said.

"We do, too!" the principal said, and stood. Everyone followed suit. "Well, take care and keep in touch!"

He extended a hand for a shake. I took it.

"What will you all do if the situation doesn't improve?" I asked, kind of offhandedly, looking at each of them in turn. After I said it I felt the impact of the words. How difficult it would be for them to consider relocation if it came to that. They all did the same thing though I'm sure they hadn't noticed.

They each bowed their heads pensively and then looked up with pleasantly pained expressions on their faces. It was kind of spooky.

"We will stay here," the vice-principal said. "It will be difficult."

I nodded, pretty certain he didn't understand my Japanese correctly. So I turned to Takahashi and said in English, "I meant if, God forbid, the radiation from Fukushima becomes hazardous for people living in Yokohama, what will you do?"

"Yes," she said.

"Yes, what?"

"Yes, I understand...*we* understand."

"You're not gonna stay here?!" I said, and I'm sure a bit of the hysteria I'd been harboring escaped. "Are you?"

"My family is here and my job and..." she broke off.

I'm sure my mouth was hanging open. I looked to the principal who was nodding like he'd understood everything Takahashi and I had said to one another. I took a breath...my heart was racing, again.

"But..." I began, and saw some anguish, just a little, escape from the frozen smile on the vice-principal's face, and through Takahashi's eyes. So I swallowed my next words which would have been some polite way of saying, in Japanese, *are you motherfuckers crazy???*

I felt myself getting upset. First with pity and bewilderment, like I would have for pandas who wouldn't fuck to save their species or for people with a misplaced faith in their government's ability to protect them and handle this crisis. But that wasn't what I saw. It was something else; something that sparked sadness. Profound sadness at the prospect of them being forced to leave their homes, families in tow, moving to unfamiliar territories, perhaps even countries, to start again. And, at the principal and vice-principal's ages, that probably wasn't a very inviting option. Their best hope was that this thing got resolved or they might as well be dead.

And Takahashi...she most of all. We'd had our differences over the course of the past two years we'd been working side by side trying to tame these wild ass kids but, geezus, we were talking life and death here, from my perspective. She was young, intelligent and beautiful, 24 years old or so with her whole life ahead of her. And, I realized at that very moment, that I'd really grown fond of her. Over the past year she'd become increasingly more real to me. Not just some functionary bureaucrat but a real person! We'd chat often about non-work related stuff. She'd tell me about what she'd done over the weekend, in detail. She'd make off-color jokes, occasionally. She'd tell me what she really thought of other teachers and of certain students. She told me about goukon (mass blind dating parties) she'd attended and other personal stuff. She'd really opened up at some point, as did I, and before I knew it we had become a real team! And friends.

Now here she was, apparently choosing death over evacuation.

I bowed to the three of them. I'm sure it was stilted and awkward but I did my best to give it the solemnity that I felt what they'd just confessed to me warranted: *We are willing to die here, if it comes to that.*

I walked out of the office feeling lost...like I'd been living in some unidentified place, thinking I knew where I was, and then after eight years finally having revealed to me exactly where I was.

You are not there, you are here!

Saying good bye to the other teachers was like a repeat performance. Not one of them had any plans to leave Yokohama. Not one! Some of them even told me with tears welling in their eyes, confessing their inner desperation.

I only had one class to teach that day, some first year students.

I went to the room and stood before them trying to convince myself that I would see them again come April when they would be 2nd year students. They all seemed totally oblivious to what was happening. But they weren't. In an American school there'd probably be trauma specialists and counselors all over the place, aching to help these kids through this series of crises: numerous earthquakes on a daily basis, tsunamis killing thousands, nuclear meltdown threatening. This all had to be having some kind of effect on these kids. But the only difference I could see was that several had lost almost entirely the ability to focus on class work, so Takahashi and I ignored the lesson plan and played games.

As the class was coming to a close I told them good bye, not knowing if I'd ever see any of their beautiful faces again. Perhaps their parents were of the same mind as the teachers. And all these lovely children, like those sitting in schools in areas well outside of the blast radius of the Atomic bombs but within the radiation contaminated area that surrounded Nagasaki and Hiroshima back in WWII...like those kids they too would have their lives infected by this invisible, odorless cell invading and mutating plague.

And, like some divine exclamation point on my thoughts, at that moment, a family-sized aftershock rocked the school. Half the class whispered, "Jishin!" which made it sound like a collective hiss. (Earthquake) Their faces were frozen in that horrific wait for it to pass. Then, the vice-principal's voice came over the loud speaker, reiterating, "Jishin," and some other stuff I couldn't catch.

I was starting to get overwrought. There was just too much going on, too many thoughts to process. Public Enemy's words: *Armageddon has been in effect. Go get a late pass*, rang in my ears. I felt a rush of desperation when the bell chimed.

I gotta get outta here!

"Loco-sensei," a few of my favorite students cried, coming up to me after the bell. "Are you going back to America?"

Takahashi had announced at the beginning of the class that this would be my last day for the school year. There'd been no discussion of the next school year beginning in April, though.

"Umm," I said. "Maybe."

"Will you be back after the vacation?" another asked. "Please come back!"

"I love you, Loco-sensei!" one girl said, giggling with her girlfriend, real love was in her eyes, though.

"Earthquakes are scary, aren't they?" said another boy. He looked at me like he could read my thoughts, knew that I wouldn't be back, and believed that the persistent aftershocks and earthquakes were quite possibly the reason. "Don't be afraid, Loco-sensei! It'll be OK!"

Their messages of concern and love and understanding kept coming and coming, like a tsunami; and the impotence of my responses, the indecisiveness, the evasions, like one of those trucks tossed and shoved around like toys in the tsunami footage on TV, seemed to spurn them on.

"I...I gotta go!" I almost shouted at them over the roar of their innocent persistence. But, as a testament to the awareness of children, they seemed to understand that this was getting to be a bit too much at the moment.

On my way out of the door, three girls sang in unison, "See you again, Loco-sensei!"

I walked back to the office, looking at everything as if it were for the last time. The artwork on the walls, the water fountains, and the school's garden, all these things I'd written and blogged about and had come to adore. I touched walls and high-five'd kids in the hall. I stopped at the senior kids' classrooms. They had graduated the week before but came back to the school to clean their former home rooms, as seniors did every year. All systems normal. They were on their hands and knees scrubbing the floors with brushes, soap and water. They stopped and tossed smiles and waves of joy at me and I smiled in return, but kept walking.

By the time I got back to the office I had had enough. I couldn't take it anymore. I couldn't sit in that office all day with people who answered the probe, "you're not gonna stay here, are you?" with tears, shrugs, and syougannai (nothing can be done).

I had no more classes for the day so I bid my co-workers farewell. Standing by the door as they all looked up from their tasks to say goodbye, I didn't look at them like I'd look at the staff of the Titanic if I'd known in advance that it was going to hit an iceberg but was unable to get them to take me seriously, like some sufferer of the *Cassandra Syndrome*. Neither did I look at them as doomed delusional optimists.

I just looked at them.

On my way home, I started feeling very guilty, and cowardly to boot.

Ironically, when I first decided to move to Japan eight years ago I'd had bouts of guilt. Was I abandoning loved ones, friends and family? Was I breaking some solemn unsung obligation, some filial covenant, to always be within reach, you know, just in case? And here I was again feeling like I was about to abandon loved ones, friends, co-workers, people who have taken me into their inner circles and embraced me.

To alleviate this pang, I told myself, "this is their country, not mine! If they want to go down with this fucking ship, that's their business...NOT MINE!!!"

People were looking at me stranger than usual as I walked into the station, and I realized I had been thinking aloud.

Losing it!

On the walk from the station to my home, my Boy called again.

"Yo, where you at?"

He was starting to piss me off, too!

"In Yokohama, motherfucker! Where *you* at?"

"In Osaka."

I stopped on a dime.

"*Seriously,*" I said, kind of laughing. Osaka is to Yokohama as DC is to NY distance-wise. "Where are you, all kidding aside?"

"You slow you blow, negro...when I make a decision, I'm on it!" he boasted. "I don't dick around. Me and my girl hopped the Shinkansen (bullet train) this morning!"

I realized I was standing stark still in the street, and that my heart had dropped. I suddenly felt very alone and ill to my stomach. I lurched for the curb and tried to retch...nothing came out but the noise from my effort.

"You alright...fuck! Are you throwing up???"

"Nah, I'm alright," I lied.

"It's that radiation sickness, yo," he said, chuckling

arrogantly. "You better get outta there!!!"

"Awww, fuck you!" I said, and I hung up.

When I got to my house, I climbed the stairs to find my Thai roommate locking her door, a large suitcase stood before her, and a backpack on her back.

"Loco, I'm so sorry," she said, teary-eyed. "My father just told me to get on a plane today or he would come and get me tomorrow!"

"Really?"

"He's very angry, and he doesn't trust Japanese!"

"I see," I said. I knew exactly how he felt. Every time I logged on Twitter I read a hundred tweets echoing her father's concerns. CNN had basically become the "You Can Never Trust A Jap!!" channel, and all my friends on Facebook had become CNN reporters in the field echoing the company line.

"When are you leaving?" she asked, wiping her eyes with her sleeve.

I realized at that moment that something had changed. I had turned a corner. Maybe it was because of my Boy's escape to Osaka without me, or his quip about radiation sickness, or maybe it was because of what my soon-to-be former roommate said about her father, or the faces of my kids and co-workers. I didn't know, but something changed, right then and there.

"I don't know," I said, and gave her a hug and kiss on the cheek. "Don't worry about me. If the situation gets really bad I'll be on the first flight outta here. Get home safely and keep in touch!"

She said she would and then she was gone.

My house was empty!

All mine!

I wasn't sure why but I felt like the last man standing, the last gaijin in Japan, the final contestant on some crazy Japanese version of an American Reality Show called: Fukushima Fear Factor.

I poured me a nice tall glass of umeshu (plum wine) and club soda, drank it down, threw on some Prince (a song of his I've always loved named, *Housequake*) and danced a jig, a la Joel Goodsen.

I danced because I had gotten over the knee-jerk response (escape) which is very unusual for me. When the going gets tough, Loco has been known to get going and leave skid marks.

Another tremor hit while I was dancing; a hefty one, but thankfully short. I paused for it, standing in the doorway, let it pass, and then resumed.

Shockalockaboom!

"What was that?" Prince sang.

"Aftershock!" I answered.

I was still alive! I knew this because I could smile again.

Ok. What's next?

I could pack some stuff, get to Narita Airport somehow, hang around there with a lot of other anxious foreigners for a flight, go to NY, where all my friends and family will welcome me with "thank God" and "It's about time!" And all would be well...And if and when this thing blows over I can always come back. Sounds like a plan.

Or...

I danced my way to my computer, feeling tipsy, and pulled up the U.S. State Department website, wondering if there had been any updates. No updates. Just that same carefully worded message. I could see meetings being held for the sole purpose of getting the wording just right to avoid panic, and in anticipation of some kind of backlash down the line. It kind of made me angry. I put Prince on pause, opened SKYPE and called the hotline number from the page.

"Thank you for calling the U.S. Department of State travel..."

"Yes, my name is Loco, I'm living in Yokohama, Japan, and I have a question regarding your most recent travel advisory."

"Yes?"

"Well, I'm not sure I understand this, so maybe you can clarify something. It says here that 'The State Department strongly urges U.S. citizens to defer travel to Japan at this time and those in Japan should consider departing'."

"That's correct..."

"Does that mean the U.S. strongly urges us in Japan to consider departing? And does that pertain to the whole entire country including Okinawa?"

"Did you read the warning, Sir?" A little snooty and defensive.

"Yeah, I read it. It's right in front of me."

"Well, it clearly says in the first paragraph," she began, like she was prepared for these kinds of foolish questions, or had been getting them since the advisory was released. I heard her tap some keys on a keyboard. "...that the State Department strongly urges U.S. citizens to defer travel to Japan at this time and..."

"I just told you I read it!" I snapped. Then seeing that I was getting no answers, and attitude wasn't going to help me, I moved on. "I have another question about these flights to the U.S. Are they free?"

"The flights are *not* to the U.S., sir. They are, at this time, to Seoul or Taipei. From those destinations you need to make your own arrangements to either stay in hotels in those countries or continue to the U.S."

"I see…"

"And the ticket price must be repaid at some point."

"Great…"

"Anything else, sir?"

Shut up, already, damn!

Prince sang, when I SKYPE'd off and un-paused iTunes. Most of that exodus adrenalin that had been coursing through my bloodstream earlier in the day had run its course. That phone call had depleted the residuals, licked the batter from the bowl.

I looked around the room, clothes piled here and there around a centerpiece: the suitcase I had taken out of the closet and half-packed the day after the earthquake. It was in the same state of indecision as it had been that day. I finished packing it.

No.

Actually, I shoved all the clothes that were around it inside of it. Then I tossed it back in my closet.

It was clogging up my dance floor.

The End

EPILOGUE

ECOLOGY OF THE SOUL

Alas, the empty seat was back. No sooner had the aftershocks subsided than the love fest came to an end. Our mutual mortality and shared vulnerability to nature's seismic tantrums had, for a few precious weeks, been an awesome argument on behalf of our common humanity. Unfortunately though, it was only a short-lived distraction. Life in Japan returned to its pre-3/11 state without so much as a backward glance, and everything was back to its usual state.

Well, *almost* everything.

*****

An Empty Seat on a Crowded Train was not only the first chapter of this book, but the inaugural post on my blog, *Loco in Yokohama*, three years ago.

This was not a coincidence. There is a reason I went to the empty seat first and have returned to it again.

Actually there are several:

1- The empty seat is something that resonates, especially with the foreigners who live here. You'd be hard-pressed to find a non-Asian foreigner in Japan who hasn't experienced this phenomenon at one time or another, to some degree or another. Though its cause, and how one should respond to it (if at all) are a recurring debate, its existence is almost indisputable. Therefore, it's safe to say that before one can make peace with Japan and the Japanese, one must first make peace with the empty seat and all that it signifies; even if one ultimately judges it insignificant or decides ignoring it is in their best interest.

2- The empty seat is, quite possibly, the *most* irksome and conspicuous manifestation of the mindset here as it pertains to foreigners. Many of the qualms I have with living in Japan, I realized recently, are variations of it. For example, if I'm not sitting but standing on the train, the empty seat becomes a Japanese-free perimeter (whenever possible). If I'm having coffee in a café or even just taking a leak in a public bathroom, the empty seat often transforms into the forsaken table, or untaken urinal. If I'm walking down the street, the empty seat becomes a force field, sending the Japanese passersby scampering into the street or fanning out to give me an inordinately wide berth.

3- One's response to the empty seat, and eventual method of making peace with it, has broad implications, impacting how one will view and judge Japan and Japanese. And one of those implications is, I've learned, actually an ancillary benefit. The empty seat becomes a sort of social Litmus test that can enlighten you as to your actual views on race, and perhaps even whether or not you're a *Shit kicker*, a *Poser* or one of the *Oblivious*. Yep, it can let you know if you're a racist. It certainly enlightened me about my status. And this Litmus test is universal. It works for everyone; everywhere the empty seat, and the associated mentality, is encountered. It works for those enduring this foolishness up-close, those viewing it from a distance, those ignoring, excusing, defending, accepting or denying its existence; even those reading about it in a book.

*****

The first time, post-3/11, that the empty seat reasserted itself, I let out a deep sigh, shook my head and smiled, thinking, "Well, it was a precious hiatus, sweet while it lasted. But now it's time to get back to work, and get back to life!"

It was like a trip home to New York. I usually spend the first few days walking around soaking up normality and anonymity. No one is paying me any undue attention; no one is running from me, or hiding their belongings...no one gives a shit about me! At first, it's glorious; then, it's bittersweet.

Like some modified version of Megan's law where, for a period of time, sex offenders have to wear identifying clothing or a mark of some sort, as part of their parole, so that everyone in the community in which they live would know them for what they really are. Once this period has expired, though, he's allowed to remove this mark of disgrace and leave that city, walk the streets of his new place of residence stigma-free. Now, imagine that scenario if you were wrongly accused, in the first place, had never and would never even imagine raping children, but due to the incompetence of your court-appointed lawyer and the habitual injustice dished out by a judge who simply didn't like your face, you lost seven years of your life in a prison system where the label "sex offender" made you pretty unpopular with the inmates, but only the ones with mothers, sisters and daughters. The others were pretty cool.

That's how returning to NY from Japan feels.

Like I said, bittersweet.

And, that's how this earthquake induced hiatus felt, as well.

For the first time in eight years I caught a glimpse of the possibilities here, though. I could see that Japanese were not permanently members of the cult of *Different Therefore Dangerous*. There was hope. Something I hadn't felt significantly since Aiko passed.

So I didn't let the re-emergence of the empty seat trouble me too much.

In fact, I started a little *Back To Life Party* via my blog and invited bloggers from all over the Japan blogosphere to come do guest posts on *Loco in Yokohama* and share their thoughts, while I sorted out mine.

I reappraised the empty seat, trying to imagine that it *wasn't* inherently bad, just a victim of circumstances, a product of its environment, no more deserving of the stigma I'd branded it with than the stigma that has been branded upon me.

It's *just* a fucking empty seat, I said, and snorted.

I told myself that I ought to be thankful for it. That the Japanese had done me a big favor by leaving it empty; that their racism, xenophobia, Iwakan (a malaise or feeling of incompatibility) or whatever it is, had helped me to recognize and begin to face up to my own!

It was around then that things started getting weird...a chain of thoughts and events that I'm still trying to wrap my thick skull around.

First off, the seat ceased torturing me. It just upped and quit.

I couldn't imagine that I'd shut it up, though. Maybe it was tired, you know? Tired of my self-righteousness; maybe even got bored with it. Maybe it had run out of ammunition and was reloading. Or, maybe my sensitive ass was way too easy a mark. Not even a challenge. Whatever the reason, the taunting stopped.

At first I missed the taunts, the way a recovering alcoholic misses the bite of a shot of whiskey, that burn as it glides down the gullet. I felt like I was suffering from some sort of modified strain of Stockholm Syndrome, but instead of feeling like I'd fallen for my captors, I felt like I'd fallen for my nemesis.

Yeah, some creepy psychotic shit was going on that had my whole belief system in a free fall.

I mean, what we had, though, was *real*, you know? We had built a relationship over the past eight years, the empty seat and I. I engaged it and it engaged me, in return. We were engaged. I gave it attention, and it kept me company, kept me safe in my cubbyhole of persecution and secure in my righteousness. We had laughs and we had tears. Well, at least I had laughter and tears. It's a fucking metal bench with a cushion. Nothing more. It doesn't *feel* anything.

Sure, it pissed me off something awful, and made me feel lower than pond scum sometimes, but at the same time it inspired me to write like nothing I'd encountered in my entire life, with results that caused me to sit back sometimes and say: *now that ain't bad*! And, it practically coerced me into this frequently unpleasant exploration into what lies at the heart of my envy and hate.

Loco was born as a direct result of our relationship.

Loco belonged to *it* as much as he belonged to me. I owe my bosom buddy, the empty seat, a debt of gratitude; for if there was no empty seat, I'm pretty sure there'd be no Loco, either.

Loco has been such a blessing in my life over the past three years (and who knows how many more years to come). He's helped me tremendously, and he has even helped others figure out some things for themselves. Loco has brought me back from the brink time and time again — the brink of apathy, the brink of violence, and even the brink of insanity. Loco is my hero! But, Loco's power source *is*, at least partially, the empty seat (in all its manifestations). Sometimes one glimpse of the empty seat is all it takes, and Loco is off to the races. Volumes are written in moments, only requiring me to sit in front of a keyboard and transcribe them.

And, to make spooky even spookier, truth be told, my

closest relationship in Japan, since Aiko passed, has been with the empty seat. It's been a constant companion. It follows me wherever I go, like a faithful mangy mutt just this side of rabid.

Talk about being careful what you wish for.

Talk about a paradox

But, my warped mind was just getting started. And it still had a ways to go.

*****

One day, a couple of months after the earthquake, my *homie* and I were on the train. I was uploading pictures I'd taken on my iPhone to a photo sharing app, and he was sitting beside me silent as the grave. I still missed his haranguing. He's actually pretty cool once you get to know him.

I looked up from my editing to notice a woman sitting down — right in my buddy's lap! I looked at the woman and she took my glance as her cue to scoot over as far away from me as she could. My buddy loved it, though. All that scooching and squirming she was doing only made the impromptu lap dance all the mo' better! I almost envied him, lucky bastard.

I almost *envied* an empty seat?

But, wait! It gets weirder.

A few days later, my mangy mutt and I were headed home, when a salaryman boarded the train and headed right for us, just like we were normal. But he must have been near-sighted or something because the closer he got the slower his stride became. Then he stopped and looked around for a free seat. Maybe my mutt had scared him. He does that sometimes: growls and snarls at people. I placed my bag next to my mutt on the seat. He gave it a few good whiffs before lying on top of it.

The man stood before us. I paid him no mind until he cleared his throat with an, "anoo –"

I glanced up at him. I thought he was about to speak to me but, alas, he pointed at my bag, then at my face, then shifted his finger's aim to the baggage rack above, like something out of a Dicken's story- the *Ghost of Christmas Yet to Come*, or something. I looked up at the rack like I had no idea that trains here came with them, then back at him, and shrugged.

Then the asshole reached for my bag.

The mutt, who had been observing all the goings-on with a sleepy curiosity, suddenly sat up and snarled, hoping I'd let him have Japanese digits for dinner. That would be bad, so I slapped the offending hand instead, the way a mother might do at the dinner table when you reach for the hot sauce instead of asking for it to be passed. Then I gave him the gas face and wagged my index finger at him like a windshield wiper. He looked at the hand he'd withdrawn like it had been contaminated and he was wondering if he had time to get to a sink and wash it before it was too late. Then, he sucked his teeth (which has about the same meaning as it does in the States) and I gave him the middle finger (which also has the same meaning here, thanks to Hollywood I bet).

As he walked away, mumbling Japanese un-pleasantries, I glanced at my faithful companion to see if he was disappointed that I didn't sic him on the guy but, of course, there was no mutt there; just my old shabby ass bag.

And that's when it hit me!

Actually *hit* is not the right word. It was more like a kiss. Not a romantic one, but one from the aging mother you only see but once a year, because you're too busy splitting your time between teaching Japanese kids how to speak a language most will never use, and sitting at a computer composing commentary most will never read about a place where you've taken up refuge that most people will never visit (thanks to the radiation situation that won't be resolved in the foreseeable future).

Maybe "hit" was the right word, after all.

I do, on occasion, have flashes of brilliance, of inspired clarity. And in these moments, ideas roll out before me like a carpet of light; warm, glowing and welcoming. *God*, I love myself at these times, when that shiftless genius in me punches the clock and puts in a little work.

But, unfortunately, these moments are not only rare, but unpredictable.

Sometimes they come when I'm in dire straits, or I might be banging my head up against a wall, when suddenly it'll crack and collapse and, *whaddayaknow*, there, through the gaping hole I'd made with my thick skull, I'd find a great idea or a solution to the dilemma du jour. A flash might occur while I'm sitting on top of the world deciding which goal to tackle next, prompting me to beat my chest and bellow from my perch atop the heap, *"I'm the friggin' man!!"* Or, it might do something sordid like manifests itself in dreams as a tolerably coherent trail of archetypal images that make sense while I'm asleep, but become indecipherable gibberish at the approach of consciousness, and fade from memory altogether upon waking. *"Fuck me, I suck!"* might be the way I greet the new day after a dream like that.

Like I said, rare and unpredictable.

And, I can now add to that list that, one time, clarity *hit* me while I was sitting on the Toyoko Line beside an invisible mutt resting in an empty seat, and being over-protective of it to the point of striking relatively innocent people...

*****

Of course, there was no one sitting there, but the empty seat was *not* empty. It had never been empty! True, my mutt was a figment of my imagination, but there was something else there; something that had been sitting there for eight years! Something I felt protective of; something that finger pointing prick's presence would've distracted me from understanding. Something related to his finger pointing, in fact: *The Ghost of Christmas Yet To Come.*

The stream of consciousness that followed went a little something like this:

Yeah!

The empty seat is occupied by something like *The Ghost of Christmas Yet to Come*: A lifeless shrouded specter of dissuasion. It's not human. It isn't even a being. It is a clever facsimile of a life form, designed to blend in, disguised as our *natural* fears and inherent insecurities, capable of an honesty that humans often are not. It tells a story aloud that we would sooner bury beneath lies, half-truths, psycho-babble, and self-deceptions.

Now we're on to something

It isn't my buddy, at all. Nor is it my loyal, mangy mutt. And, for damn sure, it isn't Loco's father. That isn't possible because this thing doesn't make love. It doesn't make hate, either. It doesn't make *anything*. It lacks the power of creation, a power reserved for the Creator and His children.

It's more like a map, hoisted high for all to see. One that reveals our *actual* location as a species on the evolutionary quest, instead of the location where we deceive ourselves into believing we currently reside;

While we fixate on such petty cosmetic considerations as pigment, language and cultural differences, using them as obstacles to unity, understanding, and mutual respect, it feeds on our smugness and complacency, growing stronger with each passing day, and in turn feeds us a steady diet of fear, envy, indifference and hate.

Wait for it.

It's a black hole in the path of humanity's trek toward progress and change. On a planet changing at a faster clip than people will ever be able to keep up with, this thing occupying the empty seat serves as a gruesome reminder of where we've come from and why we need to keep it moving. It is an antiquated meme that has survived extinction; and will continue to replicate itself, generation after generation, until it declares, "All Your Souls Are Belong To Us!"

Now, hold on, Loco! Don't get silly...

It's an executioner, not a judge. It doesn't listen to the facts and view the evidence and then hand down verdicts. It doesn't care if you're persecuting or being persecuted. It simply executes. It kills communication. It devours dreams and excretes nightmares. It dispirits aspirations. And it puts a shime-waza chokehold on goodwill. Little by little it lynches love.

Yeah! Now it's coming into focus.

It doesn't care how civilized you *think* you are. It doesn't give a fuck about those inventions and advancements that you attribute to your *brand* of indoctrination. It doesn't differentiate between our concepts of villain and hero, good and evil, common sense and nonsense. And, it cares about your skin color, ethnicity and race as much as a velociraptor would.

It doesn't tabulate the money you give to charity or how many hours you volunteer a year. It doesn't care if you throw yourself in front of a whaler to save a humpback or if you eat dolphin sushi twice a week.

It doesn't care if you call your home a Mecca of Diversity or an Island of Homogeneity. It doesn't care if you erect temples to worship it or deny its existence entirely. You could even make effigies of it and stab it with pins, lynch it in the woods or build a bonfire and torch it in the town square. It couldn't care less.

Now we're cooking!

The only way to eradicate this thing is to face it head on – individually *and* as a species. Much the way we've finally begun to accept and address (as a result of education, advocacy and activism) serious environmental issues such as air and water pollution and climate change, and have taken up the mantle of ecologically remedying these threats. There needs to be a global movement to do the same for the mentality that fabricates the empty seat. *This* needs to be the goal of the global perennial PR campaign! *This* needs to be the objective of the 100%, of a global Occupy Movement! If everyone took on this task, and willingly made the extra effort with our hearts that we have with our trash — that is, recycling what is useful and productive and eliminating the rest in a way that it doesn't cause further damage — then (and *only* then) will we be truly worthy of a universal designation: WE the people; the only way we'll ever truly be free.

Think of it as ecology of the soul.

Otherwise, I'm afraid, this *Ghost of Christmas Yet to Come* will be pointing his finger not at the empty seats of Yokohama, or at Jihadist, or at white or black supremacists, but at *all* of us! Then it will shift its aim to a tombstone. And etched into this marker will be the words: *Here Lies Humanity.* And the epitaph will read, *"These Cowards Chose Death Over Change."*

*****

The empty seat is a gift. It helped me to recognize the truth about myself: I *am* a racist. I am a poser and a hypocrite. I decry racist attitudes towards blacks while often tolerating and sometimes even espousing them against Japanese, and sometimes whites, as well. And I've done so, if not knowingly, then at least suspecting that to tolerate these attitudes toward one group is to tolerate it toward any group.

It also gave me a clue as to how to engage my racism so that it can never claim dominion over me. It's an ongoing struggle, aluta continua, but at least I now know who my adversary is and where it dwells! For I need look no further than the nearest mirror. My adversary is not external. It's whatever color or nationality I imagine it is. And it doesn't dwell on the trains, in the cafes, nor in the streets of Yokohama. It's everywhere... everywhere I am! I am the architect of the arena where I choose to do battle with this adversary. And like a nemesis confident of victory, it'll always show up. But, at the end of the day, the battle is always in the same theater of war: my heart.

I believe this is an adversary most of us must and eventually will face. It will call you out, at some point. And at that time you will dig in and fight, allow your fear, envy, or hate to distract you, or worse, convince yourself that it isn't even your fight.

You will grow, stagnate, or you will wilt.

Me? I've decided to deal with mine by taking it on *every* time I encounter it, thereby letting it know that I won't be terrorized, victimized or turn the other cheek. Never again! I may take a beating more often than I'd like, but I'll never concede. I draw strength from those who came before me and sacrificed much more than I ever have, and will ever truly know. I won't let their efforts be in vain.

Besides, I made a promise to someone very important to me, that I would ganbarimasu (do my best) and I know she's at my back! I *am* a writer, Aiko. And this book is only the beginning, merely a baby step. I won't let you down. I will use what gifts I have to not only entertain and make a living, but to try to reach people, and move people to change the things that are within their control. For, as any recovering substance abuser knows, helping others is the only way to truly help oneself.

Anyone know another way to bring about genuine change?

If so, please let me know, because right about now I'm going about breaking out of this chrysalis of ours the only way I know how, in typical Loco fashion: the hard way.

ABOUT THE AUTHOR

Baye McNeil (a.k.a. Loco) is a freelance writer and blogger from Brooklyn, New York. He currently lives in Yokohama, Japan, where he teaches junior high school English. He is a fervent connoisseur of Japanese Onsen (Hot Springs) and Ramen. He spends his free time taking photos of trains and life in the subways and stations of Yokohama, Kawasaki and Tokyo. This is his first book.